The
Last Days
of
John Lennon

The
Last Days
of
John Lennon

A Personal Memoir

by Frederic Seaman

A Birch Lane Press Book
Published by Carol Publishing Group

A Citadel Press Book
Published by Carol Publishing Group
Citadel Press is a registered trademark of Carol Communications, Inc.
Editorial Offices: 600 Madison Avenue, New York, N.Y. 10022
Sales & Distribution Offices: 120 Enterprise Avenue, Secaucus, N.J. 07094
In Canada: Musson Book Company, a division of General Publishing Company, Ltd.,
    Don Mills, Ontario M3B 2T6

Queries regarding rights and permissions should be addressed to Carol
Publishing Group, 600 Madison Avenue, New York, N.Y. 10022

Carol Publishing Group books are available at special discounts for bulk
purchases, for sales promotions, fund raising, or educational purposes.
Special editions can be created to specifications. For details contact:
Special Sales Department, Carol Publishing Group, 120 Enterprise Avenue,
Secaucus, N.J. 07094

Manufactured in the United States of America
10 9 8 7 6 5 4 3 2 1

Library of Congress Cataloging-in-Publication Data
Seaman, Fred.
    The last days of John Lennon : an intimate memoir / by Frederic
Seaman.
        p. cm.
    "A Birch Lane Press book."
    ISBN 1-55972-084-0
    1. Lennon, John, 1940–1980.   2. Rock musicians—Biography.
I. Title.
ML420.L38S38 1991
782.42166′092—dc20   91-26327
[B]   CIP
                                                                  MN

All photos courtesy of Fred Seaman.

THIS BOOK IS DEDICATED TO THE MEMORY OF
JOHN LENNON.
MAY HIS MUSIC LIVE ON FOREVER.

Contents

Acknowledgments

I am most deeply indebted to Albert Goldman, a courageous and uncompromising journalist, for giving me the gift of confidence and for teaching me that where there is a will, there is a way.

I would also like to express heartfelt thanks to all my friends who, in one way or another, lent significant support to my mission: to Bill and Kuniko Sagal for setting me up with a computer, suffering through endless printouts of my manuscript and generally extending themselves above and beyond the call of duty; to Ann Cypher for her enthusiastic support and astute legal advice; to Louise Nieves for her generous assistance of all sorts, including proofreading, research, transportation and moral support; and to Stu Klein for his perceptive comments.

In addition, I am deeply grateful to all those who encouraged me over the years (with apologies in advance to those whose names should be listed here, but are not): my good buddy Tom Babbit (who helped to see me through the strange times chronicled in the Afterword), Donna Anderson (ditto), Frank Balestieri, Caroline Claiborne, Norma Cohen, Julie Collyer, Rick Dufay, Joan Field, Peter Frank, Alex Grant, Jeffrey and John Holman, Joe Kopmar, Victoria Lefcourt, Jody Linscott, Lynn & Peggy, Danielle Mead, Charlotte Nugent, Bonnie Osborne, Lenora Paglia, Perry Press, Karen Sandt, Myra Sheer, Jane Shoemaker, Michael and Norma Wendroff, Fred Yamamoto, the Eastern Athletic Club Table Tennis All-Stars, and all my friends and former colleagues from the *Observation Post*.

Special thanks to my fellow Nutopians—May Pang, Doug Mac-Dougall, Mike Tree, and Jack Douglas—for their support. I am also grateful to Daphne Merkin, a courageous and principled editor, for her generous help. Thanks, as well, to Joni Evans, Dan Weiss, and Laurence Gonzales for their efforts all those years ago. More thanks to my agent, Dan Strone; to Hillel Black, the patient and perceptive editor who took my manuscript under his wing; to Steve Schragis, a valorous publisher who dared to go against the grain, and to Melvin Wulf, Esq., who rode shotgun.

I am also indebted to Carol Publishing's copy chief, Donald J. Davidson, designer Renata Slauter, and production manager Kevin Connell for helping us to meet an impossible deadline; to sales and marketing director Gary Fitzgerald for selling this book under sometimes adverse conditions; to the publicity department, especially Ben Petrone, for helping me to get my side of the story across to the media; to Susan Hayes and Denise O'Sullivan for their all-around assistance; and to David Palmore for his photography.

I would also like to thank Sal Russo and Ellen Zindler, chief among the many lawyers who fought my legal battles over the years.

Finally, I am deeply grateful to Helen and Norman Seaman for their support and encouragement, and to my mother, Elfriede, and brother, Matt, for keeping the faith. I would also like to express my heartfelt thanks to Lenore Wolf for her loving assistance, including meticulous editing and patient proofreading.

The
Last Days
of
John Lennon

Prologue

Around 11:00 o'clock on the night of September 27, 1982, I was entering the brownstone in which I lived on Willow Street in Brooklyn Heights, New York, when suddenly I felt a hand grip my shoulder. At the same instant, a voice near my ear sneered: "How ya doin', Freddie boy?" Startled, I spun around and found myself confronting a muscular blond man wearing jeans and sneakers. Thrusting his vaguely familiar face into mine, he growled, "We've been looking for ya." It took me a few seconds to place him; then I flashed, "Bob Greve!" He was a cop who moonlighted as a bodyguard for my former boss, Yoko Ono.

"What do you want?" I asked anxiously. Greve replied by yanking my arms behind my back and locking them inside handcuffs. Only then did he announce that he had a warrant for my arrest. As I stood there speechless with shock, I saw another man emerge from the shadowy stoop of the next building. Burly and mustachioed, Barry Goldblatt was easy to recognize. He was a plainclothes officer assigned to the NYPD's Career Criminal Apprehension Unit, who also moonlighted as a bodyguard for Yoko and Sean Ono Lennon.

Timidly, I asked to see the arrest warrant. Greve told me it was in his car. Then the two men cast nervous glances up and down the quiet, tree-lined block. As soon as they were assured that no one was watching, they hustled me across the street to a brown sedan and shoved me into the back seat. When I opened my mouth to protest, Goldblatt wrapped his fingers around by throat and hissed: "Shut up!"

I barely breathed as we drove across the Brooklyn Bridge and then threaded a maze of dark streets in the West Village. Finally, Greve parked the car in a deserted alley in the meat-packing district. Goldblatt turned to face me. Scowling menacingly, he announced that he and his partner were supposed to bring back John Lennon's 1980 journal to Yoko at the Dakota, one of New York's most famous apartment buildings. As soon as I understood what they wanted, I was relieved. Though I had taken the journal out of the Dakota more than a year and a half earlier, it was no longer in my possession. Explaining what had happened to it was a long story, but I was willing to tell it down to the last detail. Then I discovered that the cops didn't want to hear me.

"We don't believe you," Goldblatt snarled as he took a raincoat that was on the front seat and carefully wrapped it around one of his beefy hands. Grabbing me by the collar, he then began punching my face and chest. *"By the time we're through with you,"* he shouted, *"we'll either have the journal, or you'll be dead!"*

Frantic with fear, I kept screaming: *"I don't have the journal!"*

Nothing I said made any difference. Goldblatt kept punching me. Soon my body was throbbing with pain. After beating me for several minutes, Goldblatt's breathing grew labored, and I could smell the alcohol on his breath. Frozen with terror, I cowered in the back seat as Greve put the car in gear and drove out to the West Side Highway. The two men carried on a hushed conversation while driving north along the river. At one point I could make out their words. They were talking about shooting me in the head and dumping my body in the Hudson River. Even though I was terrified, I now began to feel like a player in a bad gangster movie.

Soon Greve pulled over to the side of the highway and dragged me out of the car. "Where's the journal, Freddie?" he demanded angrily. Once more I explained that I did not have what he was looking for. Ignoring what I had said, he pushed me up against the side of the car. Then he hit me in the gut three times, hard. As I doubled over in pain, he made me kneel on the grass. Suddenly I felt the muzzle of his gun at the back of my head. "This is your last chance to come clean," he intoned. "If you don't cooperate, I'll blow your brains out!" Tearfully, I kept insisting I did not have the journal. Twisting my head around to look at Greve, I saw him throw a questioning glance at Goldblatt, who was standing in front of me with a grin on his face. Suddenly, Goldblatt's smile dissolved into a frown. Grimly, he warned me that if I ever told anybody about what had happened, he would track me down and "finish the job."

That night as I lay on a jail bunk, I began to recollect the circumstances leading up to my ordeal. It had started three years earlier when I went to work for John Lennon at the Dakota. With my mind endlessly churning, I must have flashed on every experience I had with Lennon. Eventually I got back to the very beginning—the day I was hired as John's personal assistant.

1

Nutopia

When I first entered the service of John Lennon, I found it impossible to distinguish the bizarre from the merely eccentric. Everything was disconcerting, beginning with my place of employment, the Dakota Mansion. Blackened by a century of accumulated soot, this grimy antique appears less like a New York apartment building than like a backdrop for a horror movie—which is exactly how it was employed in *Rosemary's Baby*. Built like a German castle with a moat, the Dakota is surrounded on three sides by a massive black iron railing that at regular intervals sprouts the menacing head of a fierce-looking, bearded Neptune flanked by pairs of sea dragons. The cavernous entrance is guarded by a uniformed doorman posted in a bronze sentry box resembling an upright coffin; at night, it is barred by an enormous wrought-iron gate.

More unusual even than the building was the kind of thinking I learned inside this forbidding fortress. Over the front gate is an Indian head carved in stone and surrounded by the digits 1-8-8-1. To a casual observer, those numbers indicate the year in which the Dakota was built, but after I had spent a couple of years working for the Lennons, I would contemplate them in a very different light: Eight plus one is nine, the highest number, denoting change and spirituality; if you add 99 to 1881, you get 1980—the year in which John Lennon was struck down by a hail of bullets in this very spot; when your good luck runs out, eight-minus-one minus eight-minus-one equals zero.

I got my job with John Lennon through a family connection and a stroke of luck. My uncle, Norman Seaman, an impresario, produced Yoko's first avant-garde performances in New York in the early 1960s. Over the years he became her trusted friend and confidant. When Yoko married John Lennon, my uncle and his wife, Helen, became part of John and Yoko's inner circle. In the mid-seventies, Norman and Helen had an active role in the fight to stop the Nixon State Department from deporting John. As cochairperson of the Committee to Save John Lennon, Aunt Helen helped organize a nationwide drive to petition the government to grant John resident status, and Norman testified on John's behalf at his deportation hearing.

I met John and Yoko for the first time in the fall of 1975, shortly after John had won his battle to stay in the United States. The Lennons attended a performance by my father, Eugene, a pianist, and Uncle Norman, who told anecdotes and played violin, at the Biltmore Hotel. Afterward the Lennons took the Seaman family to the Russian Tea Room, where John and Norman entertained us with amusing anecdotes for most of the evening, while Yoko sat silently next to John, wrapped in a white fur coat. John was dressed conservatively from head to toe in black, but his tie was emblazoned with a portrait of a nude woman.

When my uncle told the Lennons that I was born near Frankfurt, the son of a Jewish-American father and a German-Protestant mother, John quipped that I was lucky to belong to both the Chosen People and the Master Race. He then began peppering me with German phrases he remembered from his early days in the red-light district of Hamburg with the Beatles, for instance: *"Um zweiundzwanzig Uhr müssen alle Jugendliche den Saal verlassen"*—At 10:00 P.M. all minors must leave the premises—and *"Ficken, lecken, blasen!"*—fuck, suck, blow. I complimented John on his excellent German pronunciation, and told him that I remembered hearing "Instant Karma" and "Give Peace a Chance" over the loudspeakers while riding bumper cars during the Octoberfest in my German hometown of Dillenburg. This prompted Norman to recall how he and Helen had been summoned by John and Yoko to their suite at Montreal's Queen Elizabeth Hotel in May 1969, arriving at the Lennons's bedside just in time for the impromptu recording session that resulted in John's famous pacifist anthem.

John and Norman reminisced about that chaotic session and gossiped about some of its famous participants: Timothy Leary, Dick Gregory, Murray the K, and the Smothers Brothers. I listened in awe. John was a riveting speaker. He had a marvelous sense of humor and talked in a lilting Liverpudlian drawl, punctuated by quick bursts of laughter. His eyes twinkled and darted to and fro behind thick spectacles. I found his exuberance highly contagious, and was puzzled by its apparent lack of effect on Yoko. Her impassive demeanor was slightly unnerving. She looked like she was sullen and bored. During a lull in the conversation I impulsively mentioned that two years earlier, Norman had taken me to see Yoko perform at Kenny's Castaways, a raunchy Manhattan music club. My remark elicited a frosty smile from Yoko. Norman quickly changed the subject. He told John and Yoko that my father had studied Egyptology in Berlin. This succeeded in arousing Yoko's interest, as she had recently become an avid collector of Egyptian artifacts.

She turned to my father—a former child prodigy who had studied piano at the Juilliard School of Music—and asked him how he happened to become interested in Egyptology. My dad explained that he had gone to Germany in the late 1940s to continue his musical training. While studying in Berlin, he had become fascinated with Middle Eastern music, and this led him to study Egyptology. My father then talked about his 1953 class trip to the pyramids, and how he found himself stranded in Egypt when he missed the return flight to Germany. He described working his way across the Middle East by giving music lessons as well as playing the piano in hotels, eventually winding up in Aleppo, Syria.

John suggested that my father should write a musical based on his life abroad. John also said that he and Yoko were planning to collaborate on a musical about their relationship, and that they were counting on Norman to some day produce "The Ballad of John and Yoko" on Broadway. My final memory of that remarkable evening was of John warmly shaking my hand, saying, "*Auf Wiedersehen.*"

Three and a half years later, Norman called Yoko on her forty-sixth birthday, February 18, 1979, and during the course of their conversation she told my uncle that John's assistant was leaving. She said that John wanted to know what nephew Fred was up to. When my uncle told her that I had recently been graduated with honors from City College of New York and was looking for work,

Yoko immediately demanded my date of birth. No sooner did she learn that I was born on October 10 than she decided that I was ideally suited to work for John, whose birthday was October 9.

I was summoned to the Lennon residence for a job interview the next day. In anticipation of this important event, I decided to read about the famous couple as well as reacquaint myself with John's music. Unlike many Americans of my generation, I did not grow up listening to the Beatles. Having spent the late sixties in Germany, where they were popular, but not the cultural phenomenon they became in the States, I was unfamiliar with most of their records. The only Beatle albums I remembered listening to were the *White Album* and *Abbey Road*, the group's final recording. I was also familiar with some of John's solo work, for instance, "The Ballad of John and Yoko." This song, which I had first heard a decade earlier in Germany, describes the difficulties the couple experienced in getting married.

John and Yoko had their first, fateful encounter at London's Indica Gallery on November 9, 1966. Yoko told John that she was an important New York avant-garde artist in need of a patron. Soon after their initial meeting, she gave John a copy of her book, *Grapefruit*—a collection of humorous instructional poems. Then she began bombarding him with notes begging for money, even threatening suicide unless he agreed to support her work. John, unhappily married to his meek art school classmate Cynthia Powell, was titillated by Yoko's aggressive pursuit. "I always had this dream of meeting an artist that I would fall in love with," he explained later. "Since I was extraordinarily shy, especially around beautiful women, my daydreams necessitated that she [Yoko] be aggressive enough to 'save me,' i.e., take me away from all this." One day when Cynthia went to visit her mother, John agreed to a "business meeting" with Yoko, who stayed the night. Soon they began to have trysts in the back seat of his Rolls-Royce.

Their affair remained clandestine until May, 1968, when John sent Cynthia away on holiday to Greece, and Yoko immediately moved in with him. In June, John and Yoko unveiled their first artistic collaboration, a "sculpture" consisting of two acorns symbolizing peace and simplicity which were buried as an "event" in the grounds of Coventry Cathedral. John's abandonment of his wife in favor of a controversial Japanese artist, known chiefly for bizarre stunts such as wrapping white sheets around a lion statue in Trafalgar Square, caused a tremendous scandal. The British media was full of invective against Yoko. But the more she was attacked, the more John rallied to her support. The scandal grew greater in October, 1968, when the controversial couple were arrested and charged with possessing cannabis. In November, Cynthia divorced John, and Yoko, still married to second husband Tony Cox, suffered a stillbirth. That same month, the scandal revived when John and Yoko released *Two Virgins*, whose cover showed the adulterous lovers stark naked.

On March 20, 1969, John and Yoko were secretly married at the British consulate in Gibraltar. They then flew to Paris, where Yoko told the international press: "We're going to stage many happenings and events together. This marriage was one of them." Their honeymoon proved to be the first of the promised happenings. When the Lennons announced that they intended to promote the cause of peace by spending a week in bed, most of the reporters who converged on the honeymoon suite of the Amsterdam Hilton Hotel believed that the newlyweds had intended to make love in public. The press was keenly disappointed when the so-called "bed-in" turned out to be a marathon bedside press conference. A second bed-in was staged in Montreal late in May.

In the early 1970s, the Lennons moved to New York and became active in the antiwar movement. But when the Immigration and Naturalization Service demanded John's deportation in 1972, John grew alarmed. Sensing that the Nixon government was out to get him, he backed away from his political activism and curtailed his involvement with the counterculture. In 1973, he and Yoko moved from a run-down loft in Greenwich Village into the posh Dakota. That summer, John began an affair with his and Yoko's secretary, May Pang. John and May soon relocated to Los Angeles, and thus began the period John called "The Lost Weekend"—which actually lasted eighteen months. He spent the first nine months drinking, raising hell, and recording an album of rock-'n'-roll standards with several musician friends, including Ringo Starr, Keith Moon, and Harry Nilsson.

According to the official version of the Lennons' separation, familiar to those who followed their story in the media, Yoko was John's spiritual guide and teacher, and his "banishment" was part of his "training." Once John had learned his "lesson," Yoko allowed him to move back into the Dakota. It was not until much later that I learned that it had been Yoko who pressured May to succumb to John's advances, because she could not be bothered with catering to John's voracious sexual appetite. The solution was to find him a concubine. May Pang went along reluctantly at first, but soon found herself falling in love with John. When John and May moved to the West Coast, Yoko took it in stride. She had become infatuated with David Spinozza, a studio guitarist who had been instrumental in helping her to record her latest album, *Feeling the Space*. With John out of the picture, Yoko was free to pursue her solo career while developing her relationship with Spinozza.

In the fall of 1973, Uncle Norman arranged for Yoko to play at Kenny's Castaways. It was here that I had first laid eyes on Yoko, who appeared onstage wearing black leather hot pants with knee-high, spike-heel black leather boots. The music was less impressive than Yoko's provocative outfit. While Yoko was strutting her stuff in New York, John was recording with the legendary producer Phil Spector in Los Angeles. During this period John was frequently seen drunk in public, and the press had a field day with him. Nonetheless, John made an impressive comeback in 1974 with *Walls and Bridges*, which yielded his first number-one hit single since the Beatles, "Whatever Gets You Through the Night." John cleaned up his act and moved back to New York with May Pang.

Meanwhile Yoko had embarked on a tour of Japan. Convinced that she was poised on the brink of rock stardom, Yoko had flown her whole band to her native country for a series of concerts. The tour was a critical and financial disaster. When Yoko realized that her career was going nowhere, she knew that she had to get John back. She accomplished this in much the same manner she had gotten him initially—by phoning him constantly, cajoling and threatening him until she wore down his resistance. Once she had John back, Yoko appointed herself John's business representative and assumed complete control of his money. She also became pregnant. At the age of forty-two, she gave birth to a son, Sean, on John's thirty-fifth birthday, October 9, 1975. By the end of the year Yoko had John in a viselike grip.

Four years after John had moved back in with Yoko, I was on my way to a job interview with the reclusive couple. As I made my way to the Dakota on Monday morning, February 19, 1979, I could barely contain my excitement. After stating my business to the guard at the gate, I stepped into the tunnel-like entrance archway. On the right-hand wall a wood and glass enclosure masked a staircase leading to a small vestibule that served as the reception area. Behind a desk sat the concierge, a tiny old lady who, as I came to learn, had a formidable reputation for guarding the privacy of the building's wealthy and often famous residents, such as Leonard Bernstein, Roberta Flack, Lauren Bacall, and Rex Reed. Threading a long and narrow corridor, I made my way to a marbled foyer with a black staircase and an elevator with doors at least twelve feet high. When the doors parted, I stepped inside the lavish, wood-finished cab, whose call buttons were encased in gleaming bronze. Slowly I rose to the seventh floor, feeling completely overwhelmed by the scale and grandeur of the building. When the doors opened, I found myself in a small foyer, facing another massive set of doors.

I was admitted into the Lennons' apartment by Aunt Helen, who had moved in after becoming Sean's nanny the previous year. The outer doors led into a small vestibule with a table and lamp, and another set of shiny wooden doors opened into the spacious entrance hall. Directly ahead was the Pyramid Room, which contained Yoko's small collection of Egyptian artifacts, including a glass-encased sarcophagus painted in colorful hieroglyphs. Helen led me down a long hallway decorated with children's drawings and with Yoko's odd-looking avant-garde artworks, mounted on Plexiglas pedestals. Our destination was an enormous, brightly lit kitchen.

The focus of this room was a large butcher-block table surrounded by four canvas director's chairs. The table was flanked on one side by a stove and oven range, and, on the other, by a sink, dishwasher, and Mountain Valley water cooler. In one corner were two small sofas with a table between them. My aunt told me to make myself comfortable and then disappeared. I sat down on one of the sofas, set against a wall. Behind me were several framed color Xerox snapshots of Sean, John, and Yoko. Above the photos there was a large mirror, and next to it were shelves of books and magazines bearing titles like *Eat Well*, *Better Living*, *Vegetarian Times*, *New Age*, and *Coevolution Quarterly*, as well as vitamin charts and posters of Yoko's art exhibitions. A few feet from where I sat stood a solid wall of white Formica shelving that supported an array of audio and video equipment, including a thirty-inch Sony television set, videocassette recorders, a McIntosh receiver, a tape deck, a turntable, and a thousand record albums.

I was still busy checking out the audiovisual hardware when the door flew open and John strode into the room, followed by Yoko. Startled, I jumped up and introduced myself. John had a beard and wore a denim cap tilted at a raffish angle. He came over and gently placed his hand on my shoulder. "Relax, Fred," he said, noticing how nervous I was. It was a reaction to which he was accustomed.

He asked what I had been doing with myself since our last meeting. I answered that I had been editor of the student newspaper at CCNY and had begun to do some free-lance writing. Looking somewhat worried, John asked me what kind of things I had written. When I told him I wrote music reviews, he shot back: "What kind of music?"

"Jazz," I answered quickly. A look of relief crossed John's face. He told me he had been worried for a moment that I would turn out be a Beatlemaniac. I was startled by his remark. It was the first hint I had that John was conflicted about his Beatle past. I decided to avoid the subject. I mentioned instead that I had recently had an article published in a jazz magazine about some newly issued rare recordings by John Coltrane. Suddenly growing animated, John told me that Graham Nash had once played for him Coltrane's avant-garde orchestral piece *Ascensions* while both of them were high on LSD. "That's one acid trip I'll never forget!" he chuckled, adding that he had hallucinated he was flying over African landscapes. At that point, Yoko gave John an impatient look. As if on cue, he excused himself and left the kitchen.

Getting down to business, Yoko explained that she needed someone to "look after John, do a little shopping, help John cook brown rice, and answer the fan mail, etcetera." I told Yoko that dealing with the fan mail would pose no problem, and that I could shop with the best of them—but that I lacked expertise in the rice department. Yoko said not to worry, John would teach me everything I needed to know about brown rice. She said it would be more or less a nine-to-five job, and asked me what kind of salary I had in mind. When I hesitated, she offered me one hundred fifty dollars a week. I thought it over for a moment, reminding myself that many people would give their right arm to work for John Lennon. I told Yoko that I was interested, but that the salary was a bit low. I was, after all, a college graduate. We settled on one hundred seventy-five dollars per week, and Yoko informed me that I would also have a one-thousand-dollar weekly expense account. I could not imagine spending such a large sum of money every week.

When I reported for work the next morning I met the assistant I was replacing, a Japanese photographer named Nishi. He had been working for the Lennons since 1975 and was now going back to Japan to get married. Nishi told me in halting English that he did not have much time to show me the ropes and that we had better get started right away. We went to a garage located in the basement of the adjoining apartment building, the Mayfair, where we picked up the "company car," a battered, dark-green Chrysler station wagon.

We cruised around the neighborhood, slipping and sliding in the snow—the car's wheels were completely bald and the brakes were sluggish—as Nishi showed me some of the places where I would be shopping. He introduced me to the shopkeepers, explaining that John and Yoko had charge accounts at a local pharmacy, hardware store, cleaner's, stationery store, and health food emporium. We also stopped by a nondescript brownstone. Nishi jumped out of the car and disappeared into the building, from which he soon emerged clutching a small brown bag. At first he was tight-lipped about this stop, but after some prodding he confided to me that the bag contained several Thai sticks.

"Only the best for John," Nishi exclaimed, explaining that this potent form of marijuana was John's favorite. When I asked him if I would be expected to buy drugs for John, he shrugged and said, "Only if Yoko-san asks you."

Our final stop that morning was the Nevada Meat Market on Broadway, where we bought a large quantity of calf's liver at eight dollars a pound. I was astonished when Nishi told me that it was for John's cats. He explained that John was extremely fond of his feline companions and that it was part of my job to see to it that they were well fed and groomed. As we made our way back to the garage, Nishi warned me that both John and Yoko could be difficult to work for and impossible to please. He told me that neither of them went out much and that when they did, it was usually to eat or to shop. As a result, there was a steady stream of deliveries to the Dakota,

and it was my job to see to it that these items were promptly unpacked and stored in one of the numerous spaces owned by the
family.

In addition to Apartment 72, John and Yoko owned the adjoining
apartment, 71, which they used as a warehouse, as well as a large
studio apartment on the second floor, a room on the eighth floor,
two large basement storerooms, and on the ground floor, Yoko's
office, Studio One.

Studio One had been for many years the office of the famous
scene designer Jo Mielziner, who had died of a heart attack in a cab
in front of the Dakota in 1976. Yoko had acquired the two-room
suite from his estate and converted it into the headquarters of the
family's business. Lennono was the name of the company, and Yoko
was its president. Although I had been hired as John's assistant,
Yoko was in dire need of an executive secretary, and by default the
job fell in my lap. I was responsible for sorting and answering the
mail, screening visitors, and acting as an intermediary between the
Lennons and the outside world. My post was a desk in Studio One's
front room, a modern, well-equipped office bathed night and day in
fluorescent light. One wall consisted of floor-to-ceiling file cabinets,
one hundred snow-white drawers in all, with a sliding ladder to
reach the topmost files; I found out that John had scrawled the
words "Helter Skelter" with a paintbrush on the wall before the files
were installed.

My desk stood next to the door, over which Yoko had hung an
Oriental white cloth with three black stripes. A spiritual smoke
alarm, it was supposed to drop whenever someone with "bad vibes"
passed beneath it. At another desk, facing the door, sat the Lennons' young accountant, Rich DePalma, who resembled Ringo
Starr.

Rich was forever bent over his desk, writing out checks, engineer-
ing complicated money transactions involving the Lennons' numerous bank accounts, and sometimes moaning in what seemed genu-
ine pain. He had to fight constantly to get Yoko's attention,
competing with the numerous astrologers, card readers, clairvoy-
ants, directionalists, and numerologists that she relied on for business advice.

A kitchenette connected the front office with a narrow passageway leading to Yoko's private suite—the inner sanctum, as we called

it—a dark room behind a white door. There was also a lavish, mar-bled bathroom and, at the other end of the small corridor, a second, more discreet entrance to Studio One. It was used by some of Yoko's mysterious visitors and business advisors with whom she consulted early in the morning or after hours.

At the end of my first day at the Dakota, Nishi gave me a quick tour of the building's labyrinthine maze of stairways and corridors. He warned that the ancient passenger elevators were excruciatingly slow and often an unreliable means of transportation; he had gotten into the habit of using the equally ancient, although somewhat faster, service elevator. Or, one could always run up seven flights of stairs along a narrow staircase that led directly to the kitchen service entrance, which bore a small brass plaque that read NUTOPIAN EMBASSY.

That evening I found myself having dinner with Helen and Sean in the kitchen, and I asked my aunt what the sign on the door meant. Helen explained that it was a reference to John's declaration during the deportation fight that he and Yoko were both ambassa-dors of "Nutopia," an imaginary "cosmic kingdom," and were thus entitled to diplomatic immunity. When I asked Helen about John and Yoko's absence from the dinner table, she told me that they did not always join her and Sean for meals. After dinner, I sat with Sean during his nightly ritual of watching cartoons before going to sleep. Sean's cute face was framed by shoulder-length black hair. He sat in front of the TV, laughing and commenting on the pictures. He ap-peared to have inherited some of John's wit and natural curiosity. Around 9:00 P.M. he fell asleep, and Helen carried him to his room down the hall. It had a small bunk bed, and across from the bed was a television set attached to a Betamax. Among the three-and-a-half-year-old's growing collection of videotapes were copies of *Yellow Sub-marine* and *Magical Mystery Tour*.

Helen usually slept with Sean in this room, or in an adjoining walk-in closet where she had a cot. When my aunt had first been hired to take care of Sean the previous year, Yoko had asked her and my Uncle Norman to move into Apartment 4 on the second floor; but Yoko continually forgot that the Seamans lived there and would invite other people to stay in the apartment. When the guests would arrive, Yoko would go into a little fit of giggly apology, and Helen would move into Sean's room, while Norman would have to go back to his house in Westchester. This arrangement proved so inconvenient that Norman finally moved out. Helen was too devoted to the child to leave. She reasoned that Sean needed her more than Norman did.

When Helen put Sean to bed, I figured it was time to go home. Suddenly, John came bounding into Sean's room, barefoot and clad in jeans and a black T-shirt. He kissed Sean good night and then asked me to join him for a cup of tea. I followed him into the kitchen and stood around awkwardly while he filled a kettle with water. He told me to have a seat at the butcher-block table. Then he sat facing me and lit a Gitane filter cigarette. It struck me as fitting that John—who came from Liverpool and had traveled around the world before finally settling down in New York—smoked a French cigarette whose name translated into "gypsy." He took a noisy drag, and as he exhaled a white cloud of smoke, he asked me how my first day had gone. Nervously, I described my morning drive with Nishi, mentioning that the Chrysler's brakes seemed to work only part of the time. John said that even though he had an "emotional attachment" to the station wagon, it might be time to replace it with a safer, more modern vehicle. He added he would ask "Mother" about getting a new "set of wheels." It took me a few seconds to figure out that by "Mother" he meant Yoko.

By now the water was boiling and John impatiently ground his cigarette into an ashtray, leaving the short, crumpled white stub smoldering feebly in a small heap of ashes. Leaping to his feet, he reached into a nearby cabinet, from which he retrieved a pack of Earl Grey tea. Ripping open the top, John plucked out two tea bags and deposited them in two mugs. He poured in the water and placed the mugs on the butcher block. Before sitting down again, he reached into the cabinet once more and snatched a container of Ovaltine, which he swiftly tossed into a nearby trash can. Noticing my astonished expression, John told me that Ovaltine was "junk," because it contained chemical additives. Lighting a fresh cigarette, he came back to the subject of the car.

John told me that he and Yoko had once gone cross-country in the Chrysler to visit a Chinese acupuncturist who lived in San Francisco. John explained that this doctor had helped him and Yoko withdraw from heroin, turning them on to a healthy macrobiotic diet and making it possible for Yoko to get pregnant, against all odds. I was astounded by his candor. Continuing his talk, John said that although he no longer adhered to a strict macrobiotic diet, he liked to eat wholesome, organic foods. He explained that he had a strong aversion to processed foods, avoiding anything that contained sugar or artificial sweeteners. Punctuating his speech with slight hand gestures, he then launched into a passionate lecture on the dangers of sugar and told me to keep an eye out for a book entitled *Sugar Blues* at Better Nature, the local health food store, where I would buy most of his food. He extolled this book by Gloria Swanson's former husband, William Duffy, because it exposed sugar as a "poison." He asserted that he did not want Sean to become a "sugar junkie," like so many other American kids who then grew up to be overweight, pimply teenagers. Raising his eyebrows and giving me a meaningful look, John said he expected "the staff" to set a good example for Sean. He disappeared for a moment, returning with a stack of Sean's framed pictures that had been stashed in a closet. He asked me to hang them in the kitchen, pointing out a few suitable spots.

Despite John's friendly and informal demeanor, I remained awestruck in his presence. Try as I might, I simply could not pretend that John Lennon was just a regular employer. He seemed like such a mythical figure that even having a simple chat with him in his kitchen became a surreal experience. When I mumbled something to the effect that I could not help being unnerved by the fact that to me he seemed larger than life, a walking icon of the sixties, John gave me a weary look. "Don't worry," he laughed. "That'll change."

2

Nowhere Man

The next morning, Yoko summoned me to the inner sanctum. The louvered blinds were drawn, but the ceiling of the dark, opulent space was painted to look like a blue sky with puffy cumulus clouds floating by. A Napoleonic camp bed occupied the center of the room. Miniature palm trees were scattered about. There was a small black upright piano in one corner and a massive Egyptian revival desk in another corner, near the windows onto the courtyard. Next to the desk were a white couch and matching easy chair, angled around a glass coffee table. Yoko sat in the white easy chair, with one of her legs tucked underneath her. She wore blue jeans and a black shirt. She said she wanted to go over a few things and asked me to take a seat on the sofa.

Talking in soft, urgent tones, Yoko said that most days she stayed up late making calls to the West Coast, England, and Japan. She said she did not need much sleep and would usually arise early in the morning even if she went to sleep at dawn. It would be my responsibility, she explained, to open up Studio One, which meant turning on all the lights, tidying up in the inner sanctum, and checking for messages on the Lennons' answering service. Yoko said she would phone first thing in the morning to let me know she was available to take calls. When Rich DePalma arrived, I would be free to go upstairs to the apartment and get John's instructions for the day. She told me that it was my job to "keep John happy" by buying whatever he asked me to get and by generally keeping him company when he was lonely or bored. If he made any unusual requests or behaved strangely, I was to bring it to her attention. She also warned me that all kinds of people would try to contact John, and she made it very clear that I was never to put anybody through to him without her permission. She specifically cautioned me about taking calls from John's teenage son, Julian, or the boy's mother, Cynthia, as well as from Paul McCartney and the other ex-Beatles.

When I returned to my desk, the phones were ringing off the hook. In fact, the phones in Studio One rarely stopped ringing. One of the first calls I took was from someone who organized conventions of Beatle fans around the country. I had more than a passing familiarity with these events because I had written an article about one of these "Beatlefests" for my college newspaper. The caller wanted John and Yoko to contribute something to an auction taking place at a Beatlefest that weekend; the proceeds were to benefit the Lennons' One to One Foundation. I promised to get back to him. After a while, Rich showed up, and I went upstairs to hang Sean's paintings.

John sat at the butcher-block table, drinking coffee and reading the *Daily News*. I eyed him nervously out of the corner of my eye while puttering self-consciously around the room, clumsily banging nails into the wall.

"Christ, Fred!" he suddenly exclaimed. "Will you please just fuckin' *relax*? You're making *me* tense." Mortified by John's sudden outburst, I stammered an apology. "It's okay," said John when he saw how upset I was. "It's just that life is tense enough for me as it is, and I don't need you to make it worse."

He then asked me to join him for a cup of coffee. I mentioned the call about the Beatlefest auction and John said that he would not mind contributing a Christmas card from Paul McCartney, but that he would have to "check it out with Mother." He dropped a few teaspoons of instant coffee into two cups and added boiling water and milk. He complained that he had run out of his favorite coffee, Brown Gold Instant, and asked me to buy some. I made a note on a memo pad.

John lit a Gitane and asked me to be sure and find out where Nishi bought the cigarettes. He showed me a large storage drawer filled with cartons of Gitanes, as well as Yoko's Sherman's Cigarettellos, and instructed me to always keep a large supply of both in stock. Next, he began gushing about a black female singer he had seen on *The Gong Show* doing a Stevie Wonder song.

As we were on the subject of music, I decided to ask John if he had any plans for future recordings. He threw me an annoyed look and stated matter-of-factly that for the first time in his life he no longer had a contractual obligation to record. He said that he had decided to retire from the music scene. I found this news extremely disappointing. John was smoking furiously now, carelessly flicking the ashes of his Gitane into a nearby ashtray. He said that he avoided listening to rock music on the radio because most contemporary rock was quite dreadful. If he happened to hear something he actually liked, he would only get frustrated for not having written it himself. John said he preferred listening to music he was "less connected to," such as classical or even Muzak.

Remembering that my father was a classical pianist, John asked me if I had taken piano lessons as a child. I told him that I had had a few lessons from my father. As John seemed very interested in my childhood, I filled him in on my family background. I explained that my father met my mother while they were both living in a Munich boarding house. They married in 1951, and I was born a year later. John recalled my father talking about his ill-fated trip to the pyramids during our evening at the Russian Tea Room in 1975, and he asked me about the eventual outcome of my dad's Middle Eastern adventure.

I told him that after founding a music school in Aleppo, my father had sent for my mother, who in the meantime had given birth to my brother, Matt. We were on a boat headed to the Middle East when, during a stopover on the Mediterranean island of Mallorca, my mother received a telegram from my father saying that he had to flee Syria because of a military coup and would meet us in Palma, the island's capital. John quickly interjected that he had once been arrested in Palma on a phony kidnapping charge involving Yoko's daughter Kyoko. I looked at John expectantly and waited for him to elaborate, but he simply told me to go on with my story. Resuming my narrative, I told John that after my father was reunited with my mother on Mallorca, we made a pilgrimage to the village of Valldemosa, where his idol, Frédéric Chopin, had spent the winter of 1838–39. My parents decided to settle down in this picturesque mountain village. We moved into a small Moorish castle, and my brother and I did our best to adapt to our new environment.

This was not easy, as we were the only non-Catholics in town. My playmates soon managed to convince me that I was doomed to rot in hell because I was a pagan. John cackled wildly when I told him this. He joked that he considered himself a "born-again pagan" precisely because he had become fed up with the dogmatism and hypocrisy of institutionalized religions.

After ten years on Mallorca, my parents decided to move to the U.S. in 1964. So at the age of eleven—without being able to speak a word of English—I was placed, along with my brother, in a predominantly black junior high school in Washington, D.C. By the time we moved to a suburb in Arlington, Virginia, six weeks later, my brother and I were fluent in English, largely as a result of watching television constantly. John erupted again in boisterous laughter at this point. He was even more amused when I explained that my mother had decided to move to Arlington because she had idolized JFK and wanted to be near Kennedy's grave, which was located in the nearby national cemetery. However, my mother soon soured on America, and, in 1967, my brother and I moved back to Germany with her. For two years we lived in Garmisch, an idyllic Bavarian resort situated at the foot of the Alps. We also lived in Berlin for a few months before moving back to my hometown of Dillenburg.

When I mentioned that I had played drums in a local rock band in 1970, John immediately asked me what kind of music we had played. He rolled his eyes when I told him that we mostly played songs by the Ventures, Jethro Tull and the Rolling Stones. I concluded my talk by telling John that since moving to New York in 1973, I had thoroughly immersed myself in the jazz and rock music scene as a listener and occasional critic. John asked me which clubs I frequented. I told him my favorite hangout was CBGB, a rock club on the Bowery that had launched such local groups as the Ramones, the Talking Heads, and Blondie. John said he was a fan of Blondie's lead singer, Debbie Harry. He also said he liked Donna Summer, Todd Rundgren, and the band Devo. He asked me to get Devo's remake of the Stones' classic "Satisfaction" for his jukebox. He jumped up and signaled me to follow him into an adjoining room. This was Sean's playroom, but it looked more like a playground, with its jungle gym, trampoline, rope ladder, and big hollow cubes full of every kind of toy imaginable. The floor was littered with Sean's latest doodles. John instructed me to always date them and make sure Sean had signed them—and if he had not, to sign his name myself—and then have them framed.

Sean's playroom also contained a massive Wurlitzer jukebox .

"Go ahead, take a look," John said proudly, while gathering up some of Sean's crayon drawings that were scattered about.

I examined the spectacular jukebox. John said it was a gift from the Record Plant, a studio where he had recorded in the early seventies. I could see that the jukebox was filled mostly with rock and roll singles from the fifties and sixties, including many classic recordings by Elvis Presley, Chuck Berry, Little Richard, Jerry Lee Lewis, and Buddy Holly, as well as a handful of more recent hits by Blondie and Donna Summer. John pushed a few buttons and Jerry Lee Lewis' "Great Balls of Fire" came blasting over the speakers.

Catching my surprised expression, he asked, "You've heard this before, haven't you?"

When I confessed that I had not, he gave me a horrified look.

"Jesus, Fred." John shook his head.

One of my regular assignments, he said, would be to keep the jukebox well stocked with his favorite singles, such as B. B. King's "The Thrill Is Gone," a song he had been dying to add to his collection. I promised to look for it at Bleecker Bob's, a record store specializing in oldies.

When we returned to the kitchen, John kept saying how surprised he was that I was so ignorant of the rock classics. He found it very amusing that three-and-a-half-year-old Sean, who grew up listening to his daddy's favorite tunes, was more familiar with the early rock and roll hits than I. In my defense, I pointed out that I had spent my adolescent years in Germany, where "classic" rock meant Hendrix, Cream, the Rolling Stones, and a handful of other British and American groups, including, of course, the Beatles. John gave me a baleful look and then asked me what kind of jazz I listened to. When I mentioned Ornette Coleman, John proudly told me that Yoko had done some recordings with Ornette. He rummaged through his record collection, complaining all the while that his albums were in such disarray that it proved impossible to find anything.

After searching further, John found the album for which he was looking, and placed it on the turntable. A few seconds later Yoko's voice could be heard, wailing and moaning softly as Ornette played short bursts of trumpet in the background. John explained that the piece we were listening to was a rehearsal for a concert at the Royal Albert Hall. He then flipped the record over and looked at me expectantly. Suddenly, a bloodcurdling shriek came blasting out of the speakers. I almost jumped out of my seat. Pleased with my stunned reaction, John flashed a wicked grin. Yoko's voice created a nerve-shattering screeching sound, backed by frenetic guitar riffs and propulsive drumming.

"That's me and Ringo!" shouted John over the music. I told him that it was an amazing piece and that Yoko's screaming vocals reminded me of a jazz saxophonist's freewheeling improvisation.

"Yeah," John nodded. "It's one of the best things she's done." He held up the album cover—a black and white photo of Yoko as a little girl gazing apprehensively past the camera—and bubbled: "Isn't she cute?"

Indeed, little Yoko in a black sailor suit looked adorable, but her large eyes were sad and forlorn. John told me that his first solo album, recorded at the same time as Yoko's, had a photo of him as a little boy. He kept rummaging through his records and seemed annoyed that he could not find it. He told me that extra copies of his albums were stored in the basement, and he asked me to find them and bring them to Apartment 71 next door.

The two basement storerooms looked like the warehouse of an old movie studio. Strewn about was a mind-boggling collection of objects, some of them junk and some priceless: John's large surreal oil paintings, collages, and drawings, gold Beatles records, posters, props and sound equipment from concerts, bongo drums and other percussion instruments, pianos, old furniture, damaged antiques, file cabinets, Sean's discarded toys, cardboard boxes and shopping bags full of fan mail, as well as a toilet seat and a bathtub with claw feet.

After a thorough search I managed to locate several cartons containing John and Yoko's recordings. I loaded them on a dolly and took the service elevator to Apartment 71, whose layout was similar to 72. There was a long entry hall decorated with old photos of John and mementos from the Beatle years. Branching off from the central corridor were numerous rooms filled to varying degrees with miscellaneous bric-a-brac and boxes of all sizes. Scattered around were many pieces of furniture, both modern and antique, stereo equipment—some of it brand-new and still in boxes—sound amplifiers, microphones, guitars, and an electric piano. I was thrilled at the sight of the instruments; they were the first evidence I had seen of any kind of musical activity involving John. Later I discovered that he occasionally used this room as a retreat if life in Apartment 72 became too hectic; from time to time he would get stoned here, and maybe even record a demo tape. A large adjoining room with a soiled blue wall-to-wall carpet was littered with Sean's old toys and John and Yoko's new clothes.

John and Yoko appeared to be compulsive shoppers, like kleptomaniacs who paid. Most of what they bought was neither needed nor ever used. Clothes, antiques, art, hi-fi equipment, electronic gadgets, pieces of furniture—all were delivered, stored away, and promptly forgotten. Apartment 71, part of Apartment 4, Room 265 on the eighth floor, the two basement storerooms, and even a portion of a West Side warehouse were jammed with John and Yoko's acquisitions. It never ceased to amaze me that the man who had penned the classic verse "Imagine no possessions" had become a slave to them. The only real value of many of these items was the mere fact they were owned by John Lennon.

I spent the rest of the day in Studio One going through the mail. I discovered there were file drawers full of unopened letters and unheard tapes. Rich told me that Helen, who was nominally responsible for answering the fan mail, had fallen hopelessly behind. Stacks of mail were routinely deposited into empty file drawers. As I began sorting through the piles of letters and tapes, I gradually began to distinguish between the various types of fan mail. There were requests for autographs; invitations to weddings, bar mitzvahs, and all kinds of parties; appeals for help by struggling musicians, many of whom sent along demo tapes of their work; requests for interviews; and business propositions.

Some of the fan letters were rambling, often incoherent or vaguely threatening notes from people who appeared to be drugged or delusional. A few of these fans imagined themselves to be characters from Beatle songs, for instance one who signed his name "Billy Shears," a character from the *Sergeant Pepper* album. It was hardly surprising that some of these strange letters had been sent by people confined to mental institutions.

Many fans appeared to be stuck in some kind of time warp, pretending the Beatles were still a unit. Fans even sent John letters addressed to his former bandmates. Once, John came across a letter from a Brazilian girl who wrote a postscript requesting that an enclosed second letter be forwarded to Ringo. John was not amused. "What does she think we are," he groused, "a messenger service?"

In addition to the fan mail, there was a steady stream of envelopes from a press clipping service, containing the latest media articles mentioning John and Yoko's names. These clippings were supposed to be sorted and then pasted into scrapbooks. For a while, one of my cousins had the job of bringing the scrapbooks up to date, but it had proved to be a hopeless task. John and Yoko's low profile during the past few years apparently had not diminished the worldwide media interest.

As 6:00 P.M. approached and Rich still seemed overwhelmed with phone calls and paperwork, I asked him how late he normally worked, and mentioned that Yoko had described my position as a nine-to-five job. The accountant laughed. He told me he often worked ten-hour days and predicted the same fate for me. As it turned out, he was right. Yoko's job description had been more than a little misleading.

I began my third day on the job by making the rounds of local stores, shopping for groceries and health foods, dropping off Sean's latest drawings at a frame shop, and buying some office supplies. On my way back to the Dakota I ran into John on Seventy-second Street. He was wearing jeans and a sweater, and had on black cowboy boots that made him look six feet tall. Peering at me from behind his prescription sunglasses, he asked cheerfully, "What you got?"

I fished a jar of Brown Gold Instant Coffee out of the shopping bag, and John looked very pleased. He thanked me for hanging Sean's artwork in the kitchen, but said they were a bit too high and asked me to lower them. He then instructed me to stop by the bedroom later in the day because he had a "special assignment" for me. By now, a few curious passersby had begun to stare at John, who scrutinized these strangers out of the corner of his eye. Suddenly, a chubby, buxom teenager who had been following John appeared next to him. "Hi, John," the girl cooed. "Wanna party?"

John threw her a withering glance and muttered under his breath: "Asshole, get thee behind me!" He then turned on his heel and abruptly marched off.

Looking bewildered, the girl asked me if I was John's friend. When I told her I worked for him, she begged me to give him a note and in the same breath invited me to smoke some pot with her. Mumbling with embarrassment, I collected my shopping bags and quickly strode into the Dakota.

That afternoon I made my first trip to the bedroom, where John appeared to spend most of his time. The entrance to this room was located in a corner of the foyer, near a large fireplace above which hung a colorful Japanese drawing depicting a geisha girl strumming a guitarlike instrument. On the mantel of the fireplace were life-sized busts of John, Yoko, and Sean; each had a different hat, and sometimes John changed the hats or tied scarves around their necks. A few feet from the fireplace an inconspicuous white door opened into a small, angled corridor decorated with photos of Sean, Julian, and Yoko's daughter, Kyoko. Entering this narrow passageway, I confronted a full-length mirror; then, making a left, I ran into a curtain of beads. At the other end of this short corridor was a second door, and beyond it lay the bedroom.

John's retreat appeared dark and messy. It reeked of stale air and smoke. John sat cross-legged on a queen-sized bed boxed between two old church pews that functioned as head- and footboards. Surrounded by books and magazines, he watched a soap opera on a giant Sony TV across the room. The radio was also on, emitting soft classical music. There was a large window, but its white shutters were closed. Strewn about were clothes, cassette tapes, empty coffee cups, and ashtrays overflowing with fat white cigarette butts.

As soon as John saw me, he asked me about the overweight female fan who had invited him to "party." He wanted to know if I had talked to her and cautioned me about "volunteering" information. "She'll try to sweet-talk you, bribe you, or even fuck you to get to me," he warned. "Don't be tempted!"

I was still digesting John's warning when he leapt up from the bed and rushed past me into the angled passageway that connected the bedroom with the rest of the apartment. I followed him into the Egyptian room. Seeing him strain to open a set of massive sliding doors, I pushed hard and practically fell into a dark room whose floor was covered with thick wall-to-wall black carpeting. John made a beeline for a door that opened into a large storage space. Inside were all of John's guitars from twenty-five years of performing and recording, piled helter-skelter in the closet. John pointed out his favorite, a black Rickenbacker guitar he had used during the Beatles' first tour of America. It still had the song list from the Shea Stadium concert Scotch-taped to it.

"If you're not too busy," he said, "could you make some room next door and spread them all out? It's not good to have them lying on top of each other like that." He asked me to call him when I was done and then took off for his room, leaving me standing there staring at the guitars. The sight of the old instruments stuffed carelessly into a closet filled me with great sadness, for it reminded me of what a prolific musician John had been before he disappeared from the music scene.

I cleared a room in Apartment 71 and began the painstaking job of moving all the instruments. When I was finished, the entire floor was covered with two dozen guitars in various shapes, sizes, and colors, two banjos, and a sitar. I called John on the intercom and within minutes he was standing next to me, ruefully surveying his guitar collection. We then went over to the boxes of albums I had brought up from the basement and proceeded to open them.

The first box contained a double album from the early seventies titled *Some Time in New York City*, which consisted of a studio session with the band Elephant's Memory as well as a live recording John had made with Frank Zappa and the Mothers of Invention. John said that he preferred the "live" side, because the studio recording included mostly political songs that were "pretty awful" in retrospect. "Back then I thought we were supposed to save the world," John mused. He explained that one of the songs, "Woman Is the Nigger of the World," was intended as a feminist anthem, but that it had been banned from the airwaves because the word "nigger" was considered inflammatory. "We simply circumvented the radio blacklist by advertising a number people could dial to hear the song. It was great!"

When we came across a box of John's *Plastic Ono Band*, the album he had been looking for previously, John declared that it was his best record by far because it was "all meat and no fat." He told me that his second album, *Imagine*, although commercially more successful, was inferior to the first record because it had been "wrapped in pretty musical effects" and "watered down" with strings. Of his last three LPs, *Mind Games*, *Walls and Bridges*, and *Rock 'n' Roll*, John said dismissively: "My records became more mushy as I became less centered." I was taken aback by his harsh self-judgment.

John soon tired of opening boxes and returned to the bedroom, but not before instructing me to take a handful of albums from each carton to the kitchen. He told me I could also keep one of each for myself. When I thanked him for the records and for the crash course in his discography, John said that eventually I was to assemble a complete set of his and Yoko's recordings, in chronological order. "I've lost track meself!" he said almost apologetically.

That evening, a small farewell party was held for Nishi in Apartment 4. Among those who attended were Helen; Rich DePalma; Rosa, the Spanish maid and sometime cook; and Mike Tree, the Lennons' gardener, who looked after the numerous plants scattered about the office and the apartment. He was a tall, thin, curly-haired, bespectacled man of approximately the same age as John. His last name was actually Medeiros, but John had gotten into the habit of referring to him as Mike Tree because he could never remember his real name. Everybody waited for John and Yoko to make an appearance, but they never showed.

By the end of my first week at the Dakota, I started to feel drained. That Friday, Nishi drove with me to Tillie's, an East Village store that sold chicken and vegetables grown on an organic farm in New Jersey. I met Tillie and her husband, the cheerful farmer couple who twice a week sold their organic produce to the townsfolk. The Lennons were regular customers. Nishi told me that I was supposed to pick up an organic bird and a few pounds of produce every Friday. Back at the Dakota, Helen told me that John and Yoko were out shopping at Bergdorf Goodman. I had a chance to catch my breath, watching cartoons with Sean in the kitchen while Helen cooked dinner.

When the Lennons returned from their shopping trip later in the evening, John "modeled" some of the many clothes he had bought, including a flamboyant satin nightgown. He acted goofy and clowned around with Sean. Before leaving for the weekend, I reminded John about the Beatlefest and asked him if he had made a decision about contributing Paul's Christmas card to the charity auction. It was Yoko who answered, saying that it would not be a good idea, as Paul might sue them. I thought this a puzzling notion, but said nothing more about it.

"It's probably a rip-off!" John snickered. He added that he very much doubted that any money raised at the auction would actually find its way to the One to One Foundation.

"Yes, I'm sure they only say it's for charity," Yoko immediately sec-
onded John's opinion, "but then they just keep the money."

John suggested that I should go anyway and asked me to take some
photos, because he had become curious about the exhibits as well as
the Beatles-related merchandise for sale. In particular, he asked me to
buy copies of *Two Virgins*. This recording—John and Yoko's first—
featured a notorious nude cover of the couple. John was embarrassed
by it.

"Just pretend you're a spy," he chuckled.

"Yes, don't tell them you work for us," Yoko added with a nervous
giggle.

I assured the Lennons that I understood perfectly, and promised to
be absolutely discreet.

After spending the weekend undercover at the Beatlefest, taking
photos and buying up copies of *Two Virgins*, I reported to work bright
and early on Monday morning. My second week on the job proved
no less frantic than the first.

On February 27, Fat Tuesday, John shaved off his beard. He marked
the occasion by visiting the office, hoping to pry Yoko away from her
endless meetings and perhaps go out for lunch. When he breezed into
Studio One, clad in jeans, a sports coat, and sneakers, I marveled at
how much younger he looked without the beard. While waiting
somewhat self-consciously for Yoko to receive him in the inner sanctum, he asked me to search through the files for some old correspondence with the British Society of Genealogists regarding an investigation of his ancestry. He wanted me to write the group a letter
requesting a progress report. My intercom extension buzzed and Yoko
told me to send John in to see her.

John marched resolutely into the inner sanctum, from which he
emerged a short while later looking like a whipped puppy. Yoko was
too busy to have lunch, and I could sense John's disappointment and
frustration as he hovered around my desk.

"Anything interesting to sign?" he asked.

I showed him a folder containing letters from fans who had sent
photos of John and the Beatles, requesting his autograph. John said
that as a rule he would fulfill autograph requests only if they included
a self-addressed, stamped envelope. I fished out a handful of qualify-

ing entries, and John bent over the desk and listlessly scribbled his name a few times.

"I'll be upstairs if anybody wants me," he said dejectedly on his way out.

John spent most of his days secluded in the bedroom, sometimes in the company of his three cats. Everything in the bedroom was oriented around the queen-sized bed, which was always covered with a colorful, handcrafted quilt. At its foot stood a massive chest full of *Playboy, Penthouse,* and *Oui* magazines. John also kept his marijuana there. John's reading encompassed all the news and gossip he could lay his hands on, including the *Times, Post, Daily News, Star, Globe,* and *National Enquirer, Newsweek, Time, Scientific American, Interview Magazine, Rolling Stone,* and, frequently, the British tabloids. He was fascinated by gossip relating to politicians and celebrities, and he was particularly interested in knowing which celebrities wore toupees. I was baffled by John's obsessive interest in the hair styles of the rich and famous—until I discovered that he had a growing bald patch on the back of his head.

Sitting up in bed, John could take in a panoramic view of midtown and beyond through a large window facing southeast, but most of the time what he saw was a makeshift curtain hanging in front of close-fitting white shutters. Between the bed and the window stood a Steinway spinet, and at a right angle to the piano, within John's easy reach, were a turntable, receiver, tape deck, Manhattan Cable TV control console, records, and tapes, all housed in a white Formica cabinet. Above the headboard of the bed was a shelf with a pair of black ADS speakers and whatever books John was currently reading. Like James Joyce, he often chose to read seven pages a night out of seven different books.

John read voraciously, often on weighty matters, as if he were researching some challenging subject. He was always giving me lists of books to purchase. Many dealt with religion, psychic phenomena, the occult, and especially death. Other favorite subjects were ancient history, archaeology, anthropology, and anything having to do with the sea.

A typical list of books included *Color and Personality* by Dr. Audrey Carger; *Rebel in the Soul* by Bika Reed; *The Secret Science* by Ischa Schwaller de Lubitz; *Bringing Down the Moon* by Morgana Adler; *A Slaver's Logbook* by Captain Theophilus Conmean; *The Anatomy of*

Swearing by Ashley Montague; *Working* by Studs Terkel; *The Manila Galleon*, a history of Spanish galleon trading between Manila and Acapulco; *Greek Homosexuality*, by H. T. Dover; and *How to Be Really With It*, by Father Bernard Basset, S. J.

On the ceiling above the bed, John had mounted a huge, round mirror. An oversized TV set occupied another part of the room. John had bought the set in Japan because it had a giant screen unavailable in the U.S. Being extremely nearsighted, he liked big screens. For hours on end, day in, day out, John would sit on his bed with the television on, flipping the channels. He was not particular about what he watched, but he had his favorite shows, like *Dallas*, *Three's Company*, and *The Tonight Show*. Even when he did something else, the TV would remain on with the sound turned off. As the images bubbled silently in the background, Lennon would pore over books and magazines, simultaneously listening to radio stations that played Muzak versions of his own songs.

Most days, John arose with the sun and quietly left the bedroom, marching through the angled corridor and along the main hallway that snaked through the apartment to the kitchen at the other end. A few feet from the table where John took most of his meals were several small shelves and cabinets filled with brown rice and other natural grains and cereals, honey, instant coffee, Twinings English Breakfast Tea, and Celestial Seasonings herb teas. Also nearby was a gigantic refrigerator, well stocked with fish and chicken, fruits and vegetables, yogurt, raw milk, and fruit juices.

John would spend the early morning in the kitchen, having breakfast—often shredded wheat bathed in raw milk—smoking, reading the paper, and writing memos telling me what he wanted done. A typical note would begin with a star drawn at the top and the heading "*V. Important.*" Each item would be numbered: "1. Put legs back on kitchen chairs 2. Meow Mix (hard) 3. Canned cat food (no kidney, no liver) 4. Art of Seeing (Aldous Huxley) 5. Honey Candy 6. Has portable vacuum cleaner been fixed? (ask Rosa) 7. Portable TV trade-in? 8. I have a record to be transferred to tape (ask me) 9. No more Procter & Gamble soap for kitchen, etc., only organic soap (They use it on Sean) 10. Get me some "slides" to hold hair back out of face & hair clips & rubber bands (for hair) 11. Yesterday NO SUNDAY NEWS: Today NO PAPERS AT ALL—Find out why we were chosen!" Sometimes these notes consisted entirely of a food shopping list.

John was extremely particular about what he ate, and he insisted I
follow his instructions to the letter. "Don't improvise," he once wrote
me after I deviated from his list. "Just PLAY THE NOTES!"

John had become preoccupied with his weight, and obsessional
about his diet. After a lifetime of ingesting food and drugs more or
less indiscriminately, he had finally managed to curb his unhealthy,
often self-destructive appetite. Once a robust man, tending toward
overweight, he was now so thin that his face looked hollow and
sunken in, even though it was concealed by a full beard. Standing
five-feet-ten, he weighed less than 140 pounds. John's appearance was
deceptive, however, for he possessed boundless energy. Naturally restless and high-strung, even when he sat stock-still in front of the TV,
nervous energy poured off him, like liquid oxygen off a rocket.

Because Yoko often went to bed around dawn, the early morning
was a quiet, contemplative time for John, a brief period when he was
sovereign in his domain. But his sovereignty in the kitchen never
lasted long. Yoko did not seem to need much sleep. Soon after John
had had his breakfast and coffee and a few cigarettes, she would be up
again, zinging around the house, talking on the phone, barking orders. Then Sean and Helen would show up for breakfast and were
often joined later in the morning by Sean's playmates. His favorite
was a little blonde girl nicknamed Mimi, whose mother, Marnie Hair,
became a frequent visitor.

As the morning advanced and traffic in the kitchen increased, John
would once again retreat to the bedroom. If the maid was cleaning his
room, he would cool his heels in the White Room, a large living room
overlooking Central Park. A white grand piano, the one on which
John had recorded "Imagine," dominated the room. On it were displayed various family snapshots: Yoko as a little girl; her mother and
father; John wearing short pants, straddling a bicycle when he was a
boy in Liverpool. White sectional sofas on white wall-to-wall carpeting faced each other across a chrome and glass table, and a matching
white easy chair sat opposite a window overlooking Seventy-second
Street. When John slept or watched television late at night, Yoko
would sometimes sit there and look out the window while talking on
the phone. There were several white telephones. The only color came
from a large fig tree with ferns around its base, creating an island of
green in the all-white decor. John liked to sit under this eight-foot-
high plant and gaze out at Central Park. When Rosa had straightened

up the bedroom, John would resume his routine of reading, watching TV, and listening to soft music or talk shows on the radio. Generally, he would emerge from the bedroom only for meals.

Most mornings I would get a call from John, summoning me to go over his agenda. As he would give me my instructions I would get an idea of his mood. One of the most unnerving aspects of his behavior was its unpredictability. One day he would be upbeat and witty, the next sullen and withdrawn. He oscillated between supreme self-confidence and grave self-doubt. When he was in a bad mood, he was highly irritable: the slightest grievance could provoke a stinging rebuke. At times like these, he was best left alone.

Yoko, too, was subject to erratic mood swings. She seemed to possess two basically contradictory personalities. A demanding and impatient boss, she was often aloof, abrasive, and condescending. Occasionally, however, she would display a sweet, charming, and even flirtatious character.

On Ash Wednesday, I found her sitting at Rich's desk in the outer office. She wore a black silk blouse with the top buttons opened, revealing her ample cleavage. She was on the phone, ordering someone to buy gold. When she put down the phone, I said, "Good morning," gazing at her expectantly.

"Yes, yes, good morning!" she said impatiently. Her manner was brusque and intimidating. "Look, I'm really upset about Richie. I don't know what we're going to do!" She asked me to call the accountant at home, but when I did, there was no answer. I knew that Rich occasionally bought gold and silver for Yoko, and I gathered that she was angry because she had to do this job herself. Next, she asked me to call Marlene Weiner, one of the psychics she relied on for business advice. While Yoko talked to Marlene, the intercom buzzed. It was John.

"Mother busy?" he asked in clipped tones. I threw Yoko a questioning look. She shook her head emphatically and whispered that I should tell John she was on an urgent overseas phone call. John asked me to ask her to buzz him in the bedroom as soon as she was free. He then reminded me about reactivating the investigation of his ancestry. When I told John that I had thus far been unable to locate the previous correspondence with the British Society of Genealogists, he snapped: "It's in the bloody files, okay?"

I had already spent several hours combing the files without success, and I asked him if he knew where in the files the correspondence might be found. This question only increased his irritation. "How the hell am I supposed to know?" he exploded. "Ask Mother, or ask Rich, or Helen or whoever."

As soon as Yoko got off the phone, I told her that John wanted her to call him. She picked up the intercom and I overhead her complaining that Rich was out and that she was in the middle of some difficult business transactions and could not possibly get away for lunch. When she put down the phone, she told me that John was very upset with me for not finding the old correspondence. "You better do something about it," she said nervously.

I buried my head in the files. Unfortunately, they were in complete disarray. Apart from a handful of drawers with recent business records and correspondence, they were cluttered with old fan mail, records and tapes, newspapers and magazines, clothes, and even Sean's toys. Finally, I came across a file containing correspondence from the late sixties, including a folder labeled: *J. L. ANCESTRY.* I was beside myself with joy. Inside the yellow manila folder was the old correspondence with the British Society of Genealogists. I quickly drafted a letter requesting that the investigation into John's ancestry be renewed. When I read John the letter, he asked me to make only one change: He wanted the genealogical sleuths to determine not only the age, but also the cause of death of his ancestors.

At the end of my second week on the job, Friday, March 1, 1979, I looked forward to a night out with some friends. But when I delivered Tillie's organic bird and vegetables to the kitchen that evening, John unexpectedly invited me to stay for dinner. Helen and Sean could not be with us, because Sean did not feel well. John asked me to cut up the chicken while he set the table for three. Yoko sat at a white desk at the other end of the kitchen, talking staccato Japanese into the phone. When she got off the phone, John made small talk about what color the new car should be. Suddenly, he looked pointedly into my eyes and asked, "Why do you think we hired you?"

I was startled by this unexpected question, but as I searched my brain for an appropriate answer, I realized he meant it rhetorically. John continued, saying that it was not mere happenstance that had brought me to the Dakota—it was fate. Now Yoko jumped into the conversation and told me how amazed she and John had been when they learned that my birthday was October 10, a day after John's.

They had known right away that I would be perfect for the position of assistant.

John explained further that the actual reason I was hired was not just because my birthday came a day after his own—which meant that we were highly compatible from an astrological point of view—but also because of my name. I assumed he was making a reference to the fact that I was related to Norman and Helen, whom John and Yoko regarded as Sean's surrogate grandparents, but John meant something else entirely. He pointed out that my first name was the same as his father's, Freddie Lennon, who had been a *seaman* all his life—he also mentioned in this context that "Yoko" in Japanese meant "ocean child"—and revealed further that he, too, had an uncle named Norman. Finally, John stated that there was undoubtedly an element of predestination in my working for him and Yoko.

Taken aback by this convoluted explanation, I glanced at Yoko, who calmly munched on a piece of chicken while observing John and me with cool detachment. She must have noticed the puzzled look on my face because she elaborated now on John's explanation. She pointed out that my first and last names combined had a total of ten letters, further proof that I was a "10." John interjected that it was a "good number." He said he was a "9"—a number denoting "spiritual-ity"—and went on to provide examples of instances where this num-ber had played a significant role in his life. I remembered that he had also used the number in several song titles, such as "Revolution 9" and "#9 Dream." I did not quite know how to respond to John and Yoko's talk of predestination, astrology, and numerology. Before I could think of anything to say, John told me about a book by Noël Coward's assistant, who had written of a prophecy that he would get a job with Noël Coward before midnight on his birthday. This had come to pass, and the assistant later became Coward's friend and biographer.

"Every autobiography," said John, "has some example of a predic-tion that comes true!"

He then asked me about my long-range plans. When I mentioned that I was interested in pursuing a graduate education in journalism, he scoffed at the notion of going back to school. He told me that if I was serious about becoming a journalist, I should simply write. School, John insisted, would be a step backward, a "retreat to the safety of a familiar institution." He said that I could learn more by working for him and Yoko, which would provide me with an invaluable "second education." If I learned to "go with the flow," John explained, I would have an extraordinary opportunity to acquire new knowledge and tap into a "cosmic energy." "Now you're in our energy aura," he said. "When you leave us, you'll experience an energy vacuum."

It appeared to me that the great Lennon himself was living in something of an energy vacuum—in isolation and creative stagnation in the gothic tomb of the Dakota. Still, I was excited by the thought that there might be something to astrology and numerology. I was even prepared to entertain the possibility that fate had brought me to the Dakota. When John felt upbeat and talked passionately about esoteric subjects, he could be extremely persuasive.

When John wasn't being enthusiastic, he relished playing the role of the retired superstar who has seen and done it all. More than once he told me that he felt an obligation to pass on some of his accumulated wisdom. He loved to lecture about spiritual matters, health and nutrition, the latest scientific discoveries, current events, celebrity gossip, and any number of other subjects about which he was an expert. I never ceased to be amazed at the breadth of John's knowledge. He knew more about everything than anybody I had ever met and I could not help becoming his acolyte. Indeed, I could hardly believe my luck at having John Lennon as my guru.

John was not a devotee of any philosophy: he studied them all, absorbing useful bits of knowledge from every school of thought, Western and Eastern. His restless, inquisitive mind liked to believe everything until it was disproved. Many of the ideas he tried on me were over my head, but he always suggested books that would bring me up to the mark. Unfortunately, my demanding work schedule left me little time for intellectual pursuits. All the same, I appreciated the way John shared his insights.

Besides talking up a storm and writing me daily memos, John scribbled entries in a New Yorker Diary that he always kept at his bedside. I first became aware of John's journal when he showed me a cartoon depicting a scene of family pandemonium—two parents and several kids in a cluttered room. John had doctored the drawing so that the figures were caricatures of Norman, Helen, and my cousins. The caption read: "The Seamans at Home." I howled with laughter. Suddenly turning serious, John asked me if I had ever kept a journal. I told him that I had written a diary on and off since my early teens. He gave me a piercing look, as if he were trying to ascertain something, and said that I would be well advised to keep up this practice. Actually, I had resumed my journal-keeping from the first day I stepped into the Dakota and I suspected he knew I was taking notes.

One afternoon John asked me to stop by the bedroom to pick up a copy of the *Sunday Times* Book Review section, in which he had circled the titles of several books he wanted me to buy. When I walked into the room I noticed that his diary lay open on the piano. It was full of cartoons which John had altered in a clever manner. The handwritten entries surrounding the illustrations suggested a colorful catchall log of mundane details of domestic life, philosophical ruminations, spiritual conflicts, poems, song fragments, sexual yearnings, and dreams. John appeared to have a remarkable ability to tap into his subconscious mind. Many of the entries consisted of minutely detailed descriptions of his dreams.

People and places from his Liverpool childhood; his father and mother, Julia; his Aunt Mimi; and particularly the Beatles appeared to figure prominently in John's dreams, suggesting that scenes of his spectacular and often traumatic life replayed themselves in his mind like a complicated fugue—elusive, always a beat away from resolution.

To an extent, John Lennon was held hostage by his enormous fame—not only because of his stature as the premier Beatle, but because he had chosen to live in the most conspicuous building in one of the most populous of cities. Oddly, more fans came to the Dakota when Paul McCartney was on tour or if some event brought the other ex-Beatles into the limelight. It was as if the fans still regarded the Beatles as a unit, a singular presence, and whenever one did something, it stimulated interest in the others. Crowds of fans came and went at the Dakota's front gate like so many flocks of pigeons, and John was always in a state of agitation when he had to confront them. Many times, rather than risk contact, he would simply stay inside. He even wore his paranoia like a badge of honor. "Paranoia," John liked to say, "is really a heightened state of awareness."

Paradoxically, John's seclusion inside the Dakota did not make him less vulnerable. Nobody was guarding the king. Since John had given himself over to the whims of his wife, he was at her mercy for his protection. He did not have a bodyguard, though Sean often had several. Even in his own apartment, John was in no way secure. Fans frequently tried to sneak into the building to find John. Fortunately, most people who attempted to reach the Lennons' apartment were intercepted by the Dakota's staff. As soon as strangers—particularly teenagers—were spotted in the building, Studio One would be alerted, and a "fan alarm" allowed John to cower behind locked doors.

John knew that the building's staff was sometimes no match for his most resourceful fans. For instance, one particularly persistent fan, an obese amateur photographer named Paul Goresh, gained access to Apartment 72 by posing as a video technician. Brandishing a phony work order and wearing fake uniforms, Goresh and an accomplice bluffed their way into the bedroom. When John stumbled upon the intruders, he almost had a seizure.

Another time, two young boys managed to reach the main entrance to Apartment 72 without being detected and rang the bell just as John walked past the entrance hall. He opened the doors impulsively, thinking that it was Yoko because she had forgotten her keys as usual. I was at the far end of the hallway, hanging some of Sean's latest drawings, when I heard John's voice ring out in surprise. Rushing to his side, I was stunned to find two ten- or eleven-year-old kids gaping at him. One of the boys politely asked if they might have a word with John. I was amazed when John invited them into the apartment. We all trooped to the kitchen and I served the boys some apple juice while John made tea. He must have seen that the two youngsters were quite sincere, and, not having anything better to do, he decided to spend some time talking to them. The two intrepid fans were highly intelligent and amazingly articulate for their age.

As I had some work to do elsewhere in the apartment, John cheerfully waved me along, saying that he would look after his "guests." When I returned to the kitchen a while later, one of the boys asked John what it was like to grow older. John explained to his rapt audience that life was like a movie that just goes on and on, and that the older one gets, the more it all starts to make sense. At that very moment I bent over to pick something off the floor, and a pair of sunglasses flew out of my shirt pocket. Without missing a beat, John amended his answer, winking in my direction, "Or, sometimes, you just get dumber."

Then, in response to a question about death, John theorized that one's life would simply flash by in reverse chronological order. In death, explained John, the movie of one's life is played backward, with the more recent "reels" shown first. He then gave the boys some suggestions for books to read that might help them find more answers. John spent close to an hour talking to the two kids, and it was obvious that his lecture had had a profound effect on them. He was every inch the brilliant ex-Beatle they had dreamed of meeting. But when the boys asked if they might call on him again, John quickly retreated to the bedroom, leaving me to explain that he was not in the habit of "hanging out" with his fans.

John rarely saw anyone outside of the family and staff, and he took virtually no phone calls, except over the intercom. When he did use the phone, it was always with the conviction that the FBI was listening. Thus, his insulation from the outside world seemed nearly complete. In a sense, Yoko hired me as a go-between and to give John some distraction so that he would not bother her. If he wanted something, he could ask me to get it for him. If he had something on his mind, he could say it to me. If he got mad, he could get mad at me. It did not take me long to see that John and Yoko's relationship was anything but the mythical romance they had fashioned for the media. Slowly, I came to understand that John and Yoko did not have much of a relationship.

Yoko lived at a frantic pace—submerging herself in round-the-clock meetings in her office with a steady stream of visitors during the day, and spending much of the night on the phone. John lived in slow motion, killing time in the bedroom, the White Room, and the kitchen. He lived upstairs. She lived downstairs.

As a result, all communications within the confines of the Dakota were conducted in a most peculiar fashion. There were telephones everywhere, each connected to an elaborate intercom system that enabled Yoko to keep tabs on John at all times, as well as give orders to the staff and generally supervise everyone from her headquarters, Studio One. But if John wanted to talk to Yoko, he would sometimes call me first, to ask if she appeared busy, because if she had been on the phone or tied up in a meeting and refused to talk to him, or if she were brusque with him, it might ruin his day. Calling me first was his defense. It made me sad, maybe even a little angry sometimes, that the great John Lennon was in the humiliating position of having to call me, a virtual stranger, to ask if his wife was "available" for lunch or a chat on the phone.

Occasionally when John became bored or restless, he would visit the office downstairs, read some fan mail and sign a few autographs, maybe have lunch with Yoko in the inner sanctum, or go out to a nearby café, La Fortuna. If Yoko seemed busy, he would often hang around the office for a while, hiding his frustration and disappointment with a stream of witty chatter. If it was a nice day and he felt like stretching his legs, he might take a short walk to the corner newsstand and pick up some fresh reading material or go to a nearby Japanese restaurant for lunch. Before leaving the building, he would often ask me to make sure there wasn't a gaggle of fans hanging around. One or two he could handle. He would manage to keep them at bay with a few well-chosen words, something witty and perhaps even mildly condescending. As he walked along Seventy-second Street, John's eyes would dart this way and that, anxiously scrutinizing passersby, trying to anticipate the moment when he would be recognized and approached by strangers. John hated to be caught off-guard. It was one reason why he chose to spend most of his days secluded inside the familiar environment of the Dakota.

Once, trying to impress upon me the need to keep him insulated from casual contact with the outside world, John took me aside and said: "It's like a bloody chess game, don't you see? I'm the king, and every encounter with pawns weakens me. You're my knight, and it's your job to protect me from such encounters by acting as an intermediary. As far as the public is concerned, I'm a phantom. I only exist in people's imagination. The less I'm seen, the more power I have."

I was beginning to see how John's enormous fame and his seclusion in the Dakota made it impossible for him to have normal relationships. So he always returned to isolation, hoping Yoko would spend a little time with him, maybe love him a little again.

After less than a month of working at the Dakota I could not escape the depressing realization that, although he owned more space in the building than any of its other wealthy tenants, John Lennon lived like a prisoner. He had not been kidnapped; he had committed himself voluntarily. The doors were not locked. He could walk out anytime. But he was a prisoner, not only of the massive stone walls, but of his wife, his staff, his fears and superstitions. Sometimes John did his time cheerfully, sometimes moodily. Sometimes he even lashed out at those around him, seemingly infuriated by his captivity. Perhaps some would argue with my use of the word "imprisonment," but John eventually said as much in the lyrics to one of his songs, "Watching the Wheels": "I'm just sitting here doing time."

3

Mother Superior

Yoko lived on the telephone. She apprehended the world through the medium of high-speed hookups in Pennsylvania, giant switching stations up along the Hudson, zinging her signals up into space, where they bounced off satellites and were fed around the world. She was on the phone when I arrived in the morning, on the phone when I left at night, and often on the phone to me when I got home. She talked all night sometimes, sleeping fitfully and irregularly, waking John with insistent whispering in the dark. In the daytime, I heard her myself as I waited for her attention, chattering Japanese or equally cryptic English: "Yes, yes, good idea...and also...But why?...No, no...or better yet...and the other thing is..."

The telephone. John derided it as "mind candy." Yoko embraced it as the principal device for filling the void in which they found themselves. It functioned as a protective barrier between her and John, as a drug, a symbol of her power and importance. Nothing interfered with her calls: not meals or meetings or a massage. Sometimes she lay on a rug on the floor and Kimi, the masseuse she shared with John, walked on her back while she chattered into a phone, a soldered link in the Bell system. And who was she talking to? Tarot card readers, lawyers, accountants, interior decorators, real estate agents, members of her staff, psychics, sycophants, art dealers who wanted to sell her something because she had all of John's money to spend.

One of her frequent phone partners was a Los Angeles disc jockey and tabloid journalist, Elliot Mintz. Like Yoko, Mintz was an insomniac, and he was always ready to lend an ear to Yoko's late night ramblings. He was paid a substantial retainer for his services, which included public relations advice and troubleshooting. During his occasional visits to the Dakota, Mintz would also conduct inventories of the Lennons' possessions, as well as walk around the office and apartment with impressive-looking antisurveillance equipment, searching ostentatiously for hidden electronic listening devices. He was expert at fueling the Lennons' paranoia, specializing in cloak and dagger operations that he referred to as "capers."

One rainy afternoon, Mintz called me from the Plaza Hotel and whispered conspiratorially: "I have a special assignment for you." Then he ordered me to go to Grand Central Station, from where I was to call him at precisely 1:00 P.M. to receive further instructions. It took me a while to find a cab. By the time I called Mintz it was 1:15 P.M. Somberly, he informed me that because I was late I had missed a "control" call. He said he would have to wait for a call before we could proceed, instructing me to call him at precisely 1:30 P.M. When I did so, Mintz ordered me to proceed to F.A.O. Schwarz, the Fifth Avenue toy store. There I was to call him from the second phone of a phone bank on the second floor of the store.

"And, Fred," said Mintz dramatically, "please make sure that you're not being followed!" To shake any possible "tail," he suggested taking the subway and changing cars several times just before the doors closed.

I almost laughed out loud. It seemed to me that Mintz had been watching to many spy movies. I decided to walk the fifteen blocks to F.A.O. Schwarz. When I reached the toy shop, I promptly located the designated phone booth and called Mintz.

"Are there any people around?" he asked. I told him there was an older man a few booths down, but that he was there before I arrived and could not have tailed me. Mintz seemed pleased that I was getting the hang of it. He instructed me to reach under the plastic tray beneath the phone and remove the object that was taped there. When I followed his instructions, I found myself holding a small white envelope. Mintz explained that inside the envelope was a key to a locker in the Grand Central terminal. The locker, I was told, held a plastic bag with a gift-wrapped box. I was to remove the box, but leave the plastic bag inside the locker. Then I was to rush back to the Dakota and give the box to Yoko, who was anxiously awaiting its delivery.

"What's this all about?" I wondered as I walked down Fifth Avenue engulfed by a mass of people. Perhaps Mintz had obtained an exotic antique object for Yoko, something precious and rare that had been illegally smuggled into the country. By the time I reached Grand Central Station, my nerves were tingling. Nervously, I opened the locker and removed a small, gift-wrapped box. Hopping a cab back to the Dakota, I rushed breathlessly into the inner sanctum and triumphantly presented the box to Yoko.

"Where have you been?" she asked sharply.

When I reminded her that for the past two hours, I had been carrying out Mintz's "special assignment," Yoko looked puzzled.

"What's that?" she asked, pointing to the box.

"It's from Elliot," I said.

She told me to open it. Bursting with curiosity, I tore off the gift wrapping and opened the small cardboard box. Inside were several small bottles containing GH3 Formula "rejuvenation" pills. Yoko held out her hand and asked for two of the pills. When I gave them to her, she gulped them down. "I don't know," she mumbled dubiously. "They don't seem to work."

Yoko had read about this drug in one of John's gossip tabloids. It was not approved by the Food and Drug Administration and was difficult to obtain because its distribution was illegal in most states. Delighted to be of assistance, Mintz devised ingenious, as well as costly, cloak-and-dagger operations to supply Yoko with this substance. It was, however, readily available in Rumania. When Yoko learned that my grandparents would be traveling through the Balkans, she asked Norman to arrange for them to smuggle the controversial youth serum into the United States. My grandparents reluctantly obliged.

Yoko fretted constantly about her health and obsessed about her skin, expressing the fear that it was "dying." Terrified of growing old, she was always on the lookout for a miracle drug that would arrest the aging process. For instance, she had heard that mothers who eat the placenta regain their youth. Not one to miss a possible cure for the onslaught of advancing time, Yoko had ordered that the placenta from Sean's birth be frozen. But a maid accidentally left the refrigerator door open, and as a result the rejuvenating tissue had to be discarded.

Although Yoko had told me that she would usually be upstairs when I arrived in the morning, I discovered that she was just as likely to be in her office, her glass table cluttered with cups and plates of leftover food. Often she slept on her Napoleonic camp bed. Sometimes she would spend the early morning in the bathroom, whose marble sink was littered with vitamins, bee pollen pills, garlic and grapefruit extracts, GH3 "rejuvenation" pills, and all kinds of other medicines and potions—and which had a phone by the toilet. Yoko was always gobbling large doses of the herbal laxative Swiss Kriss. She also had a disquieting habit of vomiting without warning, as if it were the most natural thing in the world. She would run to the bathroom and throw up, then resume her meeting or phone conversation.

When not on the phone, Yoko spent much of her time puttering around the office. One afternoon late in February, she approached my desk and stared absently in my direction. Frowning, she announced: "My stomach is empty." Pausing, she said, almost as if she were thinking aloud: "What are we going to do about it?" When I offered to get her something to eat, she smiled and thanked me for being so "thoughtful." Then she mumbled, "What do I want?" She briefly pondered this question and then ordered a tuna sandwich on pumpernickel bread from the local deli.

Yoko wolfed down the food, scooping up forkfuls of tuna salad without eating the bread. In between bites she boasted of multiplying John's wealth. Yoko said that after she had "kicked him out," John did "very poorly." She had felt responsible for him and so had taken John back. He had almost no money left, but when she took charge again, she managed to quadruple his assets within four years as well as reduce ten pending lawsuits to a mere four, which were in the process of being resolved. She bragged that she had made a fortune by investing in Egyptian art and precious metals. But now that gold had become too expensive, she decided she would begin to invest in real estate. She said she wanted me to drive to Virginia Beach to look at properties.

When I expressed reservations about driving all the way to Virginia in the wobbly Chrysler, Yoko offered to buy a new car for me to use on my errands. "Do you like Mercedes?" she asked. I assured her that it was a superior vehicle. Yoko then suggested I show her a Mercedes catalog so that she could choose a model. At first I thought she might be joking, but when I brought her the catalog the next day, she paged through it quickly and asked my help in choosing. I suggested a sleek new Mercedes 300 station wagon. According to the catalog, this model was being sold in the U.S. for the first time. Yoko did not need much convincing. She appeared excited by the prospect of owning the first Mercedes station wagon in New York. "Just tell Rich," she said. "Have him write a check." Still uncertain as to whether she was pulling my leg, I told the accountant that Yoko had told me to buy a Mercedes. Rich opened a drawer, took out a checkbook, and poised his pen. "How much?" he asked wearily. It was about thirty thousand dollars.

Money was no object at Lennono. Rich routinely wrote out checks for tens of thousands, sometimes hundreds of thousands, of dollars. In addition, thousands of dollars in "petty cash" were disbursed to the Lennons and their staff. At least once a week I would make my way to a local bank and pick up three to five thousand dollars. Roughly a third of this sum was for my own expense account. John would get several hundred dollars, and whenever I handed him a wad of money, he would carelessly stuff it into the back pocket of his jeans. Because he rarely went out, he had little opportunity to spend his allowance. Most of the time, I would spend his money for him. Yoko kept her cash in various drawers and pocketbooks. Rich also kept substantial amounts of money in his desk drawer as a cash reserve for Yoko, who often needed large sums on short notice.

I was earning one hundred seventy-five dollars per week, but having an expense account and driving a company car gave me the illusion of great wealth. This was one of the reasons why I did not mind working ten or more hours a day and being on call around the clock. Frequently I would come home after a long day at the Dakota only to get a call or find a message from Yoko on my answering machine with some strange last-minute request. Once, she called me late at night with instructions to drive with Rich to their SoHo loft on Broome Street—where Yoko's trusted tarot card reader, Charlie Swan (whose real name was John Green), lived rent-free. We were to pick up a mysterious object that she refused to identify, but she told me that it would be in a sitar case. Rich had a passkey, and like burglars, we traipsed around the enormous loft using flashlights. Neither Rich nor I had the slightest idea what a sitar case looked like, but when we came across an elongated wooden box, we decided that this must be it.

Nervously, we opened the box. Inside was a plain brown bag. Inside the bag was a huge rubber dildo. Rich and I dutifully delivered the dildo to the Dakota, but, of course, we could not ask Yoko about it. The accountant told me he had grown used to carrying out unusual orders without asking questions. "Yoko's the boss," he said firmly. "I just do as I'm told." Almost as an afterthought, he added, "Hey, man, I'm not sure I wanna know why I'm doing some of the stuff she's got me doing!"

Yoko's work, it often seemed, was to spend money. Though she dealt with dozens of merchants and dealers, Yoko's two main suppliers were Sam Havadtoy and Sam Green. Both men were frequent visitors to Studio One, and their appointments had to be juggled so that their paths did not cross. Yoko insisted on keeping up the pretense that the two Sams were unaware of each other, although they doubtless knew that they were in direct competition for Yoko's money and attention.

Samuel Adams Green, Jr., was a distinguished-looking, bearded gentleman in his early forties. Scion of an old New England family, he was known to readers of gossip columns as a former member of Andy Warhol's inner circle, and an escort of Greta Garbo. He specialized in esoteric commodities, such as pre-Columbian art, Egyptian artifacts, and exotic trinkets that cost twenty thousand dollars to thirty thousand dollars apiece. I always half-expected him to turn up with the Maltese Falcon. One day, indeed, he did sell Yoko an alabaster falcon for twenty-nine thousand dollars.

Sam Havadtoy was a handsome Hungarian antique dealer and interior decorator in his late twenties. In 1978, he had been hired to decorate Studio One; subsequently, he had gone on to sell Yoko antique furniture worth hundreds of thousands of dollars from his gallery on the East Side.

Yoko's life revolved around her acquisitions, but her most valuable acquisition was John. By marrying Lennon she had established herself as a celebrity and financial power to be reckoned with. It was the process of acquisition—not the object itself—that kept Yoko going. Antiques were routinely delivered, examined, and carted off to Apartment 71 or to the basement for storage. Clothes were bought and hung up, never to be worn. Once she had acquired something, Yoko lost interest in it. She lost interest in John after they were reunited and she lost interest in Sean after he was born. She treated them both with an icy reserve bordering on contempt.

Life became complicated for Yoko because John was not an inanimate object, but a human being—one with an active imagination, a strong sex drive, boundless energy, and a terrible temper. Indeed, Yoko lived in fear of John's occasional outbursts of anger and frustration. Although he remained quietly behind closed doors most of the time, she knew well that John's passive and self-absorbed behavior masked an overwhelming restlessness. Like an old lion, he could turn and bite your head off when you least expected it. Whenever John got a little stir-crazy upstairs and threatened to become "difficult," Yoko attempted frantically to appease him with vague promises, or she would scare him with ominous psychic predictions and mystical mumbo jumbo.

Usually, Yoko could keep John in line with a few carefully chosen words. One of her favorite ploys for controlling him was to tell him that the planet Mercury was going retrograde, a perilous astrological period during which accidents were likely to happen. When I asked John what Mercury being retrograde meant, he explained that it was an astrological period when the planet Mercury, "the messenger," appeared to move backward against the sun, causing massive disruptions in communications and generally creating "chaos in the cosmos."

Yoko was always to tell me that we had to keep John isolated for his own good. Once in a while, John would try to circumvent Yoko's strict rules, but he would often regret it soon afterward. For instance, one day John was listening to radio station WBAI when he heard a very eloquent, urgent plea for contributions. New subscribers were to receive a copy of a book titled *The Devil Was a Woman*. John wanted the book, and as WBAI was one of the radio stations he frequently listened to—he was particularly interested in nutritionist Gary Null's health show—he impulsively ordered me to call up and contribute one thousand dollars on his behalf. Immediately, the station announced the contribution. When Yoko heard about it, she read me the riot act. She reminded me angrily that whenever John acted impulsively, I was to bring his behavior to her attention before following his orders. I was to consult her about all matters involving John and "human relations," or his having dealings with the outside world.

"After all," explained Yoko, "I'm here to protect him." I assured her I understood perfectly.

Yoko had the key to John Lennon, and she used it to make John her sole possession by taking him out of public circulation. The old lion had pulled in his claws eagerly and agreed to give up rock and roll and its deleterious lifestyle. Because of his self-destructive behavior when he was on his own, John believed that the only sane alternative was to isolate himself.

Moreover, Yoko had offered him the opportunity to try parenthood all over again. When she managed to give birth to Sean against all odds, John took it as a sign of divine intervention. He told me that both he and Sean were "riding on Mother's good luck." His childlike dependence on Yoko was so great that he dreaded the thought of Yoko dying before he did. "I hope I go first," John had told me, "because if Mother died before me I wouldn't be able to face life on my own." He had resigned himself completely to the proposition that he could not survive without Yoko. Thus, John willingly sacrificed his freedom for the illusion of safety.

And it was part of Yoko's Faustian pact that she had to keep John, for better or for worse, and remain an appendage to John's fame and to the pervasive Beatles legend, no matter how much she craved independence and personal fame. It was no wonder that she bitterly resented John, even as she was constantly conscious of the need to retain his loyalty. Without John Lennon, Yoko Ono was just an eccentric lady with no money and no power—and for this she would never forgive him.

4

Hello Good-Bye

In March, 1979, Yoko decided that we would go to Florida for a spring break. She arranged to rent an oceanfront mansion in Palm Beach that belonged to the prominent socialite Brownie McLean. It was to be a big family vacation. Yoko's three Japanese nieces, the children of her older brother, Keisuke, were to join us in Florida. Julian Lennon, John's son by his first wife, Cynthia, would fly from his home in North Wales to spend his sixteenth birthday with us, and Helen was coming along to take care of Sean, who was to meet his half-brother, Julian, for the first time.

John, Yoko, Helen, and Sean were flying down together, and I was instructed to drive John's clothes and guitars to Florida in the Mercedes station wagon. As usual when traveling, John agonized until the last minute over what clothes to bring. He always traveled with many suits of clothes, insisting all the while that he would not think of actually going out. I knew how important clothes were to John. He had told me that he had once considered a career as a fashion designer, but in the working-class environment in which he grew up, men involved in the world of fashion were considered "fairies," and John did not want to risk being stigmatized as a homosexual. He also said that he had thought of becoming a hairdresser, but had abandoned this idea for the same reason.

On the day before my scheduled departure, John summoned me to the clothes room, where we spent hours sorting out his Palm Beach wardrobe: summer suits, sports jackets, formal wear, beach clothes, jeans, shorts, sweaters, T-shirts, shirts, ties, hats, boots, shoes, and sneakers. By the time we were done, there were enough clothes to fill a large steamer trunk. John apologized sheepishly for his neurotic need to have so many clothes and joked that if he had to go to a desert island, he would want to take a full wardrobe with him. Clothes, he said, were his disguise. He knew well that through his clothes and with his hair he could alter his appearance—his image— at will. The thought of being trapped in one image terrified John. He was always at odds with himself about his image: not only what it was and what it should be, but even whether there should be one at all.

To make the long drive more interesting, I took along a collection of Beatle and Lennon tapes. Zooming along on Interstate 95, listening to John's voice over the car's powerful sound system, I was reminded that John had once been one of the most original and prolific recording artists of his generation—which made it all the harder to understand his current state of suspended animation. It made me sad to realize that the John Lennon I worked for was a mere shadow of his former self.

I arrived in Palm Beach two days after leaving New York. It was late at night and *El Solano*, the spectacular Mediterranean-style villa on the ocean, was completely dark. I was let in quietly by the caretaker couple, Greg and Gloria, who had a cottage in the back. They showed me to my bedroom, which was decorated with green ceramic frogs. Exhausted from the 1,500-mile drive, I began to get out of my soiled clothes and was looking forward to a shower and a good night's sleep. A knock at my door made me leap about four feet across the room. I could not imagine who it might be.

When I opened the door, there stood John, in cutoff jeans and a T-shirt, wearing his thick glasses with the clear plastic frames, clean-shaven or nearly so, with his hair down to his shoulders. He looked pretty wired for that time of night.

"Welcome to our humble abode," he said, tongue in cheek. He told me that he and Yoko had worried that I might have wrecked the car, and joked that although *I* was "expendable," the thought of having his car, his guitars, or his clothes lost or damaged was simply too much to bear. He said he was glad to discover I was okay. I smiled at him. For the first time since I had come to work for him, I felt truly appreciated.

"Why don't you come to the kitchen and I'll make you a cup of tea or something?" he suggested. I wanted to say I was too tired and that I needed to sleep, but at the same time I could not pass up a chance to spend some time alone with him in this new environment. I sensed that John wanted to talk, and I thought it might be a good opportunity to get better acquainted. The kitchen was a big room with a linoleum tile floor, built-in sink and stove, moss-green cabinets, and a central island of counter space. I leaned against the counter as John lit a burner, put on a tea kettle, and searched in a cabinet until he had found a small box of Morning Thunder tea. As he prepared the tea, John talked. I was too dazed by lack of sleep to respond, but that made no difference to John. When he was flying high on adrenaline, nicotine, and caffeine, he was capable of talking, with his distinctively boyish ardor, about almost any subject for almost any length of time.

"When the Nixon government was trying to deport me," he remarked at one point, "the reason they couldn't pull if off was because Yoko knew beforehand every move they were going to make in court." I nodded, and was about to mention that I had been in the courtroom with my uncle on the day John won his green card in October, 1975. But before I could say anything, John was off and running again. "Her psychics told us what the government lawyers were planning to do. So we were always one step ahead," he chuckled. "We simply outmaneuvered the other side, since Yoko could anticipate their every move, you see!" He looked at me expectantly. I had no idea what John was getting at. "They never knew what hit 'em!" John continued with mounting enthusiasm. "At one point we brought in this ancient black woman from Chicago, Mother Gibson. She was a powerful witch, a voodoo priestess or something like that, and she was supposed to help us cast a spell on the judge to get him to rule in our favor. She brought a handkerchief that had some kind of magic scent—herbs or roots or barks or something, I don't know. If it was unfolded in court it would give off this aroma that would affect the judge." He smiled and poured boiling water over the tea bags while I gaped at him.

John explained that Mother Gibson had instructed him to unfold the magic handkerchief in a prescribed manner in court. The idea, said John, was to "open up" the heart of the judge. John next described how he surreptitiously opened the handkerchief under his defendant's table according to Mother Gibson's detailed instructions. "I was a nervous wreck," he said. "At first, I thought the whole thing was bullshit, but the judge was this nasty old buzzard who was in collusion with the prosecution and I knew that I had nothing to lose." John said that as soon as the handkerchief was opened, the proceedings were thrown into complete disarray. "Everyone in the courtroom began to wonder where 'that smell' was coming from. The judge got really upset and had all the windows opened." John told me that after he repeated the "handkerchief trick" the following day, the judge did, in fact, soften his stand.

"I guess it worked," John said. "Here I am!"

In my extreme state of fatigue, I had given up wondering if he actually believed what he had just told me. I thought, "Wow, voodoo jurisprudence! Now there's a twist!" We drank our tea, and I attempted to fill the silence with small talk. Actually, John did not care whether I talked or not. Later he would tell me, "I just like to talk, so you just being here to listen is enough. I mean, if you want to, go ahead and say something, but don't feel that you have to." Indeed, before I knew it, John was zeroing in on the subject that had been preoccupying him ever since he had arrived in Florida—his teenage son, Julian, whom he had last seen in 1977. John was overwhelmed with guilt and anxiety as he anticipated this encounter. "It'll take a week before we'll be able to touch," he said ruefully, "and another week before we're relaxed enough to hug."

John almost never saw Julian, and rarely spoke to him on the phone, in part because he detested Julian's mother, Cynthia. John always suspected that she would attempt to use Julian to reenter his life, and Yoko also did her best to fuel John's paranoid feelings toward his first wife. What's more, Yoko was resentful of John's relationship with Julian, what little of it there was, since she had been completely cut off from her daughter by her second husband, Tony Cox. Tony had gone into hiding with Kyoko, who was Julian's age, and Yoko maintained that as long as she was denied the company of her only daughter, it was only fair that John should limit his contact with his oldest son.

Although John and Julian were separated by so many barriers that communication proved extremely difficult, John wanted desperately to touch his son, before it was too late. John's father, Freddie Lennon, had been absent during most of John's childhood—and John more or less repeated the pattern when he went off to be a Beatle, leaving Cynthia and Julian to fend for themselves. Julian's birth in 1963 came at the worst possible moment for John. It was the year the Beatles made the transition from being a highly popular British band to being the single most influential musical—even cultural—phenomenon in the Western world, and John, on the manic express, could not be bothered with the responsibilities of fatherhood.

"During the early years," he mused, "when the Beatles were making it big, I led a real bachelor's life—even after Cynthia and I were married. I mean, I knew I had a wife and small child at home, but I didn't want the responsibility. It's like Julian is a semiorphan, and I was, too. It just boggles my mind that I have this sixteen-year-old kid now. He's into Rush, Led Zeppelin, and all these weird bands, and you know, I sometimes ask myself, 'Who is this stranger?' I have no idea what he's thinking or feeling." John paused to light another Gitane. "I have to admit that it's a lot like my relationship with my old man, and I wish we could be closer. I don't know where his head is at. I don't know what he feels, or what he really thinks about me. I don't know any of his friends. I have no idea if he has any girlfriends. I don't even know if I should assume he's into girls!"

I wondered why John should be telling me all this. In one sense I was delighted to be privy to his intimate personal secrets. On the other hand, I was embarrassed for him, having to open up to a virtual stranger. As his monologue continued, the tone changed. Soon he was angrily complaining that whenever he did speak to Julian, the boy would ask him for money and gifts, and John deplored Julian's current obsession with motorcycles. He had reluctantly sent him money to buy one some months earlier.

I noticed a gray luminescence about the kitchen windows. Dawn was coming. Gradually, John stopped talking. Now the ashtrays were filled with butts. The cold, dead tea bags sat at the bottom of our cups. We seemed wrapped in a malaise that came from nowhere. It was all around us, the way the sea washes around an island.

"Come on," John said, jumping to his feet. "I want to show you something."

I followed him out of the kitchen, past the dining area, and into an ornate ballroom. It was the most cavernous room I had ever seen, a misgrafted bit of Versailles left over from a grand age when people lived in ways we can no longer imagine. Strewn with antique furniture and hung with heavy oil paintings, the ballroom gave the impression of a main hall in a European museum of art, except that one entire wall consisted of floor-to-ceiling windows facing the ocean. They must have been twenty feet tall. Dawn was glimmering through these giant panes, which had not been cleaned in ages.

Soon we could see South Ocean Boulevard, with an intense light beyond it and what seemed to be another road of shining red, perpendicular to the first, stretching out to infinity—the path of the rising sun. John and I silently stared at the horizon as the sun slowly lifted out of the sea. The magnitude of the event seemed so immense, the setting so dramatic, that I gasped audibly, and tears welled in my eyes. John was so surprised to see me moved by a sunrise that he laughed, and the spell was broken. "You should get up earlier," he said cheerfully. "Sunrises rejuvenate you. It recharges the batteries!"

After this sudden rush of sunrise, I did feel revitalized. We returned to the kitchen. John made coffee and popped a few slices of bread into the toaster. When we sat down at the table to eat, he began writing out a long shopping list of things he wanted me to buy at the nearest health food store as soon as I was "back in action." I noticed that he seemed to have completely replenished his own energy supply. He looked as wired as he had been when he had knocked on my door. I thanked him for breakfast and explained that I was going to collapse if I did not soon get some sleep. John cheerfully waved me on and went out to play guitar by the pool. I slept almost the entire day. When I awoke, I discovered that Julian had arrived. He had a striking facial resemblance to his father, and he appeared to be very shy. I felt protective of him.

The morning after his son's arrival, John was floating in the pool while Julian stood around nervously waiting for John to acknowledge his presence. He did not want to ask John to get out and *be* with him, so he silently joined John in the pool. When John asked me to jump into the pool as well, I sensed that I was needed as a buffer between father and son. I was torn between wanting to leave them alone so they could sniff each other out, and feeling as if neither Julian nor John wished to shoulder the emotional burden it would place upon each of them. I would not have been surprised if John had instructed me: "Will you please tell Julian I said 'Good morning.' "

Julian did not know how to act. To him, John was a mythical superstar—a complete stranger. Yoko was even more of an enigma. She treated Julian with thinly veiled contempt, and constantly admonished me not to give him money, buy him things, or treat him as if he were in any way special. Julian had been reared in a lower-middle-class environment in North Wales, and he scarcely knew what to make of Palm Beach, the resort of the rich and famous. Even the Mercedes seemed awesome to him. When he asked me if he could have a turn at the wheel, I agreed to let him steer the Mercedes in the driveway. Just as he was getting familiar with the layout of the control panel, John happened to appear. He hollered when he saw Julian behind the wheel of his car. "Are you out of your mind? How dare you entrust a thirty-thousand-dollar car to a sixteen-year-old kid!" I took John's rebuke in stride, but I felt bad for Julian. I could see that he was very upset by his father's angry outburst, even though it wasn't directed at him. Julian told me that he was stunned because he was unaccustomed to seeing John express strong emotions.

John's relationships with Sean and Julian were a study in contrasts. John always held back his feelings with Julian. With Sean, though, he let everything come to the surface, hugging him, laughing with him, lecturing him, getting impatient with him, or even shouting at him when the occasion demanded. Julian had received few of the benefits of having a millionaire father, while Sean lived a pampered life of luxury, with every toy imaginable, bodyguards, chauffeured limousines. But despite the unfairness of it all, Julian showed no bitterness. The half-brothers seemed quite fond of each other, and romped together happily inside and around the house and in the pool.

Over the next few days Julian and I fell into a regular pattern. We cruised around Palm Beach in the Mercedes, running errands and listening to rock music. Julian talked about his hometown of Ruthin in North Wales, where he lived a typically carefree life as a teenager, chasing girls, racing his motorbike, and playing pool. Sometimes, he complained, he was picked on by jealous kids who envied him because his dad happened to be an ex-Beatle.

Julian even seemed to have inherited some of his father's musical ability. He had brought along an acoustic guitar and was eager to learn from John. In the evenings, father and son sometimes sat down after dinner with two guitars and John would begin teaching Julian new chords, passing on a little bit of the legacy hand to hand. John was easily distracted, however, and would soon lose interest in guitar picking. The mood would dissipate, and they would go back to watching television without ever speaking. Most of the time, John showed no effort to make any meaningful contact with Julian, and

Julian did not push for more attention. Often he simply appeared content to be near John. They would go bicycle riding, with Sean strapped into a plastic kiddie seat on the back of John's bike. Or they would hang around the pool—John and Sean in bare feet, Julian in Japanese sandals—surrounded by large palm trees. But they always seemed like three separate people in three separate dreams. They never meshed, no matter how hard they tried.

One morning, I found Julian and John sitting at the breakfast table. John was reading aloud a *National Enquirer* article about a woman abducted by aliens. The woman said the aliens had extracted a long, needlelike metal object from her forehead by pulling it through her nose, the implication being that they had implanted it there during childhood, made her forget about it, and had now returned to retrieve it. John was convinced that many people had had some sort of previous contact with aliens during early childhood, but had been hypnotized into forgetting it.

"It can be traced through hypnotic regression," John said to me, while Julian stood nearby, listening with widening eyes as his father speculated about having had such an encounter as a child. "That would explain why I've always seen things so differently," John went on. He wondered aloud if these aliens might be humans of the future who had mastered time travel. They might, he said, have a separate molecular makeup and coexist with us right here on earth. Julian's jaw hung down. I thought he might start to drool if he did not close it. Later, when Julian and I went out for a ride, he expressed real concern for John's mental health. I had to laugh myself, remembering how I had felt in the beginning, and wanted to say, "Don't worry, kid, you'll get the hang of life in Lennono Land soon enough."

"I wonder if Yoko puts all these weird ideas in his head," Julian said, looking bewildered.

"I doubt it," I said. "John really believes this stuff. Anyway, it never hurts to keep an open mind. You never know—there might be something to it." Julian looked at me as if I had flipped, too.

One night when we were sitting by the pool, John saw a light in the sky and began speculating excitedly about the possibility that it might be a UFO. He stared at the light for a while, then talked animatedly about a sighting he had had in early August of 1974, during the period when he had left Yoko and was living with May Pang. "I was watching the sunset from a window overlooking the East River when

I suddenly noticed this large shiny object slowly moving south against the Brooklyn skyline. At first, I thought, 'It's the cops!'—because I'd seen a police helicopter whizzing around earlier. But then it struck me that this thing was gliding over the river without making a sound!"

John said he stared out the window, transfixed by the mysterious object, while he frantically worked through all the rational explanations he could think of—none of which fit. "While I was busy trying to rationalize what it could be, in my gut I already knew." He said the hair on the back of his neck stood up. "But my mind was still fighting it, so I called May, shouting, 'Come over here! Look at this fuckin' thing!' At first she thought I was putting her on, but then she saw it, too." John said he had rushed up to the roof and had watched as the object melted into the Brooklyn skyline. "I was so disappointed!" he laughed. "I kept shouting, 'Over here! Take me with you! I'm ready!' "

John had no doubt that he had seen a real vehicle from another world. He speculated that the lone UFO was part of a fleet stationed in upstate New York, near the reservoirs and power plants, from which the craft could siphon energy to counteract Earth's gravitational pull. "UFOs were probably responsible for the last blackout," John said. "It's possible they drained off too much juice from Con Ed all at once." He also suspected that there was a high-level conspiracy to cover up verifiable UFO sightings and close encounters with aliens. "If the masses started to accept UFOs, it would profoundly affect their attitudes toward life, politics, everything," he explained. "It would threaten the status quo." He added that whenever people came to realize that there were larger considerations than their own petty little lives, they were ripe to make radical changes on a personal level, which would eventually lead to a political revolution in society as a whole.

"Christ, Buddha, Krishna, Mohammed were all messengers of the Supreme Being," John continued. "They were all saying basically the same thing, laying down the laws of the universe in language appropriate to their culture." Besides these major prophets, John believed, there were lesser messengers—the gurus, great poets, scientists, artists, musicians. "There's nothing they know that we don't know right now at this moment as we're talking," he insisted. "The trick is to make all this subconscious knowledge conscious."

John was deeply religious, though in a most unconventional fash-

ion. He viewed the Bible as a universal symbolic drama that was en-
acted daily in front of our eyes. In particular, John was fascinated by
the life of Jesus Christ. He had gone through a phase in the late sixties
when he had actually thought he was a reincarnation of Christ, and
that it was his mission on Earth to spread peace, love, and enlighten-
ment. He had even called a board meeting at Apple, the Beatles'
business company, to announce that he was the Messiah, and had
insisted that a press release to that effect be sent out. By the time I met
him, he had regained all of his original irreverence for Christianity.

One night John, Julian, and I were watching *Jesus of Nazareth* on
television and John began working himself up into a tirade against
Christianity, saying that it had virtually destroyed what was left of
pagan culture and spirituality in Europe—a great loss to civilization.
"I'm a born-again pagan," John said with pleasure at the turn of
phrase. Julian looked at him, puzzled at first, and then aghast, as John
kept saying, "Let's have the main event, let's get to the Crucifixion
already!" Although I could sense Julian's discomfort, I knew John was
not being cruel. It was simply his sarcastic nature, his liking for the
outrageous. When we watched *Deliverance* on TV, for instance, John
kept saying, "I can't wait to get to the butt-fucking scene!"

Needless to say, it was edited out.

On April 1, we chartered a small yacht for a cruise around Palm
Beach. We all went out for the day: Yoko and her nieces Reiko,
Akiko, and Takako; John, Julian, Sean, Helen, and I. Ben Johnson,
the prominent Palm Beach real estate agent who had found the house
for us, sent his twelve-year-old daughter along for the day. His Rolls-
Royce headed up the convoy to the docks that morning, followed by
John and Yoko's black Cadillac limousine and the rest of the gang in
the Mercedes.

We all scrambled aboard the spacious white cabin cruiser. From the
moment we set foot on the vessel, Sean ran around the boat as if he
had been charged up with Methedrine. Helen struggled to keep up
with him and was very worried that the little dynamo might manage
to accidently fling himself overboard. He was quickly outfitted with a
fluorescent orange life vest that he was made to wear during the entire
trip.

John and Yoko installed themselves at the rear of the boat, and
then posed for a family photo with Sean and Julian. As I trained my

camera on the Lennons, I could not help but marvel at what a motley crew they were. Yoko wore black trousers, no shoes, and a short-sleeved men's dress shirt with small black checks. John had on a colorful cap and red T-shirt, and Julian wore a blue T-shirt. He livened things up with a set of plastic fangs that he had inserted in his mouth. John found it amusing, but Yoko seemed annoyed at Julian's prankishness. In fact, she looked tense and ill at ease the entire time we were on the boat.

After we had cruised around for a while, I was sent off in a dinghy to take the kids away to a nearby island—a distraction that would enable John to get the boat ready for a surprise party to celebrate Julian's sixteenth birthday, although his actual birth date was still a week away. The small island was deserted, and we traipsed aimlessly around, Julian and I in the lead, followed by Sean and his Japanese cousins. The "Japanieces," as John called them, were aged eight, eleven, and fifteen and spoke hardly a word of English, but giggled a lot. They seemed to have a wonderful time no matter where we went. The three girls seemed particularly fond of their little cousin, Sean, chattering at him in Japanese, some of which he seemed to understand because he had spent the previous summer in Japan. Sean was delighted by all the attention he was getting.

When we returned, the boat was decorated with party favors, and there was a cake with sixteen candles. John rushed around documenting the event for the family album with a Polaroid camera. Later, John and Julian sat next to each other at the front of the boat. Out of nowhere, a speedboat suddenly appeared and began circling our yacht. It was occupied by several teenage girls, who must have been tipped off somehow about John's presence on our boat. Their screams of "We love you, John!" could be heard above the din of their motor. When John saw that he had been recognized, he decided to beat a hasty retreat, and we sped back to shore under full power. The party was over.

I sat on top of the boat with Julian, watching our wake, sad about the abrupt end to his birthday party. I glanced at him. He wanted it to work so badly, and now I could see in his face the pain, the frustration and disappointment at the unfulfilled promise of his long voyage to see his father. It had been a perfect day on the ocean, eighty degrees and sunny. We had a cake with sixteen candles. But even before the fans chased us away, the outing had been rife with tension. There were too many people on the boat, too many barriers between father and son.

A few days after his birthday Julian was sent back to England. We had become close and I assumed I would drive him to the airport. But a limousine was ordered instead, and Julian and I said an emotional good-bye. Then Yoko and John took him to the airport.

John and Julian would never see each other again.

5

Beautiful Boy

A few weeks after we returned to New York from Palm Beach, John and Yoko were off again, to spend the summer in Japan. It was a peaceful season for the staff at the Dakota. Yoko phoned only occasionally to check on business, and John sent me a postcard on which he scribbled a riddle: "What's the sound of one maid cleaning?"

I spent the time catching up on the fan mail, organizing the files, and alphabetizing John's record collection, attempting to bring some order to the chaos of Studio One and Apartment 72. I also took the time to read up on John and the Beatles. I had become thoroughly fascinated by my enigmatic boss. I also began to realize that I had formed an emotional attachment to him. I missed him, and I wanted to know more about his life. I thought that the key to understanding him was his childhood and his Beatle past. As often as possible I went to the beach armed with books about John and the Beatles, which I read while listening to Beatle tapes on a portable cassette player. At the end of this crash course on Beatles history I thought I had gained a much better understanding of John Lennon.

John's mother, Julia Stanley, was a pretty, twenty-seven-year-old free spirit who for over ten years had been dating a ship steward named Freddie Lennon. They were secretly married in 1938, and John Lennon was born two years later. Soon after John's birth, Freddie joined the merchant marine and Julia moved into a cottage owned by her older sister Mimi's husband in the suburban village of

Woolton. Julia frequently went dancing in the village, whose pubs were full of men in uniform, and sometimes she would pick up men during her nightly pub crawls and bring them back to the cottage, where little John would become distraught with these strangers.

In 1946, Freddie Lennon reappeared and in front of six-year-old John came to blows with his wife's lover, an alcoholic waiter named John Dykins. Traumatized by his mother's chaotic domestic situation, John frequently ran away to Mimi's house. Soon John, who was never disciplined by Julia, began to exhibit hostile behavior toward other children. He terrorized his classmates at the Mosspits Infants' School and was expelled from kindergarten. Later that year, Freddie took John on a holiday to Blackpool, a beach resort up the coast from Liverpool. Freddie planned to emigrate to New Zealand with John, but when Julia showed up unexpectedly and wanted to take John back, the boy was forced to choose between his parents. He chose his father, but as soon as his mother went out the door he impulsively ran after her. No sooner did Julia return to Liverpool with her son than she turned him over to her sister Mimi.

While he was grateful to Mimi for providing him with a home, John also felt a deep resentment against his aunt. Mimi was a cold, stern disciplinarian who at first tried to keep John in line by shaming or humiliating him. When John failed to respond to these psychological tactics, Mimi resorted to conventional beatings. John later blamed Mimi for bullying him and suffocating him with her insistence on discipline and routine. He never forgave his aunt for discouraging his creative pursuits. Once she even threw out some of his drawings. John's lonely and emotionally deprived childhood caused him to retreat within himself. For instance, he learned to put himself into a hypnotic state at an early age by staring at his eyes in a mirror until he began seeing hallucinatory images of his face changing. By the time he was nine, John knew that he was very different from other boys, but he wasn't sure if he was crazy or a genius. Once he began reading about Vincent van Gogh and other eccentric artists, John saw himself as a mad genius. His personality developed along two separate tracks. On the one hand he was a passive introvert, on the other, an aggressive show-off. John later encapsulated this dichotomy by describing himself as one-half "monk" and one-half "performing flea." By the time I went to work for John, the monk in him had won out.

In 1952, twelve-year-old John entered Quarry Bank Grammar School, whose motto was *Ex hoc metallo Virtutem*—"Out of this rough metal, we forge excellence." Strict discipline was enforced by student prefects, and canings were administered by the black-gowned headmaster. John, who quickly established himself as one of the rowdiest pupils at the school, received more than his share of beatings. Mimi's efforts to discipline John had long since failed, and his headmaster's canings merely inspired John to commit new and greater outrages. He soon found an ally in his revolt against school and Aunt Mimi—his mother, Julia, who re-entered his life around this time.

At age fifteen John heard Elvis Presley's "Heartbreak Hotel" and was galvanized into becoming a rocker. Julia, who played piano and banjo and loved rock and roll, bought her son a used guitar and taught him how to play it. Predictably, John's passion for rock music did not sit well with Mimi, but she was powerless to curb John's new obsession. Night after night, John would take his radio to bed with him and listen to Radio Luxembourg, Europe's premier rock and roll station. At sixteen, John Lennon was already hip to Little Richard, Carl Perkins, Jerry Lee Lewis, Chuck Berry, Buddy Holly, Eddie Cochran, Ray Charles, Fats Domino, Ike Turner, B. B. King, and other early American rock, rockabilly, blues, and R&B artists. Eventually, John Lennon became one of the foremost connoisseurs of rock and roll in England. Along with Mick Jagger, Ray Davies, Van Morrison, Eric Burdon, Jimmy Page, Pete Townshend, and other seminal, first-generation British rockers, John understood early on that the challenge lying ahead was to adapt this black American music to the tastes of contemporary British kids.

Skiffle music was the rage in England in 1957, so John formed a skiffle band. As most of the members of the group attended Quarry Bank School, John named his band the Quarry Men. The group played its first professional engagement on June 21, 1957. Equipped with acoustic guitars, and using a microphone hooked up to a radio serving as an amplifier, the Quarry Men performed two sets from the back of a flatbed truck at a block party. Two weeks later, the band played at the annual St. Peter's Church garden fete in Woolton. It was here that John Lennon met his musical alter ego, Paul McCartney. Although two years younger than John, fifteen-year-old Paul was a more sophisticated and accomplished musician, and when he joined the Quarry Men in the summer of 1957, he started pressing to have his mate, George Harrison, admitted to the group. Soon the Quarry Men included three-fourths of the future Beatles.

In 1958, Julia was killed in a traffic accident when an off-duty police officer plowed into her as she was crossing a street. The death of his mother had a devastating effect on John. He began to drink heavily and for the next two years he was, as he put it, "drunk or angry." John was by now enrolled in the Liverpool Art College, and it was there that John met his future wife, Cynthia Powell. Cynthia had a crush on John, and when her feelings were made clear to him, John wasted no time in getting intimately acquainted with his timid, pretty classmate.

Early in 1960, John moved in with Stu Sutcliffe, Liverpool's most promising painter. He persuaded Stu, who had no musical ability, to drop out of art school and buy a bass guitar so that he could join Lennon's new band—Johnny and the Moondogs. The group, soon renamed Longjohn and the Silver Beatles, consisted of Paul McCartney and George Harrison on guitars, plus a shifting cast of drummers. That summer, the Silver Beatles, now including Pete Best on drums, performed at the Club Indra, a strip bar on the Reeperbahn, Hamburg's notorious red-light district. The audience at the Indra was composed of bewildered-looking men who had come to the club anticipating the usual sex show. Overnight John had to come up with a show. Not only that, but the group was expected to play an average of six hours every night, virtually without a break. Accustomed to working one-hour sets and repeating the same tunes in every show, the Silver Beatles were compelled to drastically revamp their repertoire. They added new material on the spot while stretching out their old numbers far beyond the usual length.

Spurred on by John, who began gobbling powerful amphetamines called "Prellys" as well as guzzling great quantities of beer, the boys habitually worked themselves into a frenzy, stomping their feet and horsing around onstage—anything to capture the apathetic audience's attention. One of John's favorite stunts was to take a flying leap into the audience, a tradition that was to be carried on by future generations of rockers. As John got more and more crazed and drunk, he would begin taunting the house with reckless abandon—for instance, goose-stepping up and down the stage while shouting *Sieg heil!* The Germans apparently loved it. After seven weeks, the owner of the Indra, a dwarfish former circus clown named Bruno Koschmider, moved the Beatles to the larger Kaiserkeller. Originally a basement club catering to mostly young people, the Kaiserkeller had become, by the time the Beatles arrived, a hangout for British and American sailors as well as the local version of the Hell's Angels. Also in the audience were a group of German students—Klaus Voorman, Jürgen Vollmer, and Astrid Kircherr—who soon became the group's most devoted fans. At the Kaiserkeller, the Beatles shared the bill with another Liverpool group, Rory Storm and the Hurricanes, whose drummer, Richard Starkey, a/k/a Ringo Starr, later replaced Pete Best as the Beatles' drummer. The group's Hamburg stay came to an abrupt end in November, 1960, when the Beatles were deported after Paul accidentally started a small fire in the movie house behind whose screen they had their living quarters. Back in Liverpool, the group began playing local dances, as well as lunch-hour sessions at the Cavern. Stu stayed in Hamburg because he fell in love with Astrid, a fellow artist. On the eve of the Beatles' third trip to Hamburg, in early April, 1962, twenty-two-year-old Stu died of a brain tumor. When John heard the news he became hysterical. He assumed that the deadly brain tumor was a direct result of a head injury Stu had sustained during a fight after a Beatles concert two years earlier, and he blamed himself for his friend's death.

In April, 1961, the Beatles returned to Hamburg for an extended engagement at the Top Ten Club. That spring Bert Kaempfert, a well-known German orchestra leader and producer for Polydor Records, hired the group to back the British singer Tony Sheridan on a record aimed at the German pop market. The tracks released by Polydor later that year were "My Bonnie Lies over the Ocean" and "When the Saints Go Marching In." In October, a kid walked into a Liverpool record store and asked Brian Epstein, who managed the family-owned business, for the Beatles' "My Bonnie" single. Unable to find the record, Epstein did some checking and learned that the group in question frequently played at the Cavern Club. That winter, Epstein became the group's manager. The following spring he arranged for the Beatles to take a recording test with George Martin, the head of A&R at Parlophone Records, a subsidiary of the giant EMI entertainment conglomerate. John stood in awe of Martin, who had worked with Peter Sellers and Spike Milligan, the founding members of John's favorite radio program, the subversive "Goon Show."

The Beatles' first recording session took place at EMI's Abbey Road recording studio in September, 1962. The first song they recorded, a Lennon-McCartney original titled "Love Me Do," reached number 17 on the British hit parade. Their second single, "Please Please Me," reached the top position on *Melody Maker*'s hit chart in March, 1963.

Meanwhile, John had reluctantly married Cynthia because she was pregnant. Cynthia gave birth to Julian on April 8, 1963. A week later John finally appeared at his wife's bedside. However, John was not prepared to accept the responsibilities of fatherhood. Cynthia saw very little of her husband in 1963. John never forgave her for becoming pregnant and "forcing" him to marry, and he was never a proper father to Julian. Indeed, John had every reason to feel guilty for his abandonment of Julian, the innocent product of this relationship turned sour.

By the end of the summer, tanned and much better informed about my employer, I began to look forward to his return. When John and Yoko came back from Japan in September, they brought with them a Japanese servant named Uneko Uda. She had been their personal maid at Tokyo's exclusive Hotel Okura, and the Lennons had convinced her to come to work for them in New York. Uda-san, as John and Yoko called her, was a diminutive former policewoman whose parents were Buddhist priests. She had been reared in a Buddhist temple, and though her English was poor, she managed to make herself understood by gesticulating forcefully. Uda-san was the ideal servant. She doubled as a maid and cook, and was also able to look after Sean when Helen needed to take a day off. My aunt was, after all, a grandmother with an extended family of her own.

Only a few days after the Lennons' return, their life at the Dakota was in full swing again. It was as if they had never left. The first order of business was a big joint birthday celebration for John and Sean. Both had been born on October 9. When I first found out, I said something to John about what an amazing coincidence it was.

"It wasn't a coincidence," he said, giving me a significant look. "Mother's always trying to have babies on my birthday."

Indeed, I recalled having read that Yoko had had several miscarriages in earlier attempts to have children on John's birthday. She lost their first baby on October 9, 1969. On October 9, 1975, John's thirty-fifth birthday, Yoko gave birth to Sean by a caesarean section.

It was not until much later, when I learned that among the many superstitions John and Yoko shared was an ancient Hindu belief that a son born on his father's birthday inherits his soul when the father dies, that I finally understood why Yoko would go to such lengths to deliver a child on John's birthday. Sean had been surgically removed from Yoko Ono prematurely so that he would inherit his father's soul when John died! Yoko was proud of finally having pulled it off.

The joint birthday party for thirty-nine-year-old John and four-year-old Sean was held at Tavern on the Green in Central Park on October 9, 1979. The restaurant was owned by Warner LeRoy, who was the Lennons' downstairs neighbor at the Dakota and whose children were Sean's playmates. On that crisp and sunny autumn afternoon, the glass-enclosed atrium of Tavern on the Green resembled a fairyland where children and adults ate and laughed and sang all day long. A dozen large, round tables draped with blue tablecloths were elaborately set up and decorated with scarlet flower arrangements. A small army of uniformed waiters carved and served from an endless supply of meats and pies, while colorful helium-filled balloons floated and bounded this way and that. Sean screamed with delight, running around the big room, ricocheting off the guests like a pinball going for the big score. He was only four years old, and had spent the spring in Palm Beach, followed by a summer in Japan. Now he had one of New York's most spectacular restaurants as his playground. He was beside himself.

Yoko had T-shirts made up for all the guests, each with his or her own name printed under a blood-red heart. John sported a full beard, which he had begun to grow upon his return from Japan, and he had let down his shoulder-length hair. He was dressed in black and wore yellow plastic sunglasses. At the climax of the party, Yoko presented John and Sean with their birthday gifts—a pair of life-sized dummies, hand-sewn in the image of father and son. Sam Green had overseen the production of the two mannequins, which had been outfitted with T-shirts and blue denim jackets. John's had reddish hair and horn-rimmed glasses, while Sean's showed his shoulder-length black hair topped by a railroad engineer's cap. John appeared to be amused by Yoko's unusual gift, but Sean seemed disappointed.

After the birthday party John returned to seclusion inside the Dakota. He didn't come out again until Halloween, when he emerged to take Sean to a matinee of *Peter Pan*. It was supposed to be a family outing, but Yoko begged off, saying she was too busy. While John made a last-minute attempt to persuade Yoko to join them, Sean waited in the outer office and watched Rich with mischievous dark eyes. Then, as kids often do, from out of nowhere Sean threw him a question: "What's your favorite Beatles song?" Rich gave Sean a startled look. Before the accountant could respond, Sean said, "Mine is 'Yellow Submarine'!" Then Sean began to wail, "Weee all liiiive in a yellow submarine . . . Weeeee all liiiive in a yellow submarine!" until John emerged from the inner sanctum and told him to pipe down. The two of them went to the theatre, leaving Yoko on the phone.

The day after Halloween, I went up to the bedroom to bring John some mail and found him sitting on the bed with Sean. John was distractedly thumbing through a magazine. The white-painted shutters were open and the room was flooded with sunlight. The television muttered to itself in a corner, and the radio was faintly bubbling in the background. Sean seemed dejected. He looked up at me when I came in, and said, "Daddy should join the Beatles again."

"You don't know what you're saying, Sean," John snapped. "We wouldn't be able to go out to see *Peter Pan*, go to the toy store, or do anything in public."

Sean screwed up his mouth as if he did not really believe that—as if it was something the adults told you to keep you from persisting with your questions. He had been growing more mature in certain ways lately. He did not throw temper tantrums anymore when Yoko left the apartment, and he was so articulate that he sounded almost like an adult on the telephone. But if he did not get his way, he could raise more hell than seemed possible from a three-foot-tall, angel-faced boy. Sometimes he would go tearing through the house, pummeling anyone who got in his way, venting his frustration, often by screaming Beatle lyrics. "Do you need anybody? I need somebody to love!" was one he latched on to, and for a time it could be heard constantly throughout Apartment 72.

John did not talk much about his Beatle past, but Sean saw the records and the videos, heard the music on the radio. He was growing more curious by the day about what the Beatles had been, what they had meant. Gradually, he began to realize that his father had been part of something very big, something magical and important and entirely out of the ordinary that had taken place long, long ago, before he was born. It must have been a little like being the son of an old knight around whom hung an aura of glory, of past victories and heroic exploits.

Sean was constantly being brought in contact with echoes of his father's past. While riding in a limousine or the Mercedes, he would hear John's voice on the radio. He would turn on the TV and the Beatles would suddenly appear ("There's Daddy!"). Or, playing in Central Park, Sean would see a bicycle approaching, a large silver radio in its wire basket, and would hear, drifting across the grass, his father faintly calling, "Why am I so shy when I'm beside you?" It was a mysterious presence and seemed to be everywhere, as if John had the magical power to speak to Sean from any point on earth, at any time of the day or night. In fact, it was a remarkable testament to the power of the Beatles that even with the protective cocoon that had been thrown up around him, Sean couldn't be insulated from the mythology, not even a decade after the fact.

While Yoko had little to do with Sean on a day to day basis, John always talked to him, praised and lectured him, sometimes losing sight of the fact that a four-year-old has a limited ability to comprehend. For example, John would attempt to explain to Sean how a guitar amplifier worked, but Sean would only get confused and restless. John would then grow frustrated, and before long the two would have a fight. Once, I ran into John and Sean on their way to eat lunch at a Japanese restaurant on Columbus Avenue, and John invited me along. Sean had not yet mastered the art of eating with chopsticks and John decided this was a good time to teach both of us. Using me as a model, John pointed to my hand to show Sean the proper way of manipulating the chopsticks. But although I managed to get them into proper position, I was clumsy using them, and a piece of sushi went flying into my soy sauce dish. Sean began to howl with glee, causing John to severely reprimand him. Sean was visibly upset.

Whenever John and Sean had a fight, John would feel guilty and would often try to make it up to Sean by buying him expensive presents. For instance, John once spent over a thousand dollars at F.A.O. Schwarz for a mini-jukebox named Disco Highboy. It operated from a tape deck and had a big set of speakers and flashing lights. Sean quickly lost interest in it, however, since the toy was no match for the big jukebox in the playroom. Sean was already skilled at programming daddy's jukebox and he loved to play deejay. The LeRoy children or Sean's other playmates would come over and spend hours in the playroom cavorting to John's favorite rock hits.

John tried very hard to be a good father to Sean. He read him children's books; they watched television together; and John would even sit and watch Sean's cartoons—*Dumbo, Mighty Mouse, Heckle & Jeckle*. But then Sean would become cranky and bored, John's patience would wear thin, and he would call for Helen to take Sean away.

If John had limited patience with Sean, Yoko could hardly tolerate him at all. He needed to be around his mother—to have her undivided attention—but, just like John, he could never seem to get it, and this seemed to fill him with rage. Whoever dared to get in Sean's way would be shoved aside or rammed amidships, and no one was allowed to stop the tiny terror. The staff spent much time rolling eyeballs heavenward when Sean went on the rampage.

Yoko was usually in her office where she could not hear the uproar, while John remained behind closed doors in the bedroom. Thus the responsibility of pacifying Sean fell on Helen's shoulders. My aunt was a kindly, sixty-year-old woman, the perfect mother figure, but she could only comfort and attempt to calm Sean. She was not allowed to discipline him as she would have her own children and grandchildren. Even when they traveled, Sean was boss, and if someone refused to go along with his wishes, word got back to Yoko, and there was hell to pay. Sean, at age four, had unwittingly managed to collect his own group of sycophants. If he went to the park, for example, he and Helen were usually accompanied by several other children and adults: bodyguards, friends, neighbors, assistants—it was like the infant king traveling around with his entourage.

Sean was very spoiled, and he also had a serious discipline problem. The basic problem was that there was no discipline.

"Whatever Sean wants, Sean gets" was Yoko's decree to the staff. John, on the other hand, worried about Sean to no end, fretting over what he ate, what he wore, what he washed with, what he felt and thought about everything. John was constantly laying down strict dietary rules for his son. He watched over Sean's diet almost as obsessively as over his own. Sean was never to have ice cream, for example, because John considered ice cream a useless food. But if Sean became unruly and John wanted to pacify him, he would think nothing of bribing him with ice cream.

John felt responsible not only for keeping Sean physically healthy but also for encouraging his son's creative efforts. Anything Sean put on paper was either framed or filed away. Believing that the mind was the key to survival, John was determined to "train" Sean's mind in the hope that Sean might someday transcend the emotional handicap of being the son of a self-absorbed ex-Beatle and an indifferent mother whose main involvement in her son's upbringing was to instruct the servants to indulge his every whim. John knew that the way Sean was being reared would not stand him in good stead when he would inevitably have to face the real world.

Almost as if he were wishing out loud, John would say: "If he makes it to the age of eight or nine, he'll be strong enough to heal himself and cut through all the crap he's had to go through in his early years. He can still grow up to become a normal adult."

6

Voodoo Justice

In the fall of 1979 the Lennons embarked on a massive real estate shopping spree. They already owned a farm in upstate New York, which they never visited, and a loft on Broome Street in SoHo, not to mention the three apartments in the Dakota. It was unclear to me why they needed to buy more property, but I suspected that Yoko wanted to send John and Sean away. Then she would have them "at home" but also out of her hair. And for his part, John talked about the pleasures of having a country house where he could occasionally take LSD and psychedelic mushrooms in peace and quiet.

The key considerations in John and Yoko's search for new properties involved seclusion, security, and safety from earthquakes, tidal waves, and other natural catastrophes. Marlene Weiner, one of Yoko's psychics, had advised her that Long Island, upstate New York, Virginia, and Florida were "safe," and so she focused her house-hunting efforts on these areas. Yoko subscribed to a glossy real estate catalog, *Holiday Homes International*, and with Marlene's help she picked out houses that might be suitable for her and John.

Living through the telephone as she did, Yoko did not like to venture into the real world unless it was absolutely necessary, so I was assigned the job of scouting potential properties. Standard procedure was to call a real estate agent and say that I represented a wealthy, "internationally prominent" couple, thus ensuring maximum cooperation by brokers and owners without giving the mighty Lennon name. John believed that it was good business sense to remain anonymous. "Once they know it's us," he complained, "the price goes up."

I spent many weekends driving around the recommended areas, Long Island, upstate New York, and Virginia, as well as Maryland, Pennsylvania, New Jersey, Rhode Island, and elsewhere, to meet with local real estate agents and to photograph houses. I even flew to Toronto to scout properties. I would return from these trips bearing voluminous notes, promotional brochures, and stacks of Polaroid snapshots that I would show the Lennons, adding my own impressions of the properties. If it had been up to Yoko, she would have brought most of the available properties. "I love all these houses," Yoko once exclaimed while poring over a stack of photos from one of my outings. "If I had more money, I would buy them all!"

John did not always share her passion.

After my debriefing by the Lennons, I would have a similar conference with Marlene, the real estate psychic, who lived with several large dogs in a cramped apartment a few blocks from the Dakota. She was a good-natured, tremendously obese woman who required a constant supply of chocolate brownies and other treats to fuel her enormous bulk. Marlene would place her hands over the photos, taking in the house's "vibe." She would then call Yoko to report her psychic impressions. Sometimes, in payment for services, Yoko would send me to Marlene with a blank check for her to fill out. Fortunately for Yoko, Marlene did not appear tempted to take advantage.

John frowned upon Yoko's habit of letting a psychic decide which properties to acquire. He often complained that this was a foolish way to go about buying real estate, and he began to insist on inspecting the properties in person. He was prepared to accompany me on my house-hunting trips, but Yoko refused to ride in the Mercedes. In fact, she had never been in the car, and that, too, was an issue for John.

One morning in late October, I was getting ready to visit a house in upstate New York, when Yoko told me to see John in the bedroom.

"Don't get too excited," John said, "but the Lennons are riding with you this time."

He told me that the two of them had been up all night arguing about whether she would go. Obviously, John had prevailed. Yoko complained and dawdled for hours that morning, and when we finally hit the road, she cowered in the backseat, huddled beneath a fur coat, virtually paralyzed with fright. "Fred, please drive slowly," she said. "This is very dangerous . . . drive very carefully."

I caught sight of her in the rearview mirror. Her hair was thick and black and shone nearly blue in the sunlight. Tucked behind her large ears, it flowed below her shoulders. Her lips were thin, her face flat and triangular, a grim mask. John sat next to me and cheerfully chatted away, repeatedly reassuring Yoko that I was an expert driver and that she had nothing to fear. But when the tool kit in the rear began rattling, Yoko immediately grew alarmed.

"What's that?" she asked nervously.

Both John and I did our best to assure her that it was nothing dangerous, only some loose tools, but Yoko remained unconvinced.

"Can't you make it stop?" she whined.

Just before we got on the West Side Highway, I pulled over and rearranged the tools. However, after a few minutes on the road the rattling commenced again.

"Please, Fred, stop the noise!" she begged. "It's driving me crazy."

I was fairly annoyed by the time I zoomed off the road at the 158th Street exit. Yoko let out a scream that could have shattered glass. She must have thought I was putting an end to her misery once and for all. The tools finally secured, I was doing sixty miles per hour in the center lane, and Yoko began insisting I drive in the right lane. John said no, that was a bad idea.

"What if we get stuck between two cars and someone recognizes us?" he worried. "We'll be trapped and won't be able to get away." When Yoko stubbornly continued to insist that I pull into the right lane, John angrily snapped, "Look, just shut up and go to sleep, okay?" Yoko seemed offended and became very quiet.

When we reached our destination, Livingston Manor in upstate New York, John saw a group of teenagers drinking in front of a store.

"Rednecks," John muttered anxiously under his breath. "I don't like the looks of this one bit. If they spot us, we'll never get out alive."

He was only half-joking. John had a fear of beer-guzzling teenagers that bordered on the phobic. By the time I reached the local real estate office, he and Yoko had managed to whip each other into a state of near-panic. They both had amazingly active imaginations about what horrors might befall them. They were too afraid to leave the car, and had me buy tuna sandwiches and chicken soup, which they ate while I went to meet the real estate agent. The man insisted that John and Yoko come into the office so that he could give his standard sales pitch on the merits of the house, a secluded cottage named Irongate. I tried to explain that my clients—I had not told him their names—were a reclusive couple and that if I told them they had to come in, they would, in all likelihood, just turn around and go home.

"Nah," said the agent with confidence: "Not after you drove 'em four hours to get here."

He did not know the Lennons. When I reported the broker's request, Yoko flipped out. "Tell him to go fuck himself!" she screeched. "Let's go!"

She eventually bought the property, sight unseen.

Going home, I took the scenic route, crossing the Verrazano Narrows Bridge. John thought the view was breathtaking. Yoko worried that we might fall into the river below. I turned onto the FDR Drive, and John suddenly decided that he wanted to have dinner at one of the South Street seafood places. One of the truly amazing things about John was that he had an unerring sense of direction. He knew things intuitively. Somehow he managed to steer us to a dark, funky old dive with wooden tables and floor. John swashbuckled his way in, with tiny Yoko wrapped in her white fur. She looked like a rotund stuffed animal on his arm. The faces turned from the bar. I could imagine what they were thinking—who's this modern-day pirate and where'd he get the koala bear?

Then they saw John Lennon and Yoko Ono.

As soon as we took a table, John started talking twice as fast as before, his old defense mechanism kicking in. Talking nonstop staved off John's anxiety while keeping potential intruders at bay. People watched, waiting for him to stop, but John knew better than to let up.

"Check out that guy over there—he's about to fall off his stool." John threw a quick glance toward a young, bearded fellow who was staring at us, transfixed. "He's going to come up and shake my hand in about five minutes. Look at that one over there—he's going to nab an autograph." The odd thing was how well he could call them.

"Mr. Lennon, your music gives me so much pleasure, I just want to shake your hand." It was the man John had pointed out a moment earlier. John was polite, but I could sense that he was annoyed by the rituals of his spectacular fame.

Ordering was a bit of a problem. Yoko changed her mind three times about what she wanted. Each time the waiter took the menu away, Yoko asked for it back and chose something else. Finally she ordered fish and chips, but when it was brought, she said she wanted sushi instead, leaving the waiter flustered and confused. At that point John stepped in, calmly in control.

"That's enough, Mother!" he said firmly. "Don't cause a commotion." John then turned to the waiter and said: "Listen, she'll have the fish and chips." Yoko sat there looking sullen, but said nothing. She looked at John with reproachful eyes and hardly touched her plate.

John and I ate heartily, and I listened with growing fascination as he told me that the restaurant reminded him of Liverpool's pubs. He talked about badgering sailors on ships bound for the United States to bring him records by then-obscure American artists whose recordings were unavailable in England. John took pride in the fact that he had had such "hip" musical tastes as a teenager and that he had been "plugged into" rock and roll at its inception. "I always suspected that me and my mates knew more about American music than most American teenagers," John chuckled. I was surprised when he told me that there had even been a small blues and country and western scene in Liverpool. It was one of the happiest times I ever had with John. He seemed so much the way I had always imagined him—strong, in control, larger than life, and at peace with himself. Yet by that evening he was back in his room at the Dakota, restless and bored, flipping through the television channels, listening to Muzak on the radio.

Of the dozens of properties that I scouted for the Lennons in 1979, none seemed more suitable than a waterfront mansion overlooking Cold Spring Harbor on Long Island's North Shore. The Tudor-style house, called Cannon Hill because of the cannon by its swimming pool, nestled at the bottom of a winding driveway and from a distance looked like a gingerbread house. From the moment I first laid eyes on the old ivy-colored wooden mansion I knew it would be ideal for John and Yoko. It had more than a dozen rooms on three floors, including a large master bedroom with a balcony that offered a spectacular view of the harbor. There was even a small beach, as well as a private dock. John had begun to hint that he wanted to buy a boat, and this looked like the perfect place for it.

I persuaded John and Yoko to visit Cannon Hill, and when Marlene gave the property her stamp of approval, Yoko began negotiating its purchase. By late November the house belonged to the Lennons, and we were going to christen it with a big Thanksgiving dinner. The day before, I drove John and Yoko to the new house. The trip took about an hour in light traffic. Sean, Uda-san, and Yoko's brother's son, Keisuke, followed in a limousine. Once we reached our destination we all wandered around the house for a while, staking out our quarters. John and Yoko moved into the master bedroom, a large suite on the second floor. I took over a small bedroom down the hall, and the rest of the gang also moved into various rooms on the second floor. The entire third floor remained unoccupied.

I unpacked and helped Uda-san set up the kitchen for the big meal, which I had arranged to have catered by a French couple who owned a restaurant in New Jersey. Soon Yoko was on the phone, Uda-san complained about the inadequate kitchen facilities, and Sean pounced on his Japanese cousin. What we had was fundamentally the same chaos we always had at the Dakota, but without the usual conveniences. There wasn't even a TV—a cruel torture for John. And Sean, of course, did not have his elaborate playroom or his cartoons to watch. He was put to bed, over raucous protests.

The evening passed awkwardly. Here we were, gaping at this virtually empty house, killing time until the big dinner the next day. None of us seemed to have settled into our proper places. We all just moved around, bored, our small talk falling flat as the evening wore on mercilessly. One thing seemed odd: Everyone had developed an itch. Everywhere I turned, I saw people scratching. It was contagious, too. After a while, I began feeling as if I had bugs crawling on me.

On the Big Day, the precooked meal was delivered by the sweet, elderly couple. They arrived with numerous containers of food, spread everything out on the kitchen table, and departed. Now our job was to create the impression that we were just your ordinary little family, having our ordinary little Thanksgiving dinner, served by Uda-san. John even carved the turkey, and asked me to document the event with my camera. It was a perfect meal. A classic Norman Rockwell Thanksgiving dinner, with an enormous turkey and stuffing, sweet potatoes, giblet gravy, broccoli, green beans, and cranberry sauce.

We sat down to eat in the cozy dining room, with its old iron casement windows. Beneath a brass chandelier, the large oval table, set for eight, was draped with a white cloth. John, his hair pulled into a samurai bun, wore a white T-shirt, black trousers, and no shoes. He talked about the virtues of locally grown foods. But somehow the mood just never got on track. The table was surrounded by people who felt awkward. What was worse, we were all scratching ourselves constantly. I felt like crawling out of my skin. Even Uda-san, who was so proper that she would rather have died than do something unseemly, scratched her ass in front of God and everybody. John could usually keep a table of people going for as long as he liked, but this time his wit failed him. Eventually he, too, fell silent, absentmindedly poking his fork into "dead bird" as he called this nonvegetarian food.

When the meal was over, we retired to the bare living room, whose long rows of shelves were utterly naked. A few pieces of furniture had been left behind by the previous owners, and John slumped into a wing chair that had been gaudily upholstered in an orange nautical motif. He threw his feet onto another easy chair that was covered with a hideous chrysanthemum pattern. Staring out at the world through tinted glasses, he gave out an enormous sigh and vigorously scratched himself here and there. He asked me to have a 30-inch Sony remote TV and VCR installed in the living room, and a second set in the master bedroom, as soon as possible. "I'm going crackers without the telly," he complained.

After a while I went upstairs to my room to write in my journal. It was fairly late when I heard a knock on my door, and I was startled to see John standing there, proffering an unlit joint. "You can come down later if you feel like it," he said before he disappeared down the stairs. I smoked John's grass until I was thoroughly stoned, then lurched downstairs to see what was going on. Everyone had gone to bed except John, who sat alone in the living room, smoking and leafing through old copies of National Geographic. He gave me a sheepish smile when I entered the room.

"Ah, yes, the pleasure of the flesh," John sighed, peering at me with bloodshot eyes from behind thick spectacles. He invited me to take a seat opposite him and lit what was left of a sizable joint he had been smoking. We passed it back and forth for a while. John talked about a remote Tibetan monastery in the Himalayas that he had been reading about, a place where monks spent a lifetime in strict isolation and meditation.

"Are you familiar with kundalini yoga?" he suddenly asked. I admitted that I was not. "If you abstain from physical pleasures, especially sex"—he took a quick drag from the joint and held it for a moment, exhaling thick smoke into the dimly lit living room—"there's this substance at the base of the spine"—he coughed and passed me the joint—"it's like a tightly wound-up coil." I took a small puff, struggling to make sense of his disjointed talk. "If you fast and stay celibate for a long time," John continued, "it uncoils and shoots up the spinal column." I passed what was left of the joint, and John took another hit before resuming his rambling monologue.

"You can achieve different levels of spiritual awareness depending on how high this fluid goes up your spine, you see." I nodded. "If you abstain from food and sex for long enough," John said with mounting enthusiasm, "this stuff shoots all the way up into your head—and that's when you become clairvoyant!" I sat there, doubtless with my mouth hanging open. Not only was I very high on the excellent grass we had smoked, but I was wondering if this was something Yoko had told him in order to explain away the collapse of their sex life. John had complained on more than one occasion that he "never got any." I could just see her telling him, "Now, John, if we don't fuck, you'll become psychic. We should try it."

But I said nothing. We both went to bed, scratching.

The next morning I awoke from my drugged stupor to the sound of a loud, insistent knocking on my door. I found John standing outside once more, looking wiped out but kind of giddy, as if he'd just discovered some delightful joke.

"We have to leave right away!" he said urgently, scratching his arm. "This place is infested with fleas." He began to laugh and couldn't stop. "I mean it's fucking *crawling* with them!" John screwed up his face in mock disgust and let out a retching noise. He asked me to call Rosa, the maid at the Dakota, and to instruct her to meet us at the door with a large garbage bag into which we could deposit our contaminated clothes. John was worried about transporting fleas into Apartment 72 and had already figured out the logistics of our "quarantine." He said we would all have to take a shower. He was still laughing, scratching, as he turned away.

A short while later we all piled into the Mercedes. The Japanese contingent—Yoko, Keisuke, and Uda-san, who held Sean on her lap—squeezed into the back of the Benz, while John made himself comfortable in the front passenger seat. During the ride home John appeared to be in an exceptionally good mood. It was almost as if all the bad karma, as he would have called it, of the Thanksgiving scene had been explained away or somehow justified by the existence of the fleas. Sean, however, was bewildered by our sudden exodus. I knew it was only a matter of time before he would begin peppering us with questions. When John instructed me to call an exterminator and arrange to have the house fumigated, Sean immediately asked, "Daddy, what's an exterminator?"

John patiently described the fumigation process to his inquisitive four-year-old. When John explained that fleas were so tiny that they could not be seen, Sean demanded to know how something invisible could produce such a strong itch. Undaunted, John explained that the itching sensation was due to the fleas' "tickling" the skin, which sent Sean into a fit of hysterical laughter.

"But what do the fleas look like, Daddy?"

"I dunno, sweetheart," John sighed. "You'd have to look at them under a microscope."

"What's a microscope, Daddy?"

John threw me a helpless look, and so I tried to answer Sean's question myself. I told the little guy that a microscope was like a very powerful magnifying glass.

"Daddy, is Fred going to live with us forever?" Sean suddenly asked.

"Yeah," John said. "We've adopted him."

By the time we approached the Queensboro Bridge, John's initial giddiness had turned into mild annoyance. He was irritated not only by Sean's endless barrage of questions, but also by Yoko's indifference. She spent most of the ride slumped against the side of the car, nodding off. I assumed she had been up late making phone calls. As first John seemed content to let her sleep, but as we approached the Dakota he examined her reflection in the rearview mirror several times and tried to get her attention. When Yoko failed to respond, John snickered, "I think Mother's left us."

Suddenly Yoko came alive. As I drove up to the Dakota, she ordered me to fetch a bottle of witch hazel. I managed to find some at the Oliver Cromwell pharmacy across the street, and then rejoined the others upstairs. We took turns undressing in the Apartment 71 vestibule, depositing our contaminated clothes into a large garbage bag, and changed into one of Yoko's robes for the trip to the shower. John left a pair of jeans, a T-shirt, and underwear—all of them his—in the entrance hall for me to wear.

"What a day!" John chuckled after we had showered and changed.

To him it was all a great cosmic joke that we should make an enormous effort to go out to Long Island, order a turkey dinner from New Jersey, and try to be like a typical American family—and then be attacked by nine trillion fleas. John, I think, felt it served us right.

One morning in mid-December I took the mail to John's bedroom and found him all excited about a "guru" he had seen on cable TV. "This guy is really amazing!" John enthused. "He conveys these heavy, abstract concepts through very simple images. It's great; just watch." He got down on his knees, and asked me to do the same. Staring at me intensely as we faced each other at the foot of the TV set, John made a tight fist. "You see," he said, "the trick to getting out of a tense and uptight state is to realize that it's just part of a normal process." He gradually opened his fist. Then he picked up a piece of paper with a square hole in it and held it to his right eye. "Most of the time we allow only this much of ourselves to be expressed," John continued, looking at me through the hole. "We present a mask to the world. The trouble is, if we limit what we put out, it also automatically limits what we can take in from others—from the outside world. For most of us it's sometimes an ordeal just to say 'Good morning'!"

He got up and sat on the bed, while I stood a few feet away. Making a connection between this "lesson" from the TV guru and his own life, John now talked about the early Beatle years during which "it came"—meaning his creative powers. "When it stops coming," John said ruefully, "the trick is to accept that, too, and not try to force 'it,' because the harder you try, the more elusive it becomes. Most people can't let go. They fall apart, and simply disintegrate when 'it' no longer flows. Howard Hughes is a good example of somebody who lost it, then lost control of his entire life. He was taken over by his servants." I sensed the irony of what John was saying, but I was not sure he did. I knew, for one thing, that he felt he was totally in control at all times through Yoko; whereas in fact, he had abdicated his own authority by delegating it to her.

John told me that just before the Beatles really made it big, he had had absolute control over his songwriting muse, eventually coming up with a magic formula of sorts that enabled him to write hits with the efficiency of an assembly line. He took bits and pieces from the various popular styles of the day, recycling them into infectious pop songs designed to appeal to the widest possible audience. John said that in the early days of the Beatles, when he was "hot," it was like magic. He felt strong all the time, exhilarated, in control of his destiny, high on life. It seemed as if all he had to do was set a goal, and it would happen. Every song he wrote was a hit. Everything he touched turned to solid gold.

"Playing an instrument and writing music is a gift," John continued. "You give it all you've got—it takes a lot of hard work, a lot of practice—but once you've got those basic skills worked out and you're in the proper frame of mind, then you're in a position to allow yourself to be inspired . . . by God, by whoever it is. Then the music just flows. When it comes, it's like magic. And when it doesn't," he rounded off sadly, "there's nothing you can do to force it."

As Christmas approached and my first year as John's assistant drew to an end, life at the Dakota escalated to a feverish pitch. There was, for one thing, the monumental task of assembling Christmas gift baskets for a few dozen of the Lennons' friends and business associates. We had two lists, one for the A crowd, another for the B group. The A list included the two Sams (Green and Havadtoy); Marlene Weiner and John Green (the psychics); David Warmflash and Eli Garber (chief among the Lennons' numerous lawyers and accountants); Leon Wildes, the lawyer who had successfully defended John from the Nixon government's efforts to deport him; Dr. Hong, the San Francisco acupuncturist who had gotten John and Yoko off heroin; Loraine and Peter Boyle; Helen and Norman; the LeRoys; and Marnie Hair. Each member of this group received a basket with fruit, nuts, chocolate, and cheese. Nestled inside it all was a bottle of wine worth approximately two hundred dollars.

The B crowd included various friends and acquaintances of the Lennons, many of them artists that Yoko had been involved with in the sixties—Charlotte Moorman, Jonas Mekas, John Cage, and Merce Cunningham—as well as a handful of favored journalists, such as *Rolling Stone* publisher Jann Wenner, and members of the Dakota's staff and board of directors. They all received the same gift basket, only the bottle of wine was worth closer to forty dollars. As Christmas approached I spent much of my time typing up and revising the two lists and tracking down addresses. The task seemed endless.

In addition to the gift baskets going out, another organizational challenge was posed by the avalanche of gifts that came pouring in. Toys for Sean, presents for Yoko and John, anything one can imagine, legal and illegal, valuable and valueless, would arrive around Christmas. Mostly, these unsolicited items were left lying around the office because we were all so busy trying to get the Lennons' gift baskets sent out. Not only that, but for some reason the Christmas season prompted a flood of artwork by fans. Beatles fans had always created and sent in drawings of the group, and now they turned their efforts to John and Yoko. Some of these works were elaborate, finely drawn portraits, while others were hacked out with childlike crudity. Most of them projected a romantic, mythological view of John and Yoko's relationship. The fans could be a nuisance, but most of them were quite sincere in their devotion.

John was both flattered and embarrassed by the fans' adoration. For the most part, he did not mind being worshiped from a distance. What John dreaded were confrontations with belligerent fans. No matter how cautious, or even paranoid, he was, John could not avoid an occasional "close encounter of the fourth kind," as he once described an unnerving incident involving an aggressive fan.

One day late in December, for instance, there was an ugly incident triggered by Paul Goresh, the same fan who had previously gained access to John's bedroom by posing as a repairman. The day had begun normally enough. John called me downstairs in the office that morning to ask me to get him *The Zionist Connection*, a controversial book he had heard discussed on a talk show. Just before noon, John stopped by the office on his way out to do some Christmas shopping. He admired the latest collection of Sean's framed drawings while waiting for Yoko to decide if she wanted to join him shopping. After waiting around impatiently for a few minutes with no word from the inner sanctum, John decided to go by himself. A few minutes after John left, I went out to buy the book he had requested.

When I returned, Studio One was in an uproar. Apparently Goresh had stalked John, taking photos against his wishes. John had confronted him and demanded the film. A young female fan was present when Goresh had refused to turn over his film. John grabbed the girl's camera and threatened to smash it on the sidewalk. Goresh handed John his film.

"You can't do that," Yoko said. "What if they sue us? You shouldn't go near these people. Think of all the trouble it could cause!"

"That fat slob scared the shit out of me!" cried John, trying to justify his violent reaction. "But you're right, I shouldn't have lost my temper. This'll only encourage him."

After his run-in with Goresh, Yoko asked me to buy John a can of Mace, along with a self-hypnosis tape called *Stop Being Angry*. John did not want the Mace. "I know I would never be able to use it," he said, "so it would only give me a false sense of security."

On Tuesday afternoon, December 18, John and I were in the kitchen opening some of the cards sent by fans when word came from the front gate that the tree was being delivered.

"Does that mean there will be a lot of strong men hovering around?" John asked anxiously.

There was no quicker way to get rid of John than to announce that burly strangers would be arriving. But when he returned to the kitchen later on to help decorate the tree, he was just like a kid. We had enough lights and ornaments to decorate four or five trees. When we were finished, the tree looked overengineered.

"I wonder how this compares to the LeRoys'," John frowned.

If Warner LeRoys' taste in Christmas tree decorations was anything like his taste in clothes and furniture, his tree would be far gaudier than ours. "Maybe you should stop by the LeRoys' to see what their tree looks like," John suggested, in all seriousness. I dutifully went one floor below to inspect our neighbors' tree, and I was hardly surprised that it, too, was decorated to the hilt. I reported to John that our tree had more "soul." This idea filled him with satisfaction.

Around this time, John was moved to send a Christmas message to the world:

THIS IS THE GREAT WOK SPEAKING TO YOU FROM THE HEART OF THE WEST SIDE OF MANHATTAN, NEW YORK. I AM PLEASED TO GIVE MY ANNUAL YEARLY MESSAGE TO MA PEOPLE FOR THE NEW YEAR. I MYSELF HAVE MADE MY RESOLUTION TO

RENOUNCE COMPLETELY EVERYTHING BUT COM-
PLETE SELF-INDULGENCE AND LUXURY.

If John had planned to include this unusual message in the gift
baskets, he was talked out of it. One of Sean's drawings was made
into a Christmas card and included instead.

By Christmas Eve I was exhausted and exalted at the prospect of
being released for an entire day. Ten months of working for John and
Yoko had drained me to the core. Christmas Eve I had messengers
running all over Manhattan, Brooklyn, Queens, and Yonkers, deliv-
ering the gift baskets as fast as I could put them together. I was also
stuck with the job of wrapping all of the Lennons' gifts. When I was
done, I carried everything upstairs to the kitchen, where I arranged
the gifts under the Christmas tree.

I did not make it out of the Dakota and back to my apartment until
the stroke of midnight. Christmas morning, John called to thank me
for the Elvis Christmas record I had given him, and for a gold ashtray
I had presented to Yoko. That night I went out with my family, whom
I hardly saw anymore. Wednesday, the day after Christmas, I awoke
feeling utterly exhausted, but was back at work by 9:00 A.M. That was
my vacation for the year.

"What was life like before I entered the service of Lennono?" I
would ask myself. I couldn't seem to remember. I was on call twenty-
four hours a day, and it went without saying that I could never be out
of touch. Moreover, the Lennons did not like the idea that I might
have a private life outside the Dakota. It was assumed that if I had any
friends, they would buttonhole me to reveal intimate details of John
and Yoko's lives. John warned me frequently about being tempted by
nubile teenage fans, who, he said, would only want to use me to get to
him. Once I went out to dinner with a real estate agent, a young
woman, and John and Yoko nearly had seizures.

Gradually, what was left of my personal life was whittled away, until
I could not really remember how normal people lived. Looking back
at that time, I am reminded of the undercover agent, who cannot
even tell his neighbors for whom he works. Making matters even
worse was the fact that life at the Dakota was becoming increasingly
bizarre and oppressive. Keeping a journal helped me cope with my
isolation. Sometimes it kept me from going mad.

A few days after Christmas, I entered the bedroom to bring John some self-hypnosis tapes from Potential Unlimited, titled *Improve Your Vision* and *I Love My Body*. I found John propped self-consciously behind a white plastic bed tray, a Christmas gift from Sam Green. John began complaining that someone in another apartment was playing Beatles music very loud and that it was driving him crazy. Unfortunately, the acoustics of the Dakota were such that we were never able to locate the culprit. Or perhaps John was imagining it. I never heard the music myself. When I had returned to my desk in Studio One, John called me on the intercom to say that no one should be put through to him under any circumstances—"Not even if it's my dead mother!"

I knew that meant John wanted to get stoned in peace. Surrounded by his staff in the Dakota, he felt self-conscious about getting "high." If he was called upon to act, to decide, to speak, to be coherent, it would spoil his fun. There he would be, ripped to the gills, unable to string five words together to make a sentence, and someone would come knocking on the door or one of Yoko's sycophants would phone, asking whether Italian black marble would be all right for the new bathroom. I promised John I would keep the world at bay for a while.

Meanwhile, Sean was blazing around the Dakota screaming, "We all live in a yellow submarine!" He buzzed me on the intercom to cancel his "appointment" to play with his little friend Teddy, and I dutifully did so. Yoko gave me a letter to file from a woman who claimed that she was the mother of Paul McCartney's teenage son, begging for Paul's address. Paul, like John, had had great difficulty keeping his pants zipped in the early days; women were always claiming to be the mothers of his children. I even kept a special file labeled *Paul's Wives* for future reference. Yoko also asked me to remind her to check the pregnancy test kit in the bathroom in an hour and a half, and to order some more cranberry juice, because she was not getting enough urine for her sample every morning.

I thought we were headed for a suitably bizarre New Year's Eve and could see us collectively building to some sort of dramatic climax. I had recurring nightmares about how it might come out. John, stoned, hallucinating old Beatles songs, is finally driven mad by them and hatchets up the old woman a little bit. Or: Yoko, crazed with delusions of grandeur, imagines herself to be as wealthy as McCartney and, without telling John, buys the World Trade Center, plunging him into bankruptcy.

Indeed, by New Year's Eve, things had reached a pitch of humming weirdness. Yoko was apparently trying to get pregnant, and the Studio One bathroom was cluttered with pregnancy test kits, ruined by her forgetfulness. She could never seem to remember what time she was supposed to look for the little orange ring to appear in the bottom of the test tube supplied with the biological agglutination kits. Then a letter arrived from her doctor stating that Yoko was manopausal and had no chance of becoming pregnant again. To console herself she got on a caviar kick and starting spending a hundred dollars a day on fish eggs at Zabar's and the Caviarteria.

Yoko's behavior became increasingly weird and was accompanied by a marked deterioration in her physical appearance. Her face was haggard, her eyes glassy around pinned pupils, and she began to spend much of her time in the bathroom making loud snorting noises, frequently followed by frightful retching. At first I thought Yoko was ill, but then I realized that she was simply strung out on heroin. She began to spend virtually all her time downstairs. Her day started at dawn with a visit by Bart Gorin, a lanky young man who worked for Sam Green. It was an open secret that Sam's assistant supplied Yoko with her daily dose of the drug.

Oddly enough, the heroin made her easier to deal with. Yoko seemed friendlier and more relaxed. Her frantic pace slowed down considerably, and she would spend the day puttering lethargically back and forth between her office and the bathroom, bumping into the furniture, cigarettes dropping out of her fingers.

On the rare occasions John met Yoko, they circled each other wearily. John would harangue Yoko about her vampire hours and her disheveled, zombielike appearance. Naturally, John's outbursts caused Yoko to avoid him even more. For instance, one morning after breakfast he blew up at Yoko for spending so little time upstairs with him and Sean. When Yoko quietly shuffled out of the room, John was instantly seized with guilt and remorse. He even wrote her a poignant, humorous memo apologizing for his angry outburst.

John sensed the pressure everyone was under, and when he could, he tried to lighten the mood. In a note he wrote in red, John complained that he was still not getting regular delivery of the *Daily News*, and ended with the options: "Commit harikiri, Change mind, Decide to be a monk, Change mind, Give up."

During the first weeks of 1980 I often wondered who would be the first to lose their mind—Yoko, John, or me. We seemed to be neck and neck, only I was always able to fall back on the comforting thought that they were giving the orders and I just carried them out.

I am not sure why January proved so difficult. Perhaps it was the bleak prospect we all saw looking ahead to the new year: another vast stretch of twelve miserable months, filled with nothing but Beluga Gold, house-hunting, fan mail, daytime TV, and gossip magazines. The turning point came from the most unexpected direction.

I found John in the kitchen on the morning of January 15—a Tuesday—hunched over a bowl of Nabisco Shredded Wheat, looking glum. I could only guess that it had to do with Paul McCartney, who had called the previous day from the Stanhope Hotel, across Central Park.

Yoko took the call, but apparently something had gotten through to John that upset him. I asked innocently what Paul had said. "Nothing much," John replied, avoiding the question. I hung around in the kitchen, rearranging some shelves, biding my time. I knew that eventually John would not be able to resist talking about it. Finally he spoke up.

Paul, it seemed, had wanted to stop by the Dakota. He said that his wife, Linda, had scored a large amount of "really dynamite weed." If this was not precisely an offer to smoke the peace pipe, it was close to it. Whatever John's problems with Paul, I knew this suggestion alone had not sent him into such a funk.

"Paul's touring Japan and he called to brag about the fact that he's going to be staying in *our* suite at the Hotel Okura," John blurted out. "Can you believe the nerve!"

During their annual visit to Japan for the past few years, John and Yoko had always insisted on staying in the Okura's Presidential Suite—the most exclusive rooms in Tokyo's most lavish hotel.

"If those two [Paul and Linda] sleep there," John said through clenched teeth, "we'll never have peace when we go back to that room. They're going to fuck up our good hotel karma!" I was flabbergasted. If I had not seen for myself how this news upset John, I would have believed he was kidding. "I already talked to Mother," he said, mysteriously. "She is trying to work it out." It seemed that John

Green, Yoko's hulking, bearded tarot card reader who was also a voodoo priest, was supposed to cast a "spell" on Paul to prevent him and
Linda from occupying the Presidential Suite of the Okura. Rich informed me that under no circumstances was Yoko to be disturbed,
because she and the card reader were working on the "Japan problem." I went home that night thinking, "Well, this is it. The Lennons
have finally flipped. The little white truck will be around tomorrow to
pick them up."

The next day something remarkable happened. Paul never did get
to the Hotel Okura, because he was arrested at the airport in Tokyo
by customs officials, who had no trouble finding a large quantity of
grass in one of his and Linda's suitcases. I rushed to the Dakota to
man my battle station. When I got there, Rich was smiling like a
Cheshire cat. "Isn't it funny," he winked, "the way Paul got busted in
Japan today? Especially since he called yesterday asking if he could
bring over some smoke?"

An amazing coincidence, indeed. As the day went on, we heard
more details of the bust through the media and Yoko's Japanese
sources. It seemed the customs officials had, in fact, been tipped off
that Paul and Linda had marijuana in their possession. Wanting to
avoid a scene, they asked Paul repeatedly if he was carrying any illicit
substances. The arrest might have been avoided if he had quietly
turned over the grass. But Paul and Linda had refused to come clean,
and so their bags were searched. Within minutes the customs inspectors found the pot. Paul took the blame and was promptly carried off
in handcuffs.

The story became front-page news around the globe. John and
Yoko howled with glee at the thought of poor Paulie wasting away in a
Tokyo jail cell, the sold-out tour ruined. Even more titillating was the
rumor we were getting through Yoko's sources that the jail guards
were forcing Paul to sing "Yesterday" over and over again. Of course,
John did not want any real harm to come to Paul. He certainly would
not have turned Paul in himself. But Paul's plight seemed harmless
enough—he was sure to be released after a few days in the slammer—
and John felt it served McCartney right.

No matter how the Japanese authorities had come to conduct the
search, John firmly believed that Yoko had managed to cast a spell on
Paul. John had always claimed that Yoko had magical powers, and
here was proof. Yoko's success in preventing Paul from moving into

the Okura's Presidential Suite thus validated his way of life. Not only was his hotel karma safe, and his wife a powerful sorceress, but Paul and the "McEastmans" were dealt a humiliating blow in public. It all seemed too good to be true.

Now the malaise that had settled upon us at the Dakota was dissipated. John was gleeful—ecstatic—and asked me to get every paper I could lay my hands on, including, and especially, the British papers, so that he could follow Paul's plight minute by minute. I rushed over to Hotaling's, an international newsstand in Times Square, and picked up all the British tabloids. I delivered them to John in his bedroom, where he sat flipping through the TV channels, looking for the latest news of Paul. "I can just picture Paul sitting in a bare jail cell," John chuckled. "They've taken away his shoelaces and his belt so he won't hang himself if he becomes despondent singing"—here John broke into song—"Yesterday, all my troubles seemed so far away." He hooted with pleasure.

"You know, it serves Paul right," John went on. "I think subconsciously he wanted to get busted." John speculated that Paul's fondness for marijuana was his way of "rebelling against this image of the 'goody-two-shoes' businessman" with which the Eastmans had stuck him. "Paul wanted to show the world—particularly the British—that he's still a bit of a bad boy," John concluded. He checked out a transsexual being interviewed by Phil Donahue, then clicked through the channels, and came full circle back to Donahue. "We could get him off just like that!" John said, snapping his fingers. "Mother has great connections over there. She could get him out tonight, but of course the Eastmans would never ask for our help. It would be beneath them."

That weekend, John and Yoko were scheduled to check out a house in Suffern, New York. During the long ride upstate in the Mercedes, John pulled out a small tin container filled with grass. Cackling demonically, he opened it up and held it under my nose. "This is dynamite stuff," he boasted as he took out a small pipe and loaded it with the moist green buds. Then he lit up, and the car quickly filled with the peppery aroma of cannabis. I could tell it was strong stuff. I had only a small toke, but it made me pleasantly relaxed for the duration of the ride. I would have had more, but I do not think Yoko considered it safe for me to drive under the influence. She gave both John and me icy, disapproving looks from the backseat, and, for once, I could not have cared less.

"You know, it's Paul's arrogance toward the Japanese that screwed him," John mused, after taking another hit from his pipe. "I just know it."

"That's right!" Yoko said.

Yes, I thought, that was one way of looking at it.

7

Gardenias for Mother

In early February of 1980, we went to Palm Beach again. The Lennons had bought *El Solano*, the villa they had rented the previous spring, and we were going to celebrate Yoko's forty-seventh birthday there. To provide some distraction, John and Yoko invited Peter and Loraine Boyle to visit. Loraine had once interviewed Yoko for *Rolling Stone*. When Loraine married actor Peter Boyle, the two couples became friendly. John, who had met Boyle in a club in Los Angeles in 1974, respected the well-known actor for his work in the movies and also because he had abandoned the order of the Christian Brotherhood to pursue an acting career. John regarded Peter as a fellow religious renegade.

The Lennons and the Boyles, who had not seen each other in a long time, had a friendly reunion at *El Solano*, and Peter quickly established a marvelous rapport with Sean, who was fascinated by this convivial houseguest. At the dinner table Peter made silly faces and entertained Sean with funny stories, to everyone's delight. After dinner the two couples went to the living room to talk and watch TV. The next day after breakfast John picked up a guitar and suggested "lounging" by the pool. Yoko picked up a book, put on a hat, and made herself comfortable under the shade of an umbrella. John casually strolled around strumming the guitar. Uda-san served refreshments. Peter and Loraine stood around awkwardly, and Peter eventually did a lumbering dance to the sound of John's guitar, while I took photos.

The Boyles shared meals and watched television with us, killing time around the house. John and Peter stayed up late into the night talking and watching TV in the living room. John relished having a captive audience for his opinionated monologues. The Boyles, anxious to break the monotony, offered to take John and Yoko to a local restaurant, but the Lennons were reluctant to be seen in public. If the local media got wind of their presence in Palm Beach, it would only be a matter of time until the fans began staking out the house. Finally, after a few awkward and boring days, John and Yoko agreed to let the Boyles take them to a fancy French restaurant. That night, John appeared, fully bearded, dressed in white pants, black jacket, white shirt, dark tie, and a straw hat with a black and red band. He sat down at the piano in the living room and improvised a melody while waiting for Yoko to come down from the bedroom. I took the obligatory photos of everyone dressed for the occasion. Then the two couples went off in a limo to *La Petite Marmite*, leaving the rented red Eldorado behind for the evening, which enabled me to have a night on the town as well.

When I returned to *El Solano* in the early hours of the morning, the house was in an uproar. I overhead John loudly berating Peter and Loraine for taking him to a place where the local social set went to see and be seen. It seemed that while they were dining, photographers had snapped their picture, enraging John. Now John took his revenge on Peter.

"Always dragging us to second-rate, trendy eateries so you can get your picture taken with us, Peter—don't you think it's a bit lame-brained?"

"What the fuck do you mean, lame-brained?" hollered Boyle.

John was exquisitely calm now.

"Well, Peter, I just mean dumb. Don't you think it might just be a little bit *stupid?*"

"Don't you call me stupid!" Boyle said savagely, his face red with rage. "Who the fuck do you think you are, calling me names? You dumb scumbag! I'll tear your fuckin' head off!"

John had a mischievous glint in his eyes as he watched Peter jump and twitch like a puppet on a string. When John started to laugh softly, Boyle slowly began to catch on. Then he felt even more stupid than before. John liked to wind people up, provoke them. He often complained that most people relate on a phony and superficial level, and he liked to uncover the primal emotions that lurked beneath their facade. Something of an expert, John had an unerring instinct for finding a person's weak spot. He knew that Boyle was afraid that his screen image—big and dumb, as in *Joe* and *Young Frankenstein*—might be real. John had touched Peter's "stupid" button and enjoyed watching the sparks fly.

All of a sudden the room filled with embarrassed silence. It was three in the morning; everyone was tired and bleary-eyed, sad and freaked out. They all went to bed. The next morning the Boyles were so upset that they boycotted breakfast.

"I really got to Peter last night, didn't I?" John said, crushing a block of shredded wheat with his spoon. "Cracked that stony facade. I mean, he almost had a fuckin' *primal!*" He let out a hearty chuckle. John was in a sparkling mood. He enjoyed the fact that Peter's getting his picture in the paper had not come without a heavy tariff: He had paid with his ego, for no one could pay John any other way.

The Boyles eventually came down for lunch, pretending with all their might that nothing had happened. Everyone was so cheerful you might have thought we were on television. By Sunday, however, John must have felt some guilt for what he had done to Peter, because he agreed to go out once more with the Boyles, who were leaving the next day. The only place to be on a Sunday in Palm Beach, if you were *anyone* at all, was The Breakers, an exclusive hotel where a lavish brunch was served in the main dining room. The Boyles wanted to go there by limousine, but John insisted on taking the Cadillac, which, he thought, would be "less conspicuous."

We all piled into the red Eldorado. John and Sean shared the passenger seat next to me, while Peter sat sandwiched between Yoko and Loraine in the backseat. At one point we passed a basketball court where some kids were playing, and Peter eagerly suggested we stop for a quick game. John gave Peter a look of incredulity, but said nothing. He simply ignored Peter, who spent the rest of the ride silently fuming in the back of the car.

When we arrived at the restaurant, the headwaiter refused to let us in. John was wearing a fringed leather jacket and a straw hat, Peter had on a sweater, the women wore pants, Sean had on shorts, and I was wearing a blue velvet jacket and faded jeans. It seemed neckties were required at The Breakers. Peter gently took the maitre d' aside and showed him the color of his money in large denominations. He also pointed out that the rabid-looking gentleman in the straw hat was none other than the globally famous multimillionaire ex-Beatle, John Lennon.

Instantly, we were transformed from undesirables into celebrities and seated at a large table near the center of the dining room, which was the size of Radio City Music Hall. Brunch was buffet style. This was the idea, of course—the ultimate opportunity to see and be seen. Soon every eye in the hall was fixed upon John, who began talking nonstop to dispel the anxiety that seized him when he was on the spot. And for John, being on the spot was a chronic condition. It was home plate.

He began a running monologue, sizing up the crowd, pointing out those who were most likely to muster the courage to approach our table for autographs. He also pointed out those who "performed" to get his attention: people who pretended not to notice him, all the while behaving very conspicuously, laughing loudly and doing tricks for their wives or girlfriends, as if to say, "Hey, we're having just as much fun over at our table as you are over at your Beatle table." Then there were those somber diners determined not to notice, who dug deep into their plates, deep into their conversations, their morning Bloody Marys. There were others who stared out of curiosity or boredom, and some who simply gaped in awe—disbelieving, hard-core fans. Having all that attention streaming in my direction made it difficult for me to keep it straight in my mind that I wasn't a star, too—I just worked for one.

We got through brunch without any mishaps, and then made a fast getaway. John spent the rest of the day sequestered in the master bedroom.

After the Boyles' departure, John asked me to drive him around Palm Beach. We went looking for interesting stores, as well as observing the "natives," one of John's favorite pastimes. He would let his eyes and mind roam during these car rides. He frequently thought aloud in a rambling, stream-of-consciousness monologue, commenting on the sights. John was very impressed by the "wealthy atmosphere" and "squeaky-clean" streets, but he also complained about the preponderance of well-dressed, clean-cut, and tanned men and women.

It was just a bit too wholesome for John's taste. He said that "a little sleaze" might give the place some much-needed "color," and he wondered what would happen if a bizarre-looking punk with spiky green or purple hair were to suddenly appear in the midst of this civilized Palm Beach scene. He speculated that it would no doubt liven up the disgustingly wholesome environment. If he were a businessman, John mused, he would start a "Rent-a-Punk" agency that would hire out exotic-looking types to spice up parties and the like. John often talked about farfetched business ventures or gadgets that he would like to invent. One "invention" he was particularly proud of was a self-coiling toothpaste tube that would eliminate the effort of manual squeezing, as well as the "waste" that resulted from it.

One morning John and I were sitting in the living room reading newspapers when he came across an ad for used books. John said he was tired of staring at the naked bookshelves in the house; he asked me to drive him to the bookstore, which was in West Palm Beach, to see if it sold occult and esoteric literature. It was a small, cramped shop, filled with row upon row of antique books on countless topics. I expected John to pick out a few books for the house, but he had a different plan. He asked me to pay close attention as he dashed around the store, pausing only briefly at various shelves, pointing to groups of books that interested him. He instructed me to come back the following day and buy all the sections he had pointed out, as well as the entire stock of occult literature.

The next day, I returned to the bookstore to carry out John's orders. The owner eyed me suspiciously from behind thick spectacles as I proceeded to collect armfuls of books. When I asked to buy his entire stock of occult books, the owner asked me if I planned to go into business for myself. I quickly assured him I had no intention of opening a rival store, and explained sheepishly that I worked for an eccentric couple who simply wished to fill their empty bookshelves in a hurry. I made him an offer he could not refuse, and he quickly produced several cardboard boxes and helped me pack up the instant library.

Back at the house, John behaved like a kid at Christmas. He was eager to help unload the car, and then got busy dusting off the old books. He inspected each one closely, expressing delight when he came upon a particularly interesting volume. Anxious to share the experience with Yoko, he excitedly showed her a book by the famous psychic Edgar Cayce. Yoko smiled at John indulgently, but her mind was clearly on her business. As she walked away John came across a slender hardcover book bound in blue.

"Look at this, Mother!" he exclaimed, running after Yoko. He showed her a book by H. P. Blavatsky titled *Practical Occultism.*

Yoko leafed through it absently and then handed the small book back to John, mumbling, "Amazing, isn't it."

John was obviously very intrigued by the small, hardbound volume. He told me that its author, Madame Blavatsky, was a leading exponent of Theosophy, an ancient occult science. John became fascinated because this particular book dealt with the difference between theoretical and practical occultism, among other topics. When he discovered that the last section of the book was titled "Some Practical Suggestions for Daily Life," he scurried off to the master bedroom with his prize. "I can't wait to read this!" he said, adding that he had always been interested in Theosophy, but that most of his reading on the subject had struck him as "intellectual masturbation."

Driving around West Palm Beach one day, John and I passed a dock where a boat named *Imagine* was anchored. His curiosity piqued, he asked me to find out if the boat was named after his famous song.

I looked up the *Imagine* in the local phone book. A brief chat with the captain confirmed John's surmise. What's more, the ship turned out to be available for a lunch cruise. When I got back to John with this information, he suggested making a reservation under my name, and then set about convincing Yoko that a cruise on the *Imagine* would be an ideal family outing. Yoko adamantly rejected the suggestion, finding countless reasons why such an excursion seemed ill-advised. Normally, John would have capitulated in the face of Yoko's opposition. This time he stood his ground. Yoko reluctantly gave in, and a date was set.

The appointed day found Yoko still whining and stalling. She and John spent the better part of the morning trying to decide what to wear for this major outing. John settled on a white outfit, capped by a straw hat. Around noon I drove toward the dock; John was sitting next to me, chattering on merrily about what fun we were going to have. He found some delicious titillation in the idea of his showing up on the boat *Imagine.* "I can't wait to blow those fuckers' minds," he chuckled gleefully as we arrived. Sean was literally jumping up and down in the back of the car, ecstatic about this exciting break in our routine. Yoko was grim-faced and silent.

The *Imagine* was a twenty-foot day sailer helmed by a rugged, handsome man in his late thirties. His blonde wife served as first mate and cook, assisted by their teenage daughter, while their teenage son slouched about looking useless. When the Lennons stepped aboard, the captain and his wife were momentarily stunned. There was no mistaking Yoko, even if John was disguised behind beard, sunglasses, and a hat. I watched the couple as their faces went through the familiar changes. First they refused to believe. Then they wanted to grab, to possess John, to touch him all over, to ask a thousand questions. But then they saw that, like a rare bird caught out of its habitat, he would fly off if they moved. Soon they were trying with all their awkward might to pretend that John and Yoko were just another tourist couple out for a spin around Palm Beach.

John tried to put his hosts at ease by asking how they happened to name their boat *Imagine*.

"We were flower children," the wife explained. "We grew up with the Beatles." Her husband then described how they had watched the *Dick Cavett Show* in the early seventies, blissfully stoned on LSD, awaiting the American broadcast premiere of the film clip from the *Imagine* movie that showed John playing the title song on a white grand piano in the huge, sun-drenched living room of his mansion in Ascot, England.

"It was a mind-blowing experience," the husband said.

"That's when we decided that when we got a boat, we'd name it *Imagine*," the wife concluded.

John sat back, smiling.

After becoming relaxed enough to talk normally, the couple began to worry about Yoko, whose demeanor gave the impression she was throwing a silent tantrum. John affectionately draped his arm over Yoko's shoulder. Yoko remained grim, saying nothing. Being on boats made her nervous. Being in cars made her nervous. In fact, being anywhere except on firm ground behind locked doors and shuttered windows made her nervous. Not only that, but she had been up all night with some antique dealer who had flown in to consult with her about buying the contents of a church. Yoko looked seasick. Our hosts redoubled their efforts to please her, but it made no difference. Finally, John took the captain aside and apologized for her behavior, explaining that it was not owing to anything he or his family had done. Then he returned to Yoko, leaning over to kiss her. He was trying so hard to make her feel more comfortable. Yet she sat there like a stone, ignoring him. I wondered what they had been like when they first met—whether she had been as tender as he—and what had changed. As they kissed, I snapped their picture. It was one of the very few times I had caught them off guard. John had a sixth sense about photographs (not surprisingly, for one of the most photographed men on earth). But this time I had caught him unawares. Of all the dozens of photos I took of John and Yoko, this snapshot of them kissing on the *Imagine* was his favorite. He asked me to have it enlarged and framed.

The couple's kids, another generation, did not realize at first who John Lennon was. When they finally caught on that he was a rock star who used to work with Paul McCartney in some band before Wings, they went a little bit crazy. The boy got out his Windsurfer and leapt into the sea, nearly drowning in his eagerness to impress John, who smiled tolerantly.

A cat jumped onto John's lap, and he kept it there, stroking it gently while the captain's wife served lunch. There was wine, cheese and fruit, a giant shrimp cocktail, and delicious bread she had baked right there on the boat. We all ate heartily, except for Yoko, who said she wasn't hungry, but who allowed John to coax her into having some of the bread. John complimented the wife on her baking skills and talked about his being a "house husband" who baked bread at the Dakota while Yoko handled the day-to-day businesss affairs.

When it came time to leave the boat, there was a moment's awkwardness. I saw it in the looks passing between the couple. It seemed as if they were asking each other: "Is this it? Are we ever going to see them again?"

A few days later John and I ran into the captain in town, and John barely acknowledged his presence. We beat a hasty retreat. Even though every now and then he could not resist, soaking up the fans' unabashed adulation, he knew too much about his admirers to prolong his contact. He once said that if you give them an autograph, they want a piece of your clothes. You give them clothes, they want a lock of your hair. If you give them a lock of your hair, they want to go to bed with you; and if you sleep with them, they devour you.

It was Sunday, February 17, 1980, and John realized that he still had not confronted the problem of what to get for Yoko for her forty-seventh birthday, the next day. It was 10:00 A.M. and I had been making a phone call in my room when I heard John's anxious voice outside my door, asking me to meet him downstairs. I found him in the kitchen, pacing back and forth, sucking furiously on his Gitane.

"Ah, good morning, Sleeping Beauty," he said sardonically. "I was afraid I wasn't going to see you today. Hurry up and get some break-fast. We've got to go out and find Mother a birthday gift." I poured some coffee and began making toast, thinking I ought to skip it, be-cause John looked so jumpy. "We better split before Mother comes down," he said. "Otherwise we'll spend the whole morning arguing about whether or not it's safe to go out." I wolfed down my toast with marmalade, feeling guilty about eating at all.

"We, um, had a little fight last night," John volunteered. "Actually, I guess it was this morning. She was on the phone half the fuckin' night and I couldn't sleep, so I kicked her out of bed," John said, chuckling nervously. "I think she was up talking on the phone until dawn, so I don't think she'll show up too soon, but one never knows with Mother, does one?"

I knew that Yoko often stayed up all night calling people in England and Japan or waking her psychics to ask them questions. I had never understood how John could stand it when she talked while he was trying to sleep.

As I washed down my toast with boiling-hot coffee, John disap-peared to another room and returned with a few hats. He tried on a straw one with a green visor. "They'll never spot me with this on," John laughed. He wore blue jeans, a red-on-white Marilyn Monroe T-shirt, and a white gabardine jacket. With the green-visored straw hat, he looked like an over-the-hill hippie tourist.

"What do you think?" he asked. I suggested he might pass for a gentleman drug dealer. John was not amused. "Well, we don't want that, do we?"

He tried on several other hats in quick succession, rejecting each in turn. Finally he settled on a floppy black one and gave me a question-ing look. Too sinister, I suggested. The straw one proved better. I was about to suggest that we ought to leave when in walked Yoko. She had made no effort to disguise the fact that she had been up all night. Her face looked haggard, her skin a ghastly shade of gray, and she wore a gray floor-length gown. Her eyes were at half-mast, and she shuffled as if she'd had a stroke.

"Good morning, my dear!" John sounded as cheerful as he could under the circumstances.

Yoko stared at him with a blank expression. Then suddenly she realized that we were up to something. "What's going on?" she asked, her speech somewhat slurred.

Hanging his head, John admitted reluctantly that we had been toying with the idea of going out for a drive. He looked at her hopefully.

"Oh, so that's it!" Yoko smiled accusingly. She scratched herself while gazing absentmindedly at John. After an interminable pause, she said, "It's Mercury Retrograde, you know."

I felt sorry for John, because I knew that when it came to astrological warning signs, Mercury Retrograde was a Biggie. Now she turned and fixed me with a bloodshot stare.

"What time is it in England?" she asked sharply.

I told her it was late afternoon.

"Get Neil on the phone," she snapped, meaning Neil Aspinall, the former Beatles road manager who became president of Apple.

"Bloody hell, Yoko!" John exploded. "You've been on the phone all night. Why don't you give us a break!" I was stunned by John's outburst. So was Yoko. I could see her make the sudden and remarkable switch from witch to five-year-old in automatic response to John's dramatic outburst.

"You better wait in the car while I have a word with Mother," John suggested.

I was glad to leave. I sat in the car for half an hour, certain the ride was off, listening to a local rock station and watching the sun play on the surface of the swimming pool. Finally, John came bounding out of the house into the driveway. He jumped into the car, and I pulled out fast, with Led Zeppelin's "Whole Lotta Love" blasting over the car's speakers. John winced and shut off the radio. As our red Cadillac turned onto South Ocean Boulevard, a battered blue sedan that had been parked near the gate roared to life. We were being tailed by a carload of hopped-up teenagers.

"Fuck a pig!" John muttered anxiously, craning his neck to see. One of his worst nightmares was to be hounded by fans, particularly if they were drunk or stoned. "Don't they have anything better to do?"

he groaned. "Maybe we should go back. Maybe Mother was right, after all."

I suggested we just lose them. It would be easy once we got to West Palm Beach.

"Can't you do something *now?*" John pleaded as I stopped at a red light with the fan-mobile right behind us. I told him to fasten his seat belt. Then I gunned the Cadillac across the intersection, running the red light. John let out a scream and drew his knees up in terror as we zipped past cars aiming right for his door. We made it safely across the intersection with inches to spare, leaving the fans trapped in heavy traffic back at the light. I drove full speed ahead for a few blocks, turned into a quiet side street, and then cruised along, making sure the fan-mobile was nowhere in sight. When I was sure that we were safe, I asked John where he wanted to go.

We made a stop for newspapers, another to buy Yoko a box of chocolates for the Big Day, and then cruised along Lakeview Avenue en route to a local health food store where John wanted to stock up on some of his favorite carob-covered peanuts and raisins. But before we got to it, John was sidetracked by a place called the Metaphysical Bookstore.

"Come on, let's check it out!" he said, intrigued by the name.

The store was jammed with obscure metaphysical texts, exotic oils, perfumes, candles, and incense. The walls were adorned with pictures of an old, distinguished-looking, white-haired man.

The shopkeeper, an emaciated-looking man in his thirties who had hair down to his shoulders, gave John a penetrating look, and John appeared transfixed by his piercing blue eyes. As we wandered around picking out things, John kept stopping in front of the photos of the white-haired old man, studying them with a curious look on his face. Whatever it was that caught his attention, I could not see it myself. We ended up buying several hundred dollars' worth of books, oils, and incense. While the shopkeeper packed everything in bags, John asked, "Who's the old man?"

"That's my master," the owner replied with a trace of an Eastern European accent. "He's a Hungarian mystic named Beinsa Duono."

John turned white. I had never seen him look that way before. I had a brief moment of panic as I considered the logistics of rushing him to the nearest hospital. But he seemed to recover as we walked outside. Unable to restrain my curiosity, I asked John what had happened.

"Years ago I was told that I would look just like Beinsa Duono in my old age," John explained. "I always wondered what he looked like. I'd never seen his picture before. It was a very eerie experience."

Our next task was to find a cake for Yoko's birthday, but we could not locate a bakery in Palm Beach that was open on a Sunday afternoon. John settled for a chocolate cake from a supermarket, remarking, "Mother loves chocolate!" It was on the drive home that he finally thought of the perfect birthday surprise for Yoko. "I've got it!" he exclaimed. "Let's buy her a thousand gardenias—they're her favorite flower. We'll set them up all over the house tonight while she's asleep. That way, first thing when she wakes up tomorrow, she'll be hit by the scent of gardenias. What a great idea. Let's do it!"

Back at the house, John retired to the bedroom to sleep off our big morning of activity and I began calling florists. Gardenias, I learned quickly, were out of season and unavailable in most places. Eventually I managed to find a local flower shop that had a handful available for three dollars per blossom. I guessed that John would balk at spending three thousand dollars for a frivolous romantic gesture, but I waited until he got up to make a decision. When I broke the news to him, he was adamant. "Money is no object!" he insisted; Yoko deserved a grand array of her favorite flowers on her birthday. I did get him to modify the plan a little bit. He agreed that a hundred blossoms would probably do the trick, "fragrance-wise," to use a Yokoism.

Yoko was busy on the phone in the bedroom. So John and I went out to the car to retrieve the shopping bags and cake. "Why don't you stash everything in your room until we figure out a way to sneak it past Mother," he suggested. Then he handed me his American Express card and instructed me to order the gardenias right away. It took quite a number of additional calls to finally locate a florist who could supply a hundred gardenias. Even then I had to explain who they were for to ensure that the order would be filled on such short notice. Since I was doing this over the phone, however, I had a slight credibility problem. When the kid at the other end of the line demanded proof, I had no choice but to ask John for his help. John picked up the phone and began woofing at this kid personally. There was no mistaking the Lennon voice, and the young florist agreed quickly to a postmidnight gardenia delivery. After dinner that night, John came up to my room and asked me to gift-wrap the box of chocolates. I was reminded suddenly that we had no wrapping paper or candles.

I jumped into the Caddy and drove around Palm Beach in search of a late-night drugstore. Along the way I stopped by the flower shop to make sure that all was well on the gardenia front. The kid I had spoken to on the phone turned out to be a friendly teenage florist who also happened to be a Beatle fan. His name was Mike. To fill the massive order he had enlisted the help of his girlfriend, Cindy. I made plans to collect the flowers after midnight. They would help me to discreetly set up the gardenias throughout the house. When I returned to the villa, John was anxiously awaiting a progress report on the gardenias. Reassured that everything seemed in order and that I would pick them up that evening, John asked me to exercise extreme caution while setting up the flowers, because of the fragile quality of Yoko's sleep. Then he stuck three candles on the cake, while I gift-wrapped the box of chocolates.

Midnight found me in front of the flower shop, with not a soul in sight. After ten minutes of unmitigated panic, I saw Mike and Cindy pull up in a station wagon. Cindy was scarcely able to contain her excitement. She kept pumping me for information about my famous employers. It was clear that she hoped to meet John. I had to remind her that the purpose of this trip was to deliver flowers to John's house—that this was a business expedition, not a social call.

Inside the shop, I discovered that the gardenias were not ready to go. They were scattered everywhere. It took at least another hour to collect them, by which time Cindy, through skillful, continuous pressure, had extracted from me the reason for this midnight caper. That really set her and Mike off, and they began speculating about getting autographs. I had visions of them sneaking up the stairs to John and Yoko's bedroom while my back was turned. I could just imagine what it would do to John's psyche to find two crazed fans breathing over him in the dead of night. He would probably never sleep again.

It was past 2:00 A.M. when we finally reached *El Solano*. Attempting to be as quiet as mice, we unpacked the flowers and cut the stems so that they would float in the large aluminum lasagna trays I had placed around the house—on tables, bookshelves, mantels, even in the bathrooms. I rushed around, filling the trays with water while the kids floated the flowers. It was nearly 4:00 A.M. when we were done.

I gave the twittering young couple a hundred-dollar tip in exchange for a vow of secrecy and sent them on their way. I then spent another hour checking the arrangement of trays around the house and making sure each was placed just right. The aroma was already overpowering. I decided not to go to bed at all, because I did not want to miss the show when Yoko got up. It would be a chance to see her and John happy. I was touched by this lavish gesture and by the strong need John had to express himself, even if it was just to say happy birthday.

I took a shower, made coffee, and sat down in the living room on one of the gaudy blue easy chairs to wait for the sun to come up over the ocean beyond the glass doors. As it exploded out of the Atlantic, I remembered the first sunrise I had seen with John the previous spring. I was reminded that I had been working for John for almost exactly a year, and I marveled at how much a part of my life he had become.

John appeared at 6:00 A.M. and thanked me for setting up the flowers, adding, "You look semicomatose, Fred." He surveyed the arrangement of gardenias. "This is great!" he said, inhaling deeply. "I could smell it all over the house. It actually woke me up, I think. I can't wait till Mother gets a whiff of it."

We stood by the window, watching the rising sun.

"Next to the sunrise in Japan," John said, "this is as good as it gets. They don't call Japan the 'Land of the Rising Sun' for nothing." When low on the horizon, the sun moves very fast. As we watched, a great golden ball came tearing out of the ocean, fracturing the misty and shimmering sky.

"I'd like to take Mother out to dinner tonight," John continued. "Maybe stop by the Metaphysical Bookstore again. She'll love the place."

On his way out, he said, "You'd better get the camera ready— Mother could wake up any minute. We'll cut the birthday cake for breakfast. Then I'll serenade her with love songs."

I climbed the stairs to my room to get the camera, and then my fatigue hit me. I don't even remember what happened. One moment I was going up the stairs, the next I was on my bed, with Sean jumping on me, yelling, "Come quick, we're going to eat Mummy's cake!"

I grabbed my camera and ran to the dining room. It was 9:00 A.M. and Yoko was getting ready to blow out the candles on the cake. John smiled contentedly while I cut the cake. After we had each had a piece, John and Yoko went into the living room, where John picked up his guitar and began serenading Yoko. They sat on twin easy chairs upholstered with a flowered print. Yoko had her heels tucked underneath her purple gown and distractedly stared at John while smoking a Cigarettello. John was barefoot, as usual, and wore jeans and a purple T-shirt. He leaned forward, picking softly on his Ovation guitar.

I kicked myself for missing Yoko's wake-up and her reaction to the gardenias. "They're so beautiful!" she kept saying. But her appreciative remarks sounded perfunctory, and she seemed uncomfortable, and I kept asking myself what had gone wrong. Everything had seemed so perfect. After a while, John stopped playing and left the room to get more coffee. When he had gone, Yoko turned to me and said, "Thank you for the flowers, Fred. I love the smell. But, you know, they're just not right for the occasion. In Japan, gardenias are the flowers of death. They're used for funerals."

8

Mercury Retrograde

April 9, 1980. 8:00 A.M. and things have already gotten out of hand. I was just out of the shower when I got a call from Yoko informing me that I would be taking John, Sean, and Helen to the Long Island house, Cannon Hill, and that I should be prepared to spend at least a few days there. I knew better than to ask any one of the many questions that were on my mind. I quickly threw together a traveling bag before heading out of my West Forty-ninth Street apartment. It was a cold and wet morning, with not an empty cab in sight. By the time I arrived at the Dakota I was soaked through.

I was surprised to see a fan, Blonde Brenda, standing in the rain. She was from somewhere in the Midwest, and had been coming to the Dakota every day for the past few weeks. I was suddenly seized with an almost overpowering urge to shake her and say: "Brenda, Brenda, what are you doing here? There must be a million people in New York who would just love to sit down and talk to a pretty girl like yourself. John Lennon puts his pants on one leg at a time, just like everybody else. You are wasting your time." But I said nothing to her. Also, I thought, "This might be your lucky day, kid."

A limousine was parked in the driveway, giving Winnie, the concierge, a fit. "Someone from your office ordered it," she said in a tight whisper. "It's been out there for an hour and the other residents are starting to complain about the obstructed drive."

I promised to take care of it. I knew the car was for Yoko's mother, Isoko Ono, whom everyone called "Baba." The old lady had arrived unexpectedly from Japan in late March to spend some time with Sean and her teenage grandson, Keisuke, who was staying at the Dakota during his Easter break from a Vermont boarding school.

A daughter of the black-sheep branch of the immensely wealthy Yasuda clan—who had been unable to raise Yoko without the help of a dozen nannies, tutors, cooks, maids, and assorted other servants— Mrs. Ono appeared to be a disarmingly sweet and gentle little old lady in her seventies. She was quietly in the way and did not really know what to say to anyone or how to act. Her presence complicated Yoko's life immensely, for just as she was about to get rid of John and Sean, she had her mother and nephew to contend with. Yoko appeared to detest them both and ordered them around like servants.

I rang the kitchen intercom to see if Baba was ready for her diurnal "apartment hunt." She was not really going to rent an apartment, but Yoko had to find some way to get her mother out of the Dakota. Aunt Helen picked up the intercom and informed me that Baba had no intention of going out, but that John seemed more than a little anxious to get started. The strain of harboring his in-laws had finally gotten to him. At breakfast, Sean had been throwing food at his Japanese cousin and Yoko and her mother were not speaking. Half-way through his meal John had retreated to the bedroom, in silent protest.

"I hope we can leave soon," Helen said, sounding like she was transmitting from a firebase in Vietnam. I could hear Sean screaming in the background, competing with the noise of a vacuum cleaner and the television set. I rang John in the bedroom.

"Are we ready to roll?" he asked, his voice sounding so tense I thought it might crack.

When I told him I had to get diesel fuel for the Mercedes, he groaned. Then he asked me to stop by a video store to stock up on movies, particularly *Kramer vs. Kramer*, *Breaking Away*, some Elvis films, classic comedy (i.e., Charlie Chaplin and the Marx Brothers), anything by Peter Sellers, some of Clint Eastwood's Dirty Harry films, biblical epics, and plenty of cartoons for Sean.

On my way out of the office to pick up the Mercedes I was intercepted by Yoko, who said that Rich was running late and she needed me in the office. When the accountant showed up around 10:00 A.M., Yoko asked us both into her office for a "conference." Rich and I took a seat on Yoko's plush white sofa, while she made herself comfortable on a matching armchair and fixed us with a penetrating look.

"This is a very difficult time for us," Yoko commenced, nervously lighting a cigarette. "My mother is driving John crazy. It's probably best if he goes to the country for a while." Yoko confided to us that during John's absence she planned to embark on a secret four-day "cleansing fast," during which time she would be in seclusion upstairs in the bedroom. "But it's very important that everybody think I'm with John in Cold Spring Harbor," she continued. "Otherwise they'll call him there and try to sell him things." She instructed Rich to tell their "closest friends" that she was with John at Cannon Hill, while "everyone else" should be told that she was "out of town." Rich and I exchanged puzzled looks on our way out of Yoko's office, but we said nothing.

I rushed to the garage, and a few minutes later I had the Turbo Wagon stuck in traffic on Columbus Avenue. I decided to stop at Harvey Electronics on West Forty-fifth Street to buy the videos, and get the gas afterward, a decision I regretted when I saw the red "Fuel Critical" warning light suddenly begin to flicker ominously while I was driving across Central Park. On Fifth Avenue I was slowed to a crawl approaching midtown. As I inched along and precious minutes slipped by, I envisioned John climbing the walls of his room, desperately flicking through the daytime TV shows while I ran out of gas.

I finally reached Harvey Electronics and frantically bought over a thousand dollars' worth of videotapes. The cashier nearly flipped while adding it all up. When I told her to charge it to Lennono, she eyed me suspiciously, then called the office to clear the purchase with Rich. The accountant assured the cashier that the purchase was in order and then asked to speak to me.

"Man, am I glad I got a hold of you," he exclaimed with a sigh of relief. He told me that Yoko's mother was "stranded" at a Howard Johnson near Times Square and asked me to pick her up. Apparently Mrs. Ono, after being badgered by Yoko into using the limousine that had been waiting for her in the driveway, had ordered her driver to cruise down Broadway, across Forty-second Street, and up Eighth Avenue, where she asked to be let out at the Howard Johnson on Fifty-second Street and then sent the car away. Fortunately, the driver called his office and they called our office to report Baba's whereabouts. I promised to give the old lady a lift.

"You better hurry," Rich said. "If Mrs. Ono disappears, Yoko will freak out." I was tempted to tell him that I wasn't at all convinced that if her mother disappeared Yoko would be too upset, but I bit my tongue and reassured him I was on my way to rescue the old lady.

I found Yoko's mother sitting in a corner of the dining room, quietly sipping coffee. She didn't seem at all surprised to see me and cheerfully invited me to have a seat at her table. She asked me if I would like some breakfast. Anxious to get back to the Dakota as soon as possible, I told her I wasn't hungry. But Baba was not about to take no for an answer and insisted on ordering some ice cream. We studied the ice cream menu. Baba decided on peppermint, while I chose pistachio nut. Then Baba began making small talk. She told me that when she first visited New York twenty-three years earlier, the streets seemed a lot cleaner. She asked me if I was from New York, and when I told her I was born in Germany, she seemed favorably impressed. She said that someday she would like to go there for a visit.

As much as I enjoyed this amiable chat with Mrs. Ono, I was growing more anxious by the minute, knowing that John was waiting for me at the Dakota. When we finished our ice cream I asked for the check, but when I pulled out my wallet, Baba firmly shook her head. "This my treat," she insisted. We walked to the Mercedes, which I had parked around the corner on West Fifty-second Street. I held open the rear door for Mrs. Ono, but she indicated that she wished to take the front passenger seat. When I started the car the red fuel light went on again, reminding me that I was still running on empty. I drove to the nearest diesel pump on Tenth Avenue. As luck would have it, it was closed.

Noticing my worried expression, Baba gave me a curious look. I explained to her that the car was very low on fuel and that diesel pumps were few and far between. I decided to drive to a gas station on West Fourteenth Street that I knew had diesel, and nervously joked with Mrs. Ono that if we ran out of gas along the way we might end up hitchhiking. The old lady didn't seem too concerned, expressing absolute confidence in the car's ability to get us back to the Dakota.

"Mercedes very good German car," Baba stated knowingly. She praised German cleanliness and workmanship, and asked me if I had been in Germany during the war. When I told her that my parents did not meet until after the war, Baba smiled and said she had not realized I was such a "young boy." Then she asked what my father did. When I told her he was a concert pianist, Mrs. Ono said that her husband had been a classically trained pianist, too, and that several of her brothers were painters and sculptors. I wondered what she thought of Yoko's creative efforts. So I asked her if she had seen any of Yoko's art. The old lady shrugged vaguely. When I asked her if she'd heard any of Yoko's recordings, she said she had not. I almost wished I'd had some tapes of Yoko's music to play for Baba.

We made it safely to the Fourteenth Street diesel station; after replenishing the car's fuel supply, I gave the turbocharger a solid workout on the way uptown, tearing up the West Side Highway at seventy mph. Baba seemed thrilled by the fast ride, and I could not help but wonder at the differences between mother and daughter.

At the Dakota I backed the Benz into the driveway, ignoring the wildly gesticulating doorman, who insisted that I couldn't leave it there. I told him that I had to load some things, that it would only take a few minutes, and that it was an emergency. Before the guard had a chance to argue, Blonde Brenda came rushing over. "Is this John's car?" she asked, flushed with excitement. "Is he coming down?" I mumbled some excuse and helped Mrs. Ono out of the car, then escorted her past the reception area while the doorman kept Brenda from following us into the building.

When I entered the office, Rich glanced at the clock behind his desk—it was close to 1:00 P.M.—and shook his head angrily. "Man, what took you so long?" he scolded. "They are freaking out upstairs. John's been calling down every half hour asking where you are. If you don't split soon, it'll be too late." He told me that Yoko had had a consultation with John Green, who had advised her that today was a really bad day to be on the road because Mercury was going retrograde. I had a feeling that Yoko would ignore her card reader's advice for once, since keeping John at the Dakota might well lead to domestic violence. John had told me once that he used to be quite a violent man, taking out his frustrations on women in particular, and that Yoko had taught him that it was not necessary to be violent to be a real man. Now, waiting to get out of the Dakota, with the tension running higher by the moment, I feared that Yoko had not fully domesticated John, that she had merely kept him in check.

Full of trepidation, I rang the bedroom intercom. "It's about time!" John snapped. I started to explain about the trouble I had finding diesel fuel, but he was in no mood to hear excuses. "Never mind all that," he exclaimed. Then he ran down a checklist of items I should not forget. Most important were a supply of cigarettes, a Polaroid camera, and plenty of film and flash bars, and the remote-control device for the new television at Cannon Hill.

I quickly filled a shopping bag with Gitanes and photographic supplies. But when I tried to find the remote-control unit for the TV, no one could remember what we had done with it. I was frantically searching through desk drawers and file cabinets when the intercom went off. Rich picked it up and shot me a grave look, which I knew meant it was John.

"What on earth are you doing in the office when I'm waiting for you upstairs?" John bellowed. I started to stammer something, but John was not interested in what I had to say. "I want you to come up here, help me get my stuff down to the car, and then let's just go, okay?" He seemed beyond anger. He wanted out.

I ran upstairs and found John sitting on the bed, nervously strumming his guitar, watching television. "Jesus H. Fuckin' Christ!" he hollered when I showed my face. "I'm going out of my skull waiting around all day. I've been ready to leave all morning!"

I thought about telling John that I had had an unexpected delay when I went to pick up Baba, but I knew that it would be useless to make excuses. I said nothing. John handed me the guitar and I placed it in its case while he jumped off the bed and began to look around for his shoes. I was about to join in the search when we heard Uda-san's shrill voice coming from the kitchen: "Please come quick! Help! Help!"

"You'd better go see what's up," John said, exasperated. "If they start screwing around, we'll never make it out of here."

I ran to the kitchen. Uda-san pointed to a large cardboard box filled with brown rice, honey bran crackers, Hain orange marmalade (John's favorite, I bought it by the carton from the local distributor), honey, dried seaweed—all John's health foods. "Take down, please," she said, smiling sweetly.

I told her there was no need to take all this food with us, since there were plenty of health food stores in Long Island and we could buy whatever John might want there. I also pointed out to her that time was of the essence because John and Sean were rather anxious to get out of this madhouse. At that very moment, in fact, Sean was running around the kitchen, punching Helen in the legs, screaming, "Helen, when are we leaving... Helen, when are we leaving?"

Meanwhile, Baba sat at the butcher-block table, munching serenely on a roast beef sandwich. She didn't seem affected by the turmoil around her.

I grabbed an armful of cartons of Gitane cigarettes, and returned to John, who had found his sneakers and was now in the clothes room trying to decide what jacket to wear. I picked up his guitar and a garment bag, then headed downstairs.

While I loaded the car, Blonde Brenda approached and fixed her gaze on the guitar case.

"Is that John's guitar?" She sensed that her many days of waiting were about to pay off. "Is he coming down? Is Yoko coming down, too? Where are they going? How long will they be away?"

I ran into the office and called the kitchen to tell the others to descend to the car; then I rushed back upstairs. John was pacing his bedroom like a caged animal. He picked up a black attaché case containing his journals, and I collected the remaining bags. I followed him out to the foyer, and pressed the elevator call button.

"I wonder if we've forgotten anything," John fretted as we waited. Suddenly, he snapped his fingers. "Do you remember my favorite pair of jeans, those Lee Riders? I can't find them anywhere. I'll bet Udasan's hiding them somewhere just to mind-fuck me. I sort of blew up at her yesterday. Maybe you can find out where they are."

I promised John I would look for them when we got back from our stay in Cannon Hill and casually asked him if he knew how long we would be there. He told me that we would probably stay in Cold Spring Harbor until Mercury went normal again, but he did not know when that might be. He also appeared to be somewhat apprehensive about "tempting fate" by traveling during Mercury Retrograde.

"It's not really your fault that we're getting off to such a late start," he said in a conciliatory tone of voice. "Delays are normal during Mercury Retrograde." I was relieved that he no longer seemed angry with me and I told him about my odyssey in search of diesel gas, which John took as confirmation of Retrograding Mercury's awesome power to disrupt plans and make life on earth more difficult. John shifted his feet impatiently. "Did you get the videos?" he asked. I assured him we had enough films to start our own video rental store. "What about Polaroid film? Do we have enough?" I told him we had plenty, as well as flash bars. "Better take an extra camera, just in case," he suggested. "And you'd better find the remote for the TV. I don't want to have to get up a hundred times a day to switch channels."

I could hear the elevator laboring up the shaft. It finally came crunching to a stop and the doors opened. John and I stepped into the lavish, wood-finished box that always smelled of furniture polish because it was constantly being rubbed to a deep lustre by unseen hands. I could just sense John beginning to breathe a sigh of relief— we were nearly out—when suddenly the doors closed and the elevator moved up instead of down.

"What in the bloody hell!" John stammered, then simply stopped, stunned, speechless.

On the ninth floor the doors opened again and a young man entered, probably one of the actors or artists who occupied the small studio apartments on the top floor of the Dakota. John was visibly alarmed by the presence of this stranger, who fixed him with an unflinching and embarrassed stare, as if he knew he was not supposed to look upon the famous visage but could not help himself. The intruder stood back in awe, looking nervous, as if he regretted the unexpected encounter even more than John did.

At the ground floor John and I stood back to let him get off first, then John motioned to me to get off ahead of him—just in case there was a security problem outside the door. I stepped out cautiously, peering this way and that. Just as I turned around to signal to John that the coast was clear, the massive door to the old elevator closed, trapping John on yet another unwanted upward ride at the alarming speed of a thirtieth of a mile per hour. Knowing that John would not be back soon, I went out to the driveway and loaded the bags into the car. It had stopped raining, but as I looked up at the sky from the courtyard I could see that it was ominously dark. I went back inside just in time to escape Blonde Brenda and catch John stepping out of the elevator. He had not, as I expected he would, torn the paneling from the walls. He was remarkably calm, and had a sad, resigned smile on his face.

"Maybe Mother was right," he said. "It seems someone up there doesn't want us to leave today."

I took him out to the car. Just as he sat down in the passenger seat, Brenda came rushing out of concealment and pointed a camera at him. I started to go into action, but John held out his hand to stop me. "It's all right, Fred," he said. "I'll handle it. Just get the others down here so we can leave."

I was amazed at how calm John became before a fan with a camera. Blonde Brenda was so dumbfounded by her good fortune that she was scarcely able to focus. I could also see that she was quite bewildered by John's un-Beatle-like appearance. He wore a blue blazer over a T-shirt, gray corduroy slacks, and white sneakers. His full beard had grown unruly, his hair was pulled into a ponytail, and his eyes were hidden behind a new pair of dark glasses.

I ran back into the office to find out what was keeping the others. Apparently Sean was having trouble deciding what videos to take. I told Helen that I had plenty of new cartoons for him, but Sean insisted on bringing along his favorite *Mighty Mouse* and *Heckle & Jeckle* tapes anyway. I got hold of an extra Polaroid camera and made sure I had a set of keys to the house; then I stuck my head in Yoko's office to let her know we were leaving in a moment.

"How is John feeling?" she asked apprehensively. Before I had a chance to answer, she whispered, "I checked with Charlie Swan, you know, and he thinks it's not a good time to go because of Mercury Retrograde."

I nodded gravely and assured her that, Mercury notwithstanding, John was better off at Cannon Hill than upstairs in his bedroom going nuts. Yoko looked worried. "It's my mother, you know," she said as if letting me in on a family secret. "She's driving John crazy, but I can't kick her out. So it's probably better if he goes to Cannon Hill for a while, and I'll try to come out and visit as much as possible. This is a very dangerous time, astrologically," Yoko warned, "so you better be extra careful." She cautioned me that by now many people knew about their Long Island house, and she said she worried about "fans hounding" John. I thought of John in the driveway, flirting with a cute teenage girl who was drooling all over him while snapping his picture. I could hear Sean making a ruckus in the outer office, but Yoko ignored it. She told me sternly that John and Sean weren't getting along very well of late and so Sean should be kept away from him until their relationship was "more normal." Lastly, Yoko forbade me to "allow" John to leave the house in Long Island.

What if John asked me to take him for a ride in the car, I asked, anticipating a problem.

"Look, I know John can be very impulsive, and if he's bored or angry with Sean, he might say, 'Fred, let's go for a drive to the health food store,' or something like that. Now, if you refuse, he'll be upset with you, but it's better than if you do what he says and something happens, so don't be tempted." She promised to keep in touch by phone, and urged me to let her know if there were any difficulties. As I exited the inner sanctum, Sean rushed inside, followed by Helen. The two of them emerged with Yoko and we all trooped out to the driveway, where John was chatting with Brenda in between taking furious puffs of his cigarette. She had really hit the jackpot.

While Helen, Sean, and Uda-san piled into the backseat of the Mercedes, Yoko nervously apologized to no one in particular for not being able to join us. "Yes, I know," John said, shooting her a re-proachful look, "business before the family." Yoko looked hurt, but remained silent. "It's okay, don't worry about it," John said tersely as Yoko leaned into the passenger-side front window for a quick, awk-ward embrace. "Fred, start the car, we're leaving," John commanded. I began to pull out of the driveway, with Yoko walking alongside the car for a few moments, waving at us. The long good-bye was almost over.

"Don't hang out here too long," John said to Yoko as I waited for a break in traffic so I could make a left turn. "People will think you're just another Beatle fan." He cast a sly glance at Brenda, who was visibly aroused by this intimate family scene. Then he waved to Yoko, who waved after us as we vanished into the blackest heart of Central Park, which just at that moment was enveloped in a titanic rainstorm.

"What a day!" John sighed. "I wonder what else is in store for us, lurking out there in the mist. You know, it's not just Mercury, but everything is going retrograde right now. I mean Venus and Mars, the whole fuckin' cosmos is backward! That's why there's so much chaos, you see."

As we approached the house, John became nervous about locating the driveway in the middle of the blinding rainstorm. But I had made the trip so many times during the past year that I had no trouble finding it. John breathed a sigh of relief as Cannon Hill came into view, barely visible at the bottom of the winding road.

"We made it, thank God!" John shouted. Helen, Sean, and Uda-san applauded. I drove under the archway in front of the main en-trance and jumped out to unlock the door to the house. A few mo-

The author today. (Courtesy *David Palmore*)

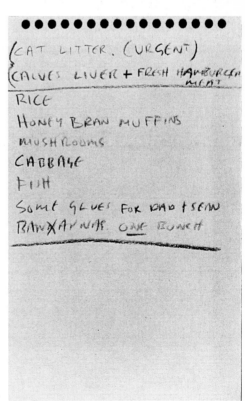

One of John Lennon's typical shopping lists.

The Lennons by the pool of their Palm Beach villa, *El Solano,*
March 1979. Left-Right: John, Sean, Yoko, Julian.

Julian shows Sean
how to use an instant camera.

Sean playing by the poolside.

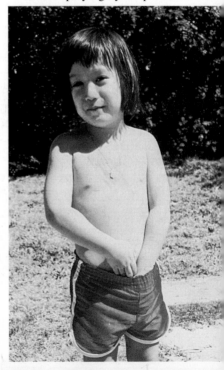

John, Sean, and Julian poolside, Palm Beach. March 1979.

Yoko prepares lunch in the kitchen of *El Solano,* with Julian
and John looking on.

John and Sean in the kitchen.

Yoko demonstrates origami to Julian.

Left-Right: A young friend of the Lennons, Sean, Julian and John in Palm Beach.

The Lennon-Onos celebrating Julian's 16th birthday with a cruise. Clockwise from top: John and Yoko; Sean, Julian, John and Yoko; Aunt Helen, Julian, Sean and two Japanese cousins.

Sean and Aunt Helen eat dinner in Palm Beach under
the watchful eye of Sean's bodyguard, Douglas McDougall.

Julian and the author in El Solano, 1979.
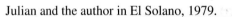

John and Ringo Starr at the Dakota during a rare visit by Ringo.

ments later I had distressing news. None of the keys seemed to fit.

John got out of the car and watched as I frantically tried different keys. "C'mon, Fred, I've got to pee!" He was getting impatient.

Again, none of the keys seemed to work.

"Hurry up before I pee in me pants!" John grimaced as I ran through all the keys once more, but the door would not budge. He threw up his hands and rushed back into the car to get his green raincoat and hat. Lurching into the woods like a green apparition, John found a likely bush and let fly. Steam rose up around him in the hissing forest.

I thought: "Brenda, if you could see us now!"

9

Cold Spring Harbor

I eventually managed to find the right set of keys, and we settled into our new quarters. The second day on Long Island the clouds broke, the sun came out, and it promised to be a beautiful and warm day. I went to the master bedroom to return a book John had lent me, *Unseen Influences*, and found him sitting at his desk writing in his journal.

"Do you remember that black Brother typewriter I had?" he asked. "Let's have somebody bring it out here. I think I'm going to start working on a book, the real *Ballad of John and Yoko*," John chuckled. "It'll blow a lot of people's minds!"

I raised my eyebrows. I did not know at that point if he and Yoko had even discussed it, but I suspected that if she knew he was going to "tell all," she might be more than a bit upset.

That afternoon he asked me to drive him to the nearby village of Cold Spring Harbor to "check out the neighborhood" and look at antiques. I decided not to call Yoko to ask her permission, knowing she would never allow it. During the ride, John mentioned that we should have a boat because we were on the water. After years of deferring to Yoko, he at times did not seem to care anymore what Yoko thought.

Our first Sunday on Long Island, April 13, John decided to go for a drive in search of flowers. Yoko had come out for a visit the night before, and John wanted to surprise her with a bouquet. We cruised around the scenic country roads, listening to taped lectures by Alan

120

Watts, the renowned British expert on Oriental philosophy and religion. John asked me to order a collection of Watts's taped talks, at a cost of over one thousand dollars. When he tired of Watts's lectures, he played tapes of Fats Waller, Noël Coward, and Willie Nelson. And just as in Palm Beach, John observed the "natives" from behind the car's darkly tinted windows, and offered a running commentary on the goings-on.

I became so absorbed in the music and John's chatter that I lost sight of the fact that the car was low on fuel. I began to worry when I realized that most gas stations were closed because it was a Sunday, and the few that were open did not carry diesel.

"Relax, Fred," he said as I anxiously studied the fuel gauge. "Let's just keep driving. Maybe we'll come across a familiar-looking road or something." Soon we ran through all of John's tapes, and I asked him if he would like to listen to some of the new-wave rock and reggae music that I kept in the glove compartment. Ignoring my suggestion, John began to tinker with the radio. Usually John would not think of touching the complicated-looking Blaupunkt quadraphonic digital radio cassette player I had installed at his request. But now he began to fiddle with the dials, and calypso music suddenly filled the car. "That sounds like the Mighty Sparrow," he said, adjusting the bass and treble, trying to get the best sound. When the announcer confirmed John's guess, his face lit up. "I should get a prize!" he said proudly.

By now we were back on a familiar stretch of Route 110, and soon I located a gas station that carried diesel. John turned down the volume and fired up a Gitane while we waited for a long-haired kid to fill the tank. When I handed the gas attendant a twenty-dollar bill, he complimented me on the car, saying he had never seen a Mercedes station wagon before. He eyed John with growing curiosity as he searched his pockets for change.

"Hey, I know you!" the youngster suddenly exclaimed, a flash of recognition lighting up his face.

"I know you, too!" John muttered anxiously under his breath and turned his face away from the excited youth.

"Keep the change," I told the kid and roared off.

Back on the highway, John breathed a sigh of relief, smoked another Gitane, and turned up the volume on the radio. John's attention span for music was short. He compulsively scanned the FM dial, never listening to a complete song unless it was something he really liked—for instance, the Rolling Stones' "Miss You." When this song came on a local rock station, John shouted with delight and cranked up the volume, commenting that Mick Jagger at least got this one great song out of his divorce from Bianca. Twice we caught snatches of Beatles songs, but John showed no interest. He told me that most Beatles songs, particularly the early ones—which he dismissed as "formula songs"—bored him. He said that usually when he heard a Beatles song he would be reminded of the recording session. His memory would dredge up details such as what he had eaten that day, what drug he had been taking, conflicts that arose at the time—mostly unpleasant memories.

We were driving past a vast shopping mall, near Walt Whitman's birthplace, when a familiar voice boomed over the four speakers.

"Fuck a pig!" John shouted. "It's Paul!"

Indeed, it was Paul McCartney's new hit single, "Coming Up," a catchy tune built around a repetitive staccato riff. John frowned, turned up the volume, and began to nod to the beat.

"Not bad," he said at the end of the song, sounding surprised and even somewhat disappointed. When the announcer mentioned that Paul played all the instruments himself, John mumbled something to the effect that it made perfect sense because Paul had always wanted to be a one-man band. John turned down the volume again and fell silent for a while. Then he asked me to get him a copy of Paul's new album and to set up a stereo system in his bedroom. I had a hi-fi system sent from New York by limousine that same day, and I had no trouble finding Paul's record, *McCartney II*, in a local music store.

I also added Paul's new release to the tape collection I kept in the glove compartment of the car. I knew that John would sooner or later shed his reluctance to listen to my tapes, and I wanted, when the time came, to have plenty of new music for him to be inspired by. Ever since I had gone to work for John more than a year ago, I had secretly hoped that he would rouse himself from his deep inertia and once again astonish the world with his songs.

The next day at breakfast, John hummed the melody of Paul's new single, which he said he could not get out of his head. "It's driving me crackers!" he exclaimed cheerfully. He said the album was uneven, but he acknowledged that it was an unusually adventurous effort by Paul, and far superior to his previous release, *Back to the Egg*, which

John had dismissed as "garbage." He gave Paul credit for trying his hand at something new.

I realized that after years of lying dormant, John's competitive nature had been aroused again. As long as Paul kept churning out mediocre "product," John felt justified in keeping his own muse on a shelf. But if Paul was writing decent music, then John felt compelled to take up Paul's challenge. It was a conditioned reflex, nurtured during years of friendly (and later fierce) rivalry in the Beatles. John told me that Paul was the only musician who could scare him into writing great songs, and vice versa. That was the nature of John and Paul's relationship: creative sibling rivalry.

In a startling turnaround, John asked me to bring him up to date on the new music scene. During the next few days we cruised around Long Island's North Shore listening to the latest new-wave groups. John was particularly impressed by the Pretenders and Lene Lovich as well as Madness, a British ska band. Ska was a style of music that had originated in Jamaica in the 1950s and became popular among London's West Indian community, where it was known as bluebeat. John told me that he had been a fan of this style of music in the sixties. I soon picked up more ska music by bands such as Selecter and the Specials.

Also around this time, our second week at Cannon Hill, John sent me out to buy a boat. I visited a local boat dealership, Coneys Marine, and bought an eight-hundred-dollar dinghy with a two-horsepower British Seagull outboard motor. On a sunny Friday afternoon in mid-April, John, Sean, Helen, and I pushed it into shallow water on the beach just beneath the house. Then we all clambered aboard. Helen and Sean huddled in the middle of the small boat. John sat at the bow, and I positioned myself at the stern. As soon as we were adrift, I yanked a cord to start the motor, and we set out into the harbor, puttering noisily.

"I want to navigate!" John said excitedly. I turned over the rudder, and he guided us around the harbor for a while, then headed toward Oyster Bay. When we reached the bay, John said, "Let's shut off the engine and just drift."

Silence enveloped us, and bright sunlight danced on the gently rippled surface of the dark green waters. Gulls screamed in the distance, and the waves lapped at the sides of the dinghy in irregular, ominous rhythms. I had never seen Sean so quiet before. When he asked if he could row, John gave the nod, and I handed Sean an oar and showed him how to use it. Then I grabbed the other oar and we started rowing toward Cold Spring Harbor.

"This is great!" John exclaimed, surveying the not-too-distant shore. "Did you ever notice how the upper classes amuse themselves with war games? They learn to sail and ride horses, shoot guns and whatnot. I want Sean to learn all those survival skills!"

John wanted to learn how to start the engine. It required a forceful tug on a cord, and at first John was unable to pull it with enough force to activate the motor. Normally, he would have become discouraged quickly and given up, but this time he persisted. After several tries, with a quick snap of his arm he started the motor. He suggested letting Sean take the helm for a while, but as we shifted around in the little boat to let Sean get next to the motor, John accidentally bumped it with his elbow and it shut off again. This time neither of us could start it. We were stranded in the middle of the harbor. John began shouting for us to "stroke!" He and I each grabbed an oar and rowed back to shore, with Sean at the helm.

"I'm sure glad Mother wasn't here to see this," John said when we were safely back at the house. "We'd never have lived it down."

That evening Yoko arrived unannounced for dinner. I joined the Lennons in the living room, where John held forth about the history of Long Island's northern shore. "Why is this called Cannon Hill, anyway?" Yoko interjected at one point. "Is it the area we're in or the name of the house?"

I explained that the area was called Laurel Hollow, a small community on an ocean inlet named Cold Spring Harbor, near a town of the same name. Then John told her that the house was called Cannon Hill because of the small cannon by the pool. Yoko did a numerological analysis of the name: "This house is a seven," she said. "The address is fourteen-twenty; and that's one plus four plus two, which equals seven."

Catching my puzzled expression, John turned to me, saying: "That's good—seven. It's a number associated with the planet Neptune, and also with the moon. So it has to do with water. But also," he continued, talking to Yoko, "the lock combination for the boat shed is thirty-five, nine, thirty-five ... which equals seventy-nine. Seven and nine is sixteen. One plus six equals seven!"

"Amazing, isn't it?" Yoko marveled.

The next morning, Saturday, April 19, she took everyone except John aside at nine in the morning to announce that John was taking a "vow of silence" for ten days. She wanted to make sure we understood what was going on so that we could cooperate as fully as possible and make the experience easier on John.

"He'll get very discouraged if it doesn't work," Yoko warned us. I took that to mean there would be hell to pay. I also could not help but wonder about the supposed aim of this "vow," but I did not dare ask. Looking pointedly at my aunt, Yoko continued, "Helen, you'll have to make sure Sean understands, okay?"

My aunt gave a quick, nervous laugh, while Sean screwed up his face and asked, "Why can't Daddy speak?"

"It's just an exercise, Sean-san," Yoko said, "like the monks sometimes do, because when you speak you don't know what you're thinking." Sean gave her a doubtful look. "And the other thing is, it's also good to clean out your head." She then turned to Uda-san. "Now, during this vow of silence you must not use any salt whatsoever in your cooking. Also, coffee must be kept away from John—he's giving it up."

I felt my heart sink. Not only was John a compulsive talker, he was also a heavy coffee drinker. I wondered what he would be like by the end of the day—or of the week.

Anyway, I knew that Yoko had it backward: Sometimes if you can't talk, you can't figure out what you are thinking.

By noon that Saturday, John was locked in his bedroom, immersed in golden silence.

Yoko was standing in the kitchen when I returned from my rounds. She gave me a note on John's *From Himself* memo paper before disappearing to the bedroom. In her handwriting, it said: "If John knocks on your door, just follow him and you will know what he wants— driving or boating. Don't communicate with him in the car or boat, since too much sign-language communication is cheating."

There was also a list of subjects that John was not allowed to read about: "No current news and fiction, no newspapers and magazines." There went the rest of John's favorite activities.

At such times I could not help but wonder if Yoko simply tormented John to maintain her hold on him or if she had other, more immediate reasons for imposing such seemingly arbitrary restrictions. In any case, I could see that John and Yoko's relationship had reached a dead end. She could not stand to have him around but she could not afford to lose him.

By dinnertime Yoko was gone. I found her "Silent Vow Poem" on the mantel in the living room. She had formulated her rules for John in poetic form, adding a suggestion that he find a "tree friend" to "talk" to at least once a day. John was also to spend an hour a day rowing the dinghy in the harbor, by himself. There was even a pre-scription for watching television without the sound. Yoko's writing style, if she could be said to have had one, consisted mostly of puz-zling, absurd instructions. This was the substances of her one book, *Grapefruit*. Sometimes she would leave short "poems" lying around here and there, and it was often difficult to determine which were meant to be "art" and which were meant to be instructions to the staff that she actually wanted carried out.

Sean and Helen were playing outside on the swing we had recently installed, and Uda-san was puttering around the kitchen, wondering how to get around John's new dietary restrictions. She also gossiped with me about some rather strange goings-on at the Dakota. Uda-san told me that Myoko, the maid, had told her that Sam Green was moving into the Dakota and was bringing great quantities of liquor with him. I was stunned by this news. Yoko's infatuation with the flamboyant art dealer was already well known to the staff, but no one dared tell John.

Dinner was tense and awkward, with everybody afraid to speak, pretending mightily that silence was normal. After the bland meal John showed me a copy of Watergate conspirator G. Gordon Liddy's new book, *Will*. He pointed to the photograph of Liddy on the back and gave what seemed to be a Nazi salute.

"He's a Nazi?" I guessed. John nodded and grinned. When he had asked me to get him the book, John had said that he had seen Liddy on a talk show. Liddy had described a time in prison when, to prove his willpower to the other inmates so they would respect him and leave him alone, he'd held his hand over a flame until his flesh burned. Now John did a pantomime routine of this hand-burning scene, indicating what tremendous willpower he, too, had.

When John and I gestured, communicating about the Liddy book, Uda-san became upset. "Not supposed to communicate with John," she said, sternly. "He silent now. Not supposed to talk."

John angrily stalked out, making a swirl with his finger at his temple to indicate that Uda-san was nuts. When he had left the kitchen, Uda-san said, "John crazy. Silence crazy." At that moment, John, having listened in on our conversation at the doorway, burst back in, snatched up a drinking glass, and hurled it into the sink. It shattered, and glass flew across the kitchen. Then John stormed out of the room. We were dumbstruck.

John managed pretty well most of Sunday. Helen and I took Sean out on the boat and John videotaped our outing. Although he had not said a word in twenty-four hours, he seemed in a lighthearted mood. During dinner that evening Sean kept asking, "Why can't Daddy speak?" and I could see the signs of strain beginning to creep into John's face. He looked tense and miserable. As soon as he finished eating, John retreated to the master bedroom, only to reappear in the kitchen a short while later with a pained expression on his face.

He snatched a honey cake from the cupboard and held it up, gesticulating, pointing at the wrapper. I gave him an inquisitive look, uncertain what he meant. He seemed frustrated, yearning to communicate, but stubbornly refused to talk. Suddenly, John savagely threw the cake in the trash can. I figured out what he was trying to tell us: The cake was a no-no because it contained additives. I was beginning to learn sign language.

The next day John embarked on another one of his food-disposal campaigns—Ovaltine being his latest target—and Uda-san began threatening to return to Japan. She periodically made these threats, but this time I thought she might actually leave. Instead, she retaliated by fixing John's food in peculiar ways. For instance, she would overcook vegetables until they were soggy. John could not complain. He was mute. I was surprised he had not learned one of the secrets of the upper classes: Never cross your servants unless you plan to dismiss them. They always have you at their mercy.

The following afternoon, I sat in the living room watching a videotape when John came down for lunch. He abruptly turned the TV set off and removed the tape. Then he pocketed the remote-control device and stalked off without explanation. He looked extremely upset. Message: If I cannot watch TV, nobody watches TV. I was learning to read John's mind.

I later found John sitting at the kitchen table with Sean, eating lunch, his nose buried in Sean's Superman comic book, trying to

conceal his frustration. Sean tried hard to be good, sensing how difficult it was for his daddy to remain silent, but he could not keep
himself from fidgeting and commenting on the comic book, asking
questions. John glared at him and sharply rapped the table with his
knuckles to silence him. Sean snapped to attention, then hung his
head, glancing at his father sideways, looking hurt.

I began to avoid any contact with John, whose behavior had become wildly unpredictable. It put us all off balance. By the end of the
first week of his silence I was really jumpy about running into him,
and I found myself trying to guess where he might be in the house so I
could avoid being there. I spent as much time as possible outside.

One afternoon I was sitting under a tree overlooking the harbor
when John rushed past me on his way to get to the dinghy for his
daily boat ride. We were both rather startled by this unexpected encounter, and John quickly gave a Nazi salute as he hurried along. A
few days later, toward the end of John's ten-day silent period, we ran
into each other in the kitchen and he promptly lit a match and held it
under his hand, writhing in mock agony. I was glad to see he had not
lost his sense of humor. Later he came to my room and handed me
the Liddy book, indicating that he had finished reading it.

On the day before he was due to talk again, I watched John playing
a puzzle game with Sean. The puzzle consisted of small, colorful, inter-
locking pieces of cardboard depicting a spaceship. Sean soon grew
frustrated at being unable to piece it together, and John, who looked
bored, was not much help. I joined in and encouraged Sean to keep
trying until all the pieces of the puzzle were in place.

"You have to keep trying until the day you're dead," intoned Sean.
John smiled and gave his four-year-old son a proud nod of approval.

On Wednesday morning, April 30, John wrote me a short note
saying: "Lend me your razor. Bring it upstairs." His ten-day silence
was scheduled to end at noon, and I gathered he would mark the
occasion by shaving for the first time in almost a year. Yoko had
promised to visit, and I was in frequent phone contact with Rich at
the office to find out when she would be arriving. Finally, Rich told
me that Yoko was not feeling well and would not be able to come out,
after all. He instructed me to tell John that Yoko was bedridden with
stomach pains, but that it was nothing serious. I gave John the message when I brought him the shaving gear. He seemed to take the
disappointing news in stride. I went back downstairs and got another

call from Rich, saying now that Sam Green's doctor had diagnosed Yoko's illness as a case of highly contagious "Russian flu" and that we would have to stay out at Cannon Hill until further notice.

John's silence ended with a call to the Dakota at five minutes past noon. He had, in fact, gone longer than the ten-day period imposed by Yoko. I sat at the kitchen table across from him, eating vegetable soup, watching him talk on the phone, listening to the renowned voice. It was over, and I could sense his relief. John was dying to talk to Yoko, but Rich told him that she was unavailable. He kept phoning the Dakota throughout the day, growing more frustrated and angry with every call.

Looking glum, he asked if I had checked into buying a sailboat, as he had requested in a note he had given me a few days earlier. I told him I had visited Coneys Marine and placed an order for a fourteen-foot sailboat, and that the young man who ran the family-owned marina, Tyler Coneys, offered to have one of his employees sail the boat to our dock and give us a sailing lesson. John liked the idea of having someone give us lessons, but he wanted Tyler Coneys to be the one. "It's always better to deal directly with the person in charge," John said. He told me it was okay to use his name if it would make things easier.

When I told Tyler Coneys that the boat I had purchased was for none other than John Lennon, the young man jumped at the opportunity to deliver it personally and show us how to sail it. The next day, May 1, I met Coneys at his store. The small sailboat was loaded on a carriage and attached to the back of his car. We drove to a sandy beach near the house and struggled to put the boat in the water. Then Coneys sailed toward the house, while I drove back to Cannon Hill to get John.

I found him waiting excitedly on the front porch, surveying the harbor. We rushed down to the dock and got there just in time to help Tyler Coneys tie the boat next to the rickety, decaying wooden structure. John and I jumped into the boat and I introduced the marina manager, who was visibly affected by coming face-to-face with the legendary star he admired since he was a teenage Beatle fan. Tyler told John that he had thought I was pulling his leg when I'd told him who the boat was for, and said that even now that he was in John's presence, he still could not quite believe it.

"Don't worry, you'll get used to it soon enough," John said, wearily.

"Try to pretend I'm just another one of your clients." We untied the rope and set out into the harbor, with Tyler showing us all the necessary steps involved in sailing the little boat. John was ecstatic. "All my life I've been dreaming of having my own boat," he bubbled. "I can't wait to learn how to sail!"

John talked manically about his rather dismal boating experiences in the past. He told of one night at the height of Beatlemania in the mid-sixties when he and Ringo had gotten blind drunk in Scotland and decided to go boating on one of the lochs. They kept right on drinking in the boat, unmindful of the sinking sun. By the time he and Ringo realized it was dark, they were hopelessly lost and totally inebriated, and John said he could just imagine the headlines the next day when their bodies were washed ashore. Luckily, John continued, he and Ringo somehow drifted ashore and survived the incident with nothing worse than a bad hangover. Another time, John related, he went sailing during a trip to New England with his friend Richard Ross. They had no trouble getting out to sea, but since neither of them had wanted to admit that they did not really know how to sail, when it was time to return to shore they were unable to turn the boat around, and had to be rescued by the Coast Guard.

Once John saw that Tyler was an expert sailor and that we had nothing to fear, he relaxed and even agreed to take the helm for a while. As we sailed around the harbor executing a few basic maneuvers, John decided to name the boat *Isis*, after the Egyptian fertility goddess. He was so pleased with our first outing on the *Isis* that he asked Tyler to return the following day.

That night John and I stayed up late watching television, and John talked about how much this sailing venture meant to him. I had never seen John so excited. After years of reading about great seamen like Eric the Red and Thor Heyerdahl, and speculating about his own Viking heritage, John was finally able to realize a lifelong dream of sailing his own boat. John told me he had spent hours on the docks of Liverpool, watching the big ships come and go, wondering if his father was on one of them. John said that he had often daydreamed about the exotic places the ships visited, and that he even thought about becoming a stowaway in order to escape whatever misery he was facing at home or in school. Sometimes he would get an almost overpowering urge to sneak aboard a ship, usually after Mimi or one of his teachers gave him a hard time. But in the end, John said, he was always too afraid of the unknown, and he never followed through on his impulse. He told me that as a boy he had often dreamed of sailing across the ocean to new, exotic lands, imagining all kinds of adventures. He talked candidly about his violent seafaring fantasies, in which he frequently saw himself as a fearless Viking, raping and pillaging with gusto.

Tyler was a frequent visitor at Cannon Hill during the early part of May, 1980, stopping by after work, and whenever he visited, John picked the young sailor's brain. John was quite serious about learning everything there was to know about sailing and he would ask Tyler many technical questions about it. He supplemented Tyler's lessons with home study, reading numerous books on the subject that I picked up at local bookstores. I had a standing order to buy all the literature on the art and craft of sailing I could find. Once John learned the basic skills involved in sailing, he began to talk about buying a larger boat with which he could embark on extended trips. He said he counted on me to be his "copilot," and that he hoped I would live up to my family name by becoming an expert seaman.

One windy afternoon, John, Sean, Helen, and I were cruising around the harbor with Tyler. John asked me to take over at the helm while he smoked a cigarette. The wind grew stronger and we picked up speed. I jerked the rudder too hard and the *Isis* slowly capsized. The next thing I knew we were swimming in Cold Spring Harbor and Sean began to cry. Fortunately he was wearing a life vest. John and Helen immediately swam toward him and comforted him. I was astounded to see Tyler standing on the side of the boat. The quick-witted sailor had managed to stay on the boat as it keeled over. He showed John and me how to help him set the *Isis* upright, and within minutes the boat was afloat again. We climbed back in. As we made our way to the shore John teased me mercilessly about my incompetence as a sailor. "You really disgraced the family name this time, *Seaman*," he said, crackling gleefully.

I had expected John to be furious with me and was relieved that he appeared to take the sailing mishap in stride. Indeed, he later told me that the accident was a useful experience for him, because having survived such a "worst-case scenario," it made him even more confident. His biggest worry was that Yoko would find out about it and forbid any further sailing trips. "Not a word to Mother," he admonished everyone.

By mid-May John had grown confident enough at the helm of the *Isis* to venture out to sea without Tyler, who, after all, did have a marina to run. I got used to John knocking on my door at all hours of the day asking me if I was up for a "spin around the harbor." The two of us would then take turns at the helm. During one of our outings I told John about Billy Joel's glass house on the harbor. I had a vague idea of where it was located, and John, suddenly intrigued by it, cruised close to the shore in search of the house. When we finally spotted something resembling Joel's house, John leapt up and yelled across the harbor, "Hey, Billy, I have all your records!"

This was not exactly true, although John did love Joel's hit single "Just the Way You Are." Once, when this famous ballad came on the radio in the kitchen at the Dakota, John asked me to get it for his jukebox because it was his and Yoko's song. Now, John became so excited about having a fellow superstar musician as a neighbor that he suggested paying Billy Joel a visit. But we never did.

Try as he might, John was unable to persuade Yoko to join us for a sail around the harbor in the *Isis*. Yoko remained steadfast in her refusal to so much as set foot on the small boat. John had better luck with Yoko's sister, Setsuko, who visited us in Cold Spring Harbor, accompanied by Baba. John wasted no time in showing off his newly acquired sailing skills for Yoko's younger sister. John asked Yoko to film one of our outings, and I set up the video camera on the terrace, from where she would have a commanding view of the harbor. I assumed she would be somewhat familiar with video equipment from her days as an avant-garde filmmaker. I was surprised that she had great difficulty in even bringing the camera into focus.

By the end of May, John began to seriously contemplate an extended sailing venture. Tyler told John that he had two cousins who were also expert sailors, and who wanted to sail to the Caribbean. The idea of such a joint sea voyage greatly appealed to John.

In recent years, John and Yoko had spent the summer visiting Yoko's family in Japan. But this year Yoko's mother was in the U.S. and John had had his fill of Japanese in-laws. A trip to the Caribbean would be a welcome change of pace. John was no stranger to the region. In 1965 the Beatles filmed *Help!* in the Bahamas, and he had made several trips to the Islands since then, most recently to Grand Cayman in the summer of 1978. The only difference would be that instead of flying, this time he would sail to the West Indies. Yoko immediately agreed to help John find a boat and crew. She saw a way of letting John have his way and at the same time have hers. His desire to embark on an extended voyage offered her a great opportunity to pursue more freely her romance with Sam Green. She liked the idea of sending John to some distant place where he would not interfere with her relationship with Sam.

The only problem was that Yoko insisted on making all the arrangements. Her plan for finding a suitable boat involved scrutinizing ads in nautical publications and then asking her psychics to do a "reading" on likely vessels. Impatient with Yoko's slow progress, John told me to get in touch with Tyler Coneys and ask him to look into obtaining a boat. "Tyler's got good connections," John said confidently. "Tell him money is no object."

Tyler quickly chartered a forty-three-foot schooner anchored in Newport, Rhode Island. Now Yoko had to come up with a destination for John's voyage. According to her Japanese directionalist, Takashi Yoshikawa, the only practical direction in which John could travel at that moment was southeast, and the only thing southeast of New York is Bermuda, unless one is planning to sail to Brazil. So Bermuda it was. John would sail there with the Coneyses. Sean, Helen, Uda-san, and I would follow later, by plane.

Early on Wednesday morning, June 4, 1980, Sean, John, and I had breakfast with Tyler and his two cousins, Ellen and Kevin Coneys. The view from the sun-drenched room was a panorama of the harbor, a dazzling, glittering sight at that time of the morning. After breakfast, I loaded the Mercedes with John's provisions for the trip, mostly miso soup, brown rice, and green tea. John had decided to go on a "cleansing fast" during his sailing trip to Bermuda, which was expected to last five days. With the three Coneyses in the back of the car and John sitting next to me with Sean on his lap, I drove for a half hour along Route 110 to Farmingdale Airport. A twin-engine Cessna had been chartered to fly John and his crew to Newport, where their boat, the *Megan Jaye*, was awaiting them.

"I love you, sweetheart," John said, planting a kiss on his son's forehead.

"I want to go with you, Daddy," said four-year-old Sean, bravely holding back tears.

"When you're older, we'll have plenty of time to sail together," John said as he gave Sean a good-bye hug. I held Sean's tiny hand while

John walked to the plane. He climbed aboard, shouting, "See you in paradise, boys!"

The Cosmopolitan Airways Cessna wheeled around on its nose gear, and the small Plexiglas windows exploded with light as they reflected the sun. The plane slowly rolled down the runway and the turbines screamed as the pilot applied takeoff power. The plane shuddered with energy as it gathered speed and then leapt into flight, its wheels sucked up inside its belly. Sean and I stood motionless and watched until it was no more than a speck in the sky. "Bye, Daddy!" Sean waved at the airplane as it disappeared from view, becoming just a faint mechanical whine in the distance.

I took the next day off, with Uda-san's blessing, and spent my free time on the beach munching psychedelic mushrooms with a girlfriend I had met in a club in Roslyn. I made it back to Cannon Hill by midnight. In the morning I awoke to an insistent knock on my door. It was Doug MacDougall, the ex-FBI agent who was Sean's bodyguard and, occasionally, babysitter. He asked me to meet him in the kitchen. I hastily threw on some clothes and went downstairs. Doug poured me a cup of coffee and explained that after I took the day off, he got a call from Myoko at the Dakota, asking him to stock the Cannon Hill refrigerator with vodka and wine. Doug grudgingly went out and bought the booze. No sooner had he stashed it in the refrigerator than Yoko showed up in a limo, carrying shopping bags full of food and clothes. She then disappeared into the bedroom, but sent the limousine back to the Dakota twice to pick up more clothes. Doug informed me that Yoko planned to spend the day at Sam Green's Fire Island house and that Sam would pick her up in a seaplane at noon.

"Now you know as much as I do," the guard said, grinning sheepishly. He drove off in his battered old pickup truck, but not before warning me that Sam Havadtoy was scheduled to deliver a truckload of furniture to Cannon Hill that morning. I immediately called the office to sound the alarm, envisioning a scenario of the two Sams converging on the house—Havadtoy rolling down the driveway in a truck while Sam Green's seaplane landed in front.

There was no answer at the Dakota. A flustered-looking Uda-san then shuffled into the kitchen and handed me a massive shopping list.

"Yoko very upset you not here yesterday," she said gravely.

I told her that would be nothing compared to the fireworks that might occur if we did not head off Havadtoy's visit. When I explained that both Sams were scheduled to arrive at Cannon Hill at approximately the same time, Uda-san let out a shriek. It was impossible to tell if it was because she found the situation amusing or alarming. She promised to contact Myoko at the Dakota, who would then tell Rich, who could perhaps find a way of intercepting Havadtoy. I jumped into the Benz and went shopping in Huntington, where I scurried around local stores in search of mussels, figs, and all kinds of gourmet foods.

Back at the house, I was relieved to learn that Rich had managed to intercept Havadtoy just before he departed. I helped Uda-san unpack the bags of food and watched as she reorganized everything into three shopping bags for Yoko to carry aboard the plane. Uda-san was both outraged and amused by Yoko's shameless romancing of "Glean Sam." Amid fits of giggling, she whispered to me that Yoko had recently been wearing sexy lingerie and even a garter belt, as well as putting on makeup for her dates with Sam. With John out of the way, Yoko no longer saw a need for discretion in her relationship. She openly flaunted her romantic infatuation with the debonair art dealer.

Sam arrived right on schedule, his seaplane emitting a faint buzzing sound before landing on the harbor in front of the house. Uda-san and I took the shopping bags to the dinghy. I began loading them into the small boat. When I walked back to the house, I found Yoko waiting anxiously on the terrace, dolled up in white jacket and shorts, looking extremely nervous. I escorted her and Sean to the boat, and helped them find a seat among the shopping bags. Yoko was petrified. She didn't have much confidence in the small craft's seaworthiness. I reassured her that it was absolutely safe, and I began rowing toward the seaplane, which was about fifty feet away. Suddenly Sean started jumping up and down, causing the dinghy to take in some water. Yoko almost fainted. She rebuked Sean angrily for his rowdiness and admonished him to sit still.

I reached the plane and gave the shopping bags to the pilot while Sam stood on one of the ballast tanks, trying to persuade Yoko to stand up and allow herself to be helped aboard. It took several minutes of delicate coaxing before Yoko finally mustered the courage to disembark.

I had lunch with Uda-san and then I took a nap by the pool. I awakened to Uda-san's shrill voice screaming from the bedroom balcony that Yoko was on her way back. Within minutes I heard the by now familiar buzzing sound that signaled the seaplane's arrival. I rushed to the beach and jumped into the dinghy, rowing forcefully toward the plane, which had drifted very close to the shore. Sam guided Yoko and Sean onto the plane's ballast tank, and I helped mother and son climb into the dinghy, and went back for the shopping bags. Back on firm ground, Yoko ran back to the house, while I stayed behind with Sean, who wanted to watch the plane take off.

Later, Sean annoyed Yoko with his persistent demands for attention, and she suggested taking him for a long drive in the Mercedes. Sean and I cruised the local roads listening to Beatles tapes—Sean knew that I kept them stashed in the glove compartment—while he told me about the day's outing, which was apparently marred by Sam Green's pet turtle "pissing and poopooing" all over Sam's place.

Yoko went back to the Dakota that evening, but the next morning she was back at the house, ordering chicken soup for lunch. Since John had thrown out all the chicken bouillon cubes in a last-minute food raid prior to his departure, a flustered Uda-san begged me to drive to town on an emergency shopping run. On my way out, Yoko handed me a tape recorder, which she asked me to get fixed. I examined the device in the car and discovered that the tape simply got mangled. When I played back the cassette I was astonished to hear an eerie, high-pitched voice talking in clipped sentences. The topic was Sam Green's relationship with Yoko. I realized that I was listening to a psychic reading. Sam could be heard in the background, asking questions as well as responding to the reading, which culminated in Sam being told that he was attracted to older women of means and that he was a "catalyst" and brought romance into their lives.

Returning to the house with a fresh supply of bouillon cubes, I was told that they were no longer needed. Yoko had apparently decided to invite Sam for lunch. She sent Doug MacDougall, who had been playing with Sean outside the house, to buy several pounds of shrimp, scallops, mussels, and sole. Doug showed up a short while later, grumbling about being used as an "errand boy." Meanwhile, Sam Green had called to cancel the lunch date, but Yoko insisted on sending him the seafood anyway. I dutifully loaded the fish-filled shopping bags into the dinghy and delivered the seafood to a waiting seaplane.

The following morning, a Sunday, Uda-san asked me to serve Yoko and Sean tea in bed. For some reason, she herself found the idea of serving mother and child in bed offensive. When I entered the bedroom, Yoko was on the phone, chain-smoking Cigarettellos. Her eyes were at half-mast. The blinds were drawn, the ashtrays were overflowing with long brown cigarette butts, clothes were strewn all over the floor, and numerous empty cups were scattered around the dark room. I placed a cup of tea on the small night table next to Yoko's side of the bed, and did the same for Sean. He was bouncing up and down, trying to get his mother's attention, but she ignored his antics. Sean then began screaming for breakfast, and between phone calls Yoko instructed me to ask Uda-san to bring Sean something to eat.

When I told Uda-san, she refused to set foot in the bedroom. A few minutes later Sean came charging into the kitchen, screaming, "I want my food!" and pummeling Uda-san with his tiny fists. When she remained adamant in her refusal to cater to Sean, the boy ran off for a short while, then came running back, still screaming for his food.

The phone rang, and it was Yoko ordering me to instruct Uda-san to "give Sean whatever he wants." When I passed Yoko's orders along to Uda-san, she angrily flung open the refrigerator door and told Sean to help himself, then stormed out of the kitchen, with Sean in hot pursuit.

Later in the day, Yoko informed me that we would be returning to the Dakota in the morning. She then instructed me to get Sam Havadtoy on the phone. I overheard her asking him to make sure there would be "stuff to sniff" upon her arrival. Uda-san was ordered to stay behind in the house to keep an eye on the painters, who had been working on the house on and off for the past two months. I felt sorry for her, having to remain in the big house alone with no work to do. Maybe she was being punished for having disobeyed Yoko and Sean. Meantime, a violent thunderstorm cut off our power. Yoko gave me a panicky call from the bedroom, asking me to "make the lights go back on."

Informed that there appeared to be a local blackout, she sulked for a while, then resigned herself to the situation and asked me to light a candle on her night table. I overheard her giggle to Sam Green on the phone how "romantic" it was in her candle-lit room.

After the storm subsided, Yoko descended to the living room and sat down at the piano. Suddenly there was a knock on the front door and everyone—even Sean—froze. I opened the door and found myself facing a tall, middle-aged man who introduced himself as Dr. James Watson from the nearby Cold Spring Harbor Biolab. He had a boy with him who I assumed was his son. He said they were just passing by and happened to see Yoko playing piano. Dr. Watson said that on a recent visit to Tokyo he had met a friend of hers, an architect. I was not, of course, allowed to let him in, but I took his number. Yoko was outraged by the intrusion. It made no difference to her that Dr. James Watson was a world-famous scientist who had received the Nobel Prize for unraveling the structure of DNA, as well as coauthoring the best-selling book *The Double Helix*.

On Monday, June 9, exactly two months after John and I were sent to Cold Spring Harbor, I was back in Studio One. I spent the morning gossiping, with Rich and catching up on the mail, which was piled high on my desk.

Yoko showed up with Sam Green in the afternoon and asked me to bring her a copy of every record she ever made. When I delivered the albums to the inner sanctum I noticed a new piece on her desk: a skull encased in a glass box. Yoko wanted Sam to hear all her songs, including outtakes from the three albums she recorded in the early seventies. She asked me to contact Roy Cicala, the owner of the Record Plant, and make arrangements to retrieve all her unreleased recordings. When I got hold of Cicala, he told me that Yoko's music was stored in a nuclear-proof underground vault in upstate New York, and that it would take time to retrieve the tapes. I stayed in the office late into the night, sorting the mail while Yoko played Sam her songs.

Tuesday afternoon, Sam and Yoko flew to Palm Beach for the day, and Yoko left strict orders to tell everyone who called, including John, that she was "unavailable."

The next day, Yoko asked me to drive Havadtoy and one of his carpenters to Cannon Hill to take some measurements, and to bring Uda-san back to the Dakota. I was to then return to Cannon Hill, where I would stay until further notice. On the way back to Long Island I stopped by my apartment to pick up some clothes and retrieve a bag of psilocybin mushrooms from my freezer. I had been saving them for a special occasion, and the prospect of spending a few days by myself in a giant mansion overlooking Cold Spring Harbor seemed like the ideal place. I made it back to Cannon Hill at dusk and walked along the deserted beach in front of the house. I was glad to finally have some time to myself.

After a good night's sleep, I got up to watch the sunrise. Then I drove into town to pick up some newspapers. Back at the house I had some psychedelic mushrooms for breakfast and waited for the painters. I settled myself by the pool with a Walkman, a handful of reggae tapes, and my bag of mushrooms. I munched on a fat stem, and scanned the front page of the *Times*, feeling the morning sun begin to warm my legs and chest. A headline announced the death of Japanese Prime Minister Masayoshi Ohira. I read about two paragraphs and my eyes began to glaze over. Then I gazed at a photo of a boat overloaded with Haitians, and was instantly reminded of the fact that exactly a week earlier John had left for Bermuda, and had not been heard from since. The sailing trip was supposed to last only five days. What if John's boat had disappeared into the Bermuda Triangle? I sat up suddenly, my head reeling. I hallucinated banner headlines proclaiming John's mysterious disappearance. With great effort, I excluded such alarming thoughts from my mind.

I put on headphones and cranked up Bob Marley's *Natty Dread* album. Soon I felt a wave of euphoria wash over me. It was as if an electric current was being run through my body. At the same time I could feel the earth's gravitational pull doubling in strength, then doubling again. I was vibrating to the beat of Rasta rhythm with an elephant sitting on my chest. Wow. The mushrooms were far more potent than I had anticipated. I sat back, trying to relax, and flipped through the paper, which by that time was crawling with green and glowing headlines. On the Op-Ed page I came across a little article by an associate director for drug policy at the White House, who opined that the best way to prevent youngsters from using drugs was "to bring about inner peace in adolescents."

I found myself cackling hysterically when all of a sudden I heard a faint, familiar voice coming through the headphones. I looked up and saw a massive figure looming over me. It was Doug MacDougall, the bodyguard, fixing me with a concerned look. Fortunately I was wearing mirror sunglasses.

"You sleeping?" Doug asked, looking puzzled.

I shook my head with great effort. I found that I could not speak, even though I was moving my mouth. When I stood up to face him, it was as if I'd had a stroke and was partially paralyzed. I lurched to the wooden fence surrounding the pool and hung there like a dying spider. Doug watched me with a frown on his face, and since I wasn't talking, he told me that he had come out to supervise the removal of some pieces of furniture, then walked away.

Relieved to be out of his sight, I slithered into the pool, hoping the water might help straighten me out. I really had overdosed on the mushrooms. I floated in the pool for a while, thinking, "I have ceased to be a biped," and feeling oddly relaxed, waited to regain full possession of my motor abilities. But then Doug called me to the house to take a phone call. As I struggled out of the pool I realized I was still semiparalyzed. I dried myself in slow motion and threw on a shirt before making my way toward the house with great difficulty. I somehow managed to reach the kitchen. I grabbed the phone and said, "Whoooaaa," or something like it.

"Are you all right? You sound very fucked up." It was Rich.

"Fiynnne," I croaked.

"Glad to hear it, because I've been instructed to tell you to get your ass back here on the double!"

"Nooowaiiee," I protested feebly.

I do not know what the rest of the conversation was like, but I hung up without resolving our disagreement. I sat in the kitchen, unable to decide what to do next. I noticed some men loading furniture into a truck parked in front of the house and was about to call the cops when Doug came in and poured me a cup of coffee, which I promptly lifted to my lips and poured down the front of my shirt. Doug pretended not to notice. I attempted to tell him about my conversation with Rich, but my words ran together. Still, I must have somehow managed to make myself understood.

"You don't look to me like you're in any condition to drive," Doug said gravely before going off.

The phone rang and I found myself on the line with Havadtoy, who was asking me if his movers had arrived. Then he began reading me a long list of furniture they were supposed to take, which went in one ear and right out the other. I muttered something about being in the middle of something, and said I would get one of his men to talk to him. Then the other phone rang. It was Rich again, and he sounded miffed. He insisted I had to come back to New York at once and that he was under strict orders not to say why. I told him that I could not come, not under any circumstances, and that I was under strict orders not to say why, too.

"Okay, you win!" Rich said, exasperated. "Himself just called from

Bermuda, and he wants you to join him A.S.A.P." I smiled. I had almost given up hope of ever seeing John again.

"Listen," Rich continued, urgently. "I was told to book you on an evening flight, so you better get your ass in gear!"

This news had a sobering effect on me, and I quickly blurted out that I didn't think I would be able to get ready on such short notice.

"Well, then you better work it out with the boss himself," Rich said, and gave a number where John could be reached. I called the overseas operator and gave her the number in Bermuda. An unfamiliar voice answered the phone, and immediately cut me off when I asked, "Is John there?"

I wondered if I had the right number, but then it occurred to me that my thoughtless question might have triggered an attack of paranoia at the other end. I tried again, this time giving my name before asking for John. A moment later, he was on the line.

"Hi, Fred!" John said cheerfully. "When are you coming?"

"Uh, I'll need a day or so to get ready."

"You sound weird, Fred," John said, perceptive as ever. "You're not sick, are you?" Concern and suspicion had crept into his voice.

I knew there was no point in continuing the charade. I could tell from the tense tone of John's voice that he was on to me, and so I blurted out that I'd had "magic" mushrooms for breakfast.

"Oh, really? How are they?" I had piqued his interest. "Do you have any left?"

I told him I had a whole bagful of the psychedelic fungi.

"Great! Maybe you can bring them with the health food Uda-san is bringing in."

That sounded like a wonderful idea.

"Listen," John continued, lowering his voice. "I've got some grass stashed in the bedroom. You better find it before the painters get their hands on it. I think it's in my desk drawer. Why don't you call me back from the bedroom when you've found it, and then I'll give you a list of clothes I want you to bring."

I crawled up the stairs to the second floor, my progress tracked by incredulous stares from the painters, and locked myself inside the master bedroom. I didn't think I could handle any more interruptions. I searched John's desk and found the marijuana in a clear plastic bag. I also came across a typewritten manuscript titled *The Ballad of John and Yoko*. I glanced through the manuscript, looking for major revelations, but after scanning a few pages I realized it was a diatribe aimed at his and Yoko's detractors. It included numerous sardonic, angry comments about the other Beatles. Beyond that it was a rambling discourse on life with Yoko, about which I felt I knew far too much already.

I took the grass and then called John back. He suggested hiding the mushrooms and marijuana among the health foods Uda-san was bringing, maybe mixing them in with the dried seaweed.

"Don't tell Uda-san," John chuckled. "That way, if you're caught, she'll put on a show of righteous indignation that will convince even the most hardened customs agent of your innocence."

John next gave me a detailed list of clothes he wanted me to bring. After a long, mind-wrenching grope through his closets, I managed to find everything except a pair of white sneakers. When I called him back, he said the sneakers might be at the Dakota. I promised to look for them and told him I would call him back from the office to let him know our exact time of arrival. I then packed John's clothes into a big leather bag and collected a few of my things before checking in with Rich at the office. The accountant informed me that Uda-san, Sean, and I were booked on a flight to Bermuda the following afternoon.

"How are you feeling?" Rich asked, his voice expressing both sarcasm and concern. "You sounded like you were really out of it this morning."

I assured him I never felt better.

In fact, my central nervous system had not only regained all of its functions, but seemed to have gone into overdrive. I felt myself vibrating with nervous energy. Perhaps, I thought, John felt this way all the time. I quickly loaded the Mercedes and drove off, right into the rush hour. Although traffic was slow-moving toward Manhattan, it was nothing compared to the mass exodus of commuters in the adjoining lanes of the Long Island Expressway, which resembled a vast parking lot. Catching a glimpse of the setting sun ahead, I was reminded that I had been up for more than twelve hours, and that in another twelve hours I would be in sunny Bermuda. I was quietly thrilled at the thought of joining John, and glad to be leaving Yoko's orbit. I asked myself if it might help John to break free of Yoko's spell if he knew that his wife was infatuated with another man and was spending a small fortune on extravagant lunches and seaplane rides.

Considering John's childlike dependency on Yoko, I decided he probably would not want to know.

When I called John from the Dakota, he gave me a new list of clothes and reminded me to look for his white sneakers, all the while apologizing for being so compulsive about his wardrobe. I found the sneakers in the clothes room, an octagonal, wood-paneled chamber located between the bedroom and the White Room, and filled from floor to ceiling with apparel. There were several mobile racks from which hung Yoko's impressive collection of furs and John's expensive European jackets and blazers, as well as numerous oversized drawers and wooden bins stuffed with sweaters, T-shirts, socks, and underwear. A large section of floor space was taken up by countless pairs of shoes. I dutifully collected all the clothes on John's list and left them in a pile in the White Room.

It was fairly late at night by the time I made it back home, I was not surprised to find a message from Yoko on my answering machine, asking me to call John in Bermuda first thing in the morning. After a few hours of restless sleep, I got up early the next day, which happened to be Friday, June 13. When I called John, he told me that not only was it Friday the 13th, but also Mercury Retrograde, and that I should forget about bringing the mushrooms and marijuana. If I attempted to smuggle drugs on such an inauspicious date, John warned, I was sure to get caught. Lastly, he instructed me to bring his favorite Ovation acoustic guitar, as well as his copy of Thor Heyerdahl's *Early Man and the Ocean*.

I quickly packed a few of my own clothes, taking along as little as possible because I knew that I would be loaded down with John's things. I made it to the Dakota just in time to take a call from John asking me to take his guitar on the plane as hand baggage, and not to let the instrument out of my sight. I found John's guitar in Apartment 71, and then stopped by the kitchen, where Yoko and her mother sat at the butcher-block table, eating breakfast in silence. Yoko told me cheerfully that the old lady was also leaving.

Suddenly Yoko asked, "What time are we going to the airport?"

"Are you coming with us to Bermuda?" I said, taken aback.

"No, silly," Yoko giggled. "I just want to see you off."

Around mid-morning, Yoko strutted into the office wearing a provocative outfit consisting of black leather hot pants and a black silk shirt unbuttoned to expose maximum cleavage. She asked me to set up a tape recorder on her piano in the inner sanctum, explaining that she wanted to record "a song for John." She spent the rest of the morning warbling in a high-pitched voice.

John called me at noon to ask for "one last thing"—his favorite tie, a black and maroon striped one he used to wear in grammar school.

When our limousine arrived, I rang Uda-san upstairs and asked her to look for John's grammar school tie and then come down with Sean. I then buzzed Yoko, who was on the phone to John, and told her we were ready to drive to the airport. We all piled into the back of a stretch limo and began driving up Central Park West. I asked Uda-san if she had all her papers, and she showed me her Japanese passport, but of course no one had remembered to bring Sean's. Yoko said it was probably in one of her desk drawers, so we turned back and she and I ran into her office and furiously searched through her desk.

"Don't worry, Fred," Yoko said, noticing my alarmed expression. "I'm sure it's here somewhere."

She emptied out several drawers, which were cluttered with miscellaneous items such as half-empty cigarette packs, lighters, pens, memo pads and money—but no passport. I was debating whether to call our travel agent to find out about the next flight to Bermuda when Yoko triumphantly held up the missing document, which had been hidden under a pile of old photos. I was so relieved that I almost hugged her. By now it was past 1:00 P.M. Yoko had a two o'clock lunch date with Sam Green, so she decided to skip the airport trip. She kissed Sean good-bye and promised to visit us in Bermuda "in a week or two."

When we checked in at the airport there was a big hassle over John's guitar. The airline personnel insisted it was too bulky to take on the plane and refused to let me take it aboard. I had no choice but to give it up, and felt my heart sink as the instrument was carried away on a conveyor belt. Sipping champagne in first class, I soon calmed down. Sean demanded a taste of the yellow bubbly and threatened to cause a commotion if I denied his request, so I let him have a sip. Uda-san was aghast, but she need not have worried, because after tasting the champagne, Sean turned up his mouth in disgust and vowed never to touch the stuff again.

Uda-san appeared to suffer from a mild case of fear of flying. She told me that the long flight from Tokyo to New York the previous year had been the worst experience of her life. Her anxiety in this case was compounded by the fact that she had no idea where we were going.

"Where this Bermuda?" Uda-san kept asking. She seemed to think it was somewhere in the Mediterranean. When I showed her our destination on a map, a tiny speck of land surrounded by a vast ocean, Uda looked disappointed. "Japan much bigger," she sniffed.

After a brief and uneventful flight we landed in the British Crown Colony of Bermuda. It was here that I finally discovered the John Lennon I had always suspected existed, hidden beneath layers of boredom and despair.

10

Bermuda

When Uda-san, Sean, and I reached Hamilton, the capital of Bermuda, we were told that Uda-san needed an entry visa. I had to buy her a seven-hundred-dollar ticket to Tokyo before they would admit her. Then I discovered that John's guitar was missing. After a frantic search, I learned that it was on a later flight. By the time we left the airport, it was early evening. Tyler Coneys, who had been dispatched to meet us, directed our cab to John's house. Tyler announced happily that he and John had become "best friends" during their trip. They had shared some potent sinsemilla along the way, and Tyler believed this had cemented their relationship. I didn't want to be the one to tell him that no one was "best friends" with John, and in any case, he would not have believed me.

John and his crew of Coneyses were ensconced on the top floor of a house in Knapton Hill. John had a bedroom to himself. Tyler, along with his cousins Ellen and Kevin, had set up a bivouac on the living room floor. John welcomed us to his "humble abode," and he and Sean had an emotional reunion. The moment I saw John, I noticed a difference in him: He had lost the pallor he had acquired over five years at the Dakota. I realized that the entire time I had known him, he had always looked like a man suffering from a degenerative illness. Now he was tanned and exuded health and vitality.

John plucked the guitar from its case and began singing Liverpool sea chanties. Sean was delighted at his daddy's impromptu performances and danced gleefully around the cramped living room. Then

John talked esthusiastically about his sailing trip. He told me that once he was out on the ocean, surrounded by water as far as the eye could see, he realized he was fulfilling some part of his destiny that he had put off for too long. "You can't imagine what it's like when you look around and all you see is water and sky," he said. "You feel both isolated and in communication with the almighty whatever. It's an overwhelming sensation of freedom."

A few days after leaving Newport, the boat had sailed into a power-ful mid-Atlantic storm and all hell had broken loose. Rocked by twenty-foot-high waves and whipped by gale-force winds, the *Megan Jaye* began a roller-coaster ride through the turbulent seas. The storm lasted for almost two days, and when by the end of the first day the Coneyses were incapacitated by seasickness, John took the helm. He attributed his unusual fortitude to his macrobiotic diet of brown rice and miso soup.

"So there I was at the wheel," John said, "the wind and sea lashing out at me, wave after wave. At first I was terrified, but Cap'n Hank was at my side, so I felt relatively safe, 'cause I knew he wouldn't let me do anything stupid! But after a while even he wasn't feeling too well and he retreated to the cabin below." John laughed, shaking his head in disbelief. All alone at the helm, with the fate of the ship in his hands, John knew it was "do or die." After overcoming his initial panic, John rose to the occasion and single-handedly steered the ship through the storm.

"Once I accepted the reality of the situation," he continued, "some-thing greater than me took over and all of a sudden I lost my fear. I actually began to enjoy the experience, and I started to sing and shout old sea chanties in the face of the storm, feeling total exhilaration. I had the time of my life. I felt like Liddy must have felt, strapped to the top of that tree during the storm, screaming at the thundering sky, 'Take me away, God! I don't give a shit!' "

The only other time he had felt as "centered" and "in tune with the cosmos," he said, was in 1961, when the Beatles were at their peak as a live band, wasting audiences in Liverpool and Hamburg night after night. "I knew then that nothing could stop me and that the Beatles would make it big sooner or later. It was the only time in my life that I felt truly in charge of my destiny." Having survived by his own skills and courage, John felt that he had once more tapped into his primal, indestructible, youthful self. Suddenly, I realized that I was looking at the John Lennon I had heard him describe once, a man in the full flush of his power, a man eager for life, not cowed by it.

John had invited Cap'n Hank for dinner, and Uda-san, still dazed from the ordeal at the airport, was faced with the task of preparing dinner for our motley crew on short notice. She made up a long shopping list, and Tyler and I jumped on two rented mopeds and raced to the nearest store. We bought a hundred dollars' worth of groceries, and Uda-san quickly whipped up a meal of fish, vegetables, and brown rice.

The captain arrived, accompanied by his friend Gretchen, an attractive young woman who had flown in from Rhode Island to assist him on the return trip. The captain, a cheerful, bearded man in his early thirties, had introduced Gretchen as his "celestial navigator," which aroused John's curiosity. John was fascinated by the idea of being able to navigate the seas simply by studying the stars in the sky. It was the way of the ancient mariners, his Viking ancestors, who crossed the ocean without the help of even a compass. While John engaged the young woman in an intense conversation about the stars, I chatted with Cap'n Hank. I learned that he was a die-hard Beatles fan who had idolized Lennon since his teenage years. By an amazing twist of fate, he had been chosen to take John halfway across the Atlantic Ocean. When he realized who he had on board, he was absolutely dumbfounded. He still seemed stunned by the whole experience, and spent much of the evening with a blissful smile on his face while listening to John reminisce about the sailing trip.

The next morning when I got up, John was out on the terrace overlooking the water, surveying the spectacular view of the harbor. Cap'n Hank and Gretchen were planning to take the *Megan Jaye* back to Newport the next day, and John had made plans for a farewell cruise around the island. We drove to the harbor in a taxi, escorted by the Coneyses on mopeds. On the way, it began drizzling, and once we were aboard, John put on a bright yellow slicker over his green-on-white Marilyn Monroe T-shirt. Sean was outfitted with a red life preserver and sat next to John as Cap'n Hank steered the ship out of the harbor.

When the rain got heavier, Sean and I followed John down into the cabin, where John recalled how he had been making tea when the storm struck its first blow. The doors to the cabinets had flown open and their contents were strewn all around the cabin. "It seems funny now," John laughed, "but at the time I was scared out of my wits. I didn't know what was happening. I thought maybe we'd been rammed by a whale or something. I was sure we would sink."

As soon as the rain let up, we went above again and Sean took the wheel, assisted by Hank and Gretchen. John sat back with the hood up on his yellow heavy-weather gear, fired up a Gitane, and surveyed the boat and the spectacular view of the Bermuda coastline. The houses appeared as irregular white specks on the lush green hills in the distance. On the other side of the boat lay the open sea. John gazed wistfully at the horizon.

After a while, Gretchen joined us, and soon she and John were deep in conversation. John seemed very taken by the pretty navigator. At the end of the cruise, John and the Coneyses said good-bye to Hank and Gretchen, making all sorts of plans for a reunion stateside, and John took us to lunch at an Italian restaurant in St. George that he and the crew had visited when they first docked in Bermuda. "We looked like survivors of a shipwreck," John chuckled, recalling how he and the crew had caused heads to turn when they'd staggered into the restaurant in their filthy clothes, stoned out of their minds because they had smoked a huge quantity of marijuana before entering the harbor. Cap'n Hank had told him that incoming boats were occasionally searched by Bermuda customs inspectors. This information had triggered John's paranoia; he had been arrested for possession of marijuana in 1968, and his subsequent drug conviction had made it difficult for him to obtain travel visas in the past. Fearing another bust, John had insisted that the crew get rid of the pot. John said that they had rolled several huge joints, which they smoked as they approached the island. At the last minute, however, John asked one of the crew to save one of the joints for him. The remaining marijuana was cast adrift in a bottle.

After lunch, the Coneyses went back to the house, while John, Sean, Uda-san, and I spent the afternoon sightseeing in St. George. When we got back to out apartment, John complained about his cramped quarters and was ready to chew off the heads of his "roommates." Resentful about sharing his space, John began treating the Coneyses with contempt. He was annoyed that Uda-san felt obligated to cook and clean up after them. She was a consummate servant, and it was unthinkable for her to simply look after John and Sean while ignoring our guests.

As soon as we had a quiet moment that evening, John called me into his room, and asked me to find larger quarters, preferably a secluded waterfront villa. There had obviously been a mix-up in communications between Studio One and a local real estate agent about what kind of accommodations were suitable for John, whose identity had not been revealed.

It did not take me long to find out that renting a secluded waterfront villa in Bermuda in the middle of June was next to impossible. Seeing that I was getting nowhere, John told me that money was no object and even authorized me to use the mighty Lennon name as a last resort. Miraculously, a promising waterfront villa suddenly became available. John scouted the property on Sunday, June 15, which happened to be Father's Day.

Villa Undercliff was situated in Fairylands, an affluent neighborhood on the outskirts of Hamilton, whose imposing mansions and the lush greenery that surrounded them reminded me of a Mediterranean resort town. It was the last house on Fairylands Drive, which ended in a circular turnaround that overlooked the sea. A flight of stone stairs led down to the partially concealed yellow stucco villa with green shutters. For John, it was love at first sight. However, he was reluctant to go inside because he did not wish to meet the owner. "The less I'm seen, the better," he said, asking me to inspect the premises and give him a full report.

I visited Villa Undercliff the next day. The property was owned by the Luthi family. Rolf Luthi managed Bermuda's largest department store, Cooper's, having married into the family that owned it. He was a handsome man of about 50 and had thinning white hair and a deep tan. Detecting a trace of a Germanic accent, I asked Luthi about it, and he told me he was originally from Belgium. His wife was a statuesque blonde, and their kids, a boy and girl in their early teens, were also blond. They seemed like an ideal family. I was given a thorough tour of the house, beginning with the elegant living room, which had a grand piano. A broad stone staircase led to the second floor, where the master bedroom and two smaller rooms were located. The kitchen was spacious and bright. The property also included a red brick terrace overlooking the ocean. I was told that we were welcome to use a Sunfish sailboat that was stored in a nearby shed.

John was thrilled when I described Villa Undercliff to him. The fact that it had a piano and even a sailboat seemed almost too good to be

ean watching a puppet show during
s fifth birthday party at
avern on the Green, October 9, 1979.

Yoko's birthday gifts to Sean and John–
a pair of life-size dolls made in their likeness.

John displaying Yoko's personalized
T-shirts made up as party favors for the
guests at Sean's party.

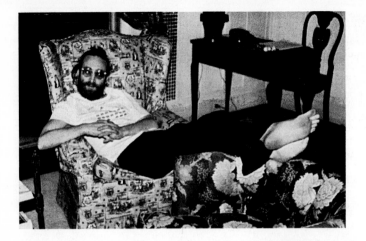

John stretches out in the living room after dinner.

The Lennons at their house
in Cold Spring Harbor, Long Island.
Thanksgiving dinner, November 27, 1979.

A Thanksgiving message from the Lennons.

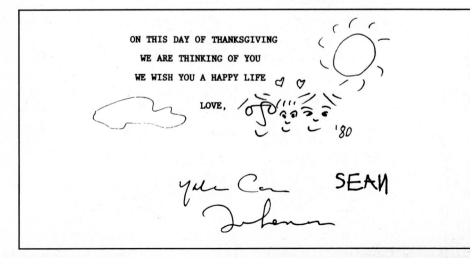

ON THIS DAY OF THANKSGIVING
WE ARE THINKING OF YOU
WE WISH YOU A HAPPY LIFE
LOVE,
'80
SEAN

Yoko, John, and Sean in Palm Beach, February 1980.

o and Sean, 1980.

The Lennons maid/cook, Uneko Uda (Uda-san) with Sean in Palm Beach.

John and Yoko with Peter Boyle and his wife Loraine
dressed up for their night out in Palm Beach.
February, 1980.

John playing piano and his guitar in Palm Beach.

John and Yoko aboard
the *Imagine,* Palm Beach, 1980.

John and Sean eating lunch
on the *Imagine.*

Left-Right: Yoko, Loraine Boyle and John
(with guitar), lounging poolside
in Palm Beach, February 1980.

Books: ① MEN IN LOVE — NANCY FRIDAY
② BEYOND THE ANDES — ? PARALLO

TV: ① T.V. TABLE FOR BEDROOM T.V. WITH WHEELS.
MUST BE AT LEAST SAME HEIGHT AS THE ONE NOW
IN USE: ie: MEASURE HEIGHT.
IF IT CAN SWIVEL ROUND — EVEN BETTER.

② I'd like to trade in the DOWNSTAIRS T.V. FOR
A SONY — 'THO I'm NOT CRAZY ABOUT THE
BIG WHITE 'BOX' AROUND THE BEDROOM ONE.
I PREFER A PLAIN T.V. (BUT BIGGEST SCREEN)
IF I'm DOUBT — CHECK WITH ME: (when I'm don't
available come
knocking

BOAT: I wanted a ONE (1.) SAIL — SAIL BOAT
ie: the 'dumbest' and simplest. 4

HOUSE: COLLECT ALL BOOKS not in my bedroom and
put them on the DOWNSTAIRS SHELVES.
EXCEPT FOR CHILDRENS' BOOKS WHICH ARE
TO BE PUT and/or LEFT IN SEANS' BEDROOM.
— SORT OUT THE REST INTO CATAGORIES AS
BEST YOU CAN.

ME GET ME RAZOR AND A ^(SHAVING) BRUSH;

PLUS: NO MORE 'YOGURT' BALLS + RAISINS: It's making
ME SICK!

ABOVE: A memo John Lennon gave the author on April 30, 1980,
during their stay at Cannon Hill. NEXT PAGE: An excerpt from the author's journal
entry for April 30, 1980.

Wed.
April 30

8³⁰ - Bath. 9³⁰ - Breakfast: Toast w. apricot butter, slice of honey cake, orange. So I'm sitting at kitchen desk eating JL walks in. Wears yellow T-shirt, hair in ponytail. Responds to my "good morning" with an awkward glance + twisted, forced smile. I return my attention to article about Heart's Wilson sisters, who were inspired by the Beatles. Article starts off with a quote from Ann Wilson's prize-winning 1966 essay about how the Beatles changed America's youth, or s.th. like that.

10 -   Watch 'Deputy Dawg' w. Sean.
10¹⁵ -   JL comes down just as kitchen phone rings. He comes up to me + makes shaving motion. "You want to shave?" I ask incredulously. He nods. "Are you sure". He gives me a playful jab from behind + follows me to kitchen. Uda-san hands me phone. Richie explains Y.O. isn't feeling to well + plans to stay in bed today. Meanwhile JL is gesticulating at me. I'm not sure what he wants, so he writes me a note: "Lend me your razor. Bring it upstairs."
        I return my attention to Rich, who says I'm to tell JL Y.O.'s stomach pains are nothing serious and that we're to stay here until further notice.
        Bring shaving stuff to JL in his bathroom + give him message about Y.O. He seems to take it in stride.
        Go back downstairs and let Sean select another tape - "Impossible Poorman".
10³⁰   Richie rings again. Says Sam Green walked in on Y.O. and insisted on having her examined by his doctor, who diagnosed a case of highly contagious 'Russian Flu'.
        We chat about movie 'Heartbeat' which Rich caught last Friday - sans Deb.
10⁴⁰   Uda hands me a note from JL 'My 10 days are over today at Noon. Ask Uda-san to make me a strong miso soup & No more funny tea!"   ☀

John, Yoko, and Sean at Cannon Hill, Cold Spring Harbor, Long Island. April 1980.

true. Later that afternoon he emerged from the bedroom and cheer-fully announced that the New York office would arrange to rent Villa Undercliff for six weeks. He instructed me not to tell the Coneyses that we were moving out, as he did not wish to feel obligated to invite them to visit us at the new house. They were welcome to stay in the apartment, which had been rented until the end of the month, but John made it clear that he had no intention of having any further contact with his crew after we left. He looked surprised when I told him that Tyler would be very disappointed because he was under the impression that he had become John's close friend during the voyage.

"I don't have any friends!" John reminded me. "Friendship is a romantic illusion!"

He said that he had learned this the hard way after the breakup of his relationship with Paul McCartney, whom he had once regarded as his close friend. John's features hardened as he launched into a terse monologue on the subject. Using his relationship with Paul McCart-ney as an example, John asserted that most "so-called friendships" were based on a symbiotic exchange of services. "The basis of our friendship was an intuitive understanding we had as musicians," he said. John explained that when he and Paul first started working to-gether, he needed Paul more than Paul needed him, because in addi-tion to being a well-rounded musician who could help John translate rough ideas into songs, Paul had a secure family background. "Being around Paul gave me a sense of stability," John said. "When I met Yoko, I knew it was time to cut myself loose. Paul hated me for turn-ing my back on him and did everything he could to turn the others against me. He saw that he couldn't compete with Yoko, so he tried to stab us in the back. He was absolutely vicious, and it shattered what-ever illusions I had about our so-called friendship."

Abruptly concluding his startling monologue, John asked me about the "TV situation" at Villa Undercliff. When I reported that there was only one TV set, and no video cassette recorder at all, John asked me to see to it that a TV and VCR were installed in the master bedroom, which also had to be air-conditioned.

John was in high spirits that evening. He clowned with Sean and serenaded us with a medley of songs, including snatches of "(Sittin' on) the Dock of the Bay" and "Take Me to the River." After a buffet-style dinner, Sean, the Coneyses, and I sat spellbound at John's feet as he continued his impromptu show with a scorching parody of Bob

Dylan's song "You Gotta Serve Somebody." "Serve Yerself!" extolled the virtues of self-reliance and even selfishness. It was a wicked parody, sung over a galloping guitar riff, that left no doubt that John had begun to reclaim his muse.

The night was still young when John retreated to his room, ignoring Tyler's attempts to make friendly conversation. Frustrated in his efforts to "hang out" with John, Tyler suggested going out to Hamilton. The Coneyses and I mounted our mopeds and soon joined the hordes of tourists drinking potent rum-based alcoholic concoctions in Hamilton's lively pubs. Tyler and I got drunk, and he told me that he could not understand why John was giving him the cold shoulder. Tyler firmly believed that he and John had become good "buddies." He felt that he had been a loyal and devoted friend to John, had sacrificed time and even money to help him fulfill his dream of sailing the Atlantic, never asking for anything in return. I told the bewildered sailor that, like royalty, John did not feel bound by the normal rules of social interaction. Loyalty was a one-way ticket with John: He demanded it from others, but he was unwilling to reciprocate.

We ended up that evening at a local discotheque, the Forty Thieves, better known at Disco 40. In the early hours of the morning we puttered back to Knapton Hill with great difficulty. After a few hours of sleep, I woke up with Sean's knees planted in my rib cage.

"Wake up, Fred," Sean urgently squeaked. "Daddy wants you!"

Groggy from lack of sleep, I stumbled out to the porch, where John was reading a newspaper. He asked to me to call the real estate agent to see if it would be possible to move into Villa Undercliff that afternoon. He also wanted me to order a limousine. We were going to Hamilton to catch a parade in honor of Her Majesty's birthday.

"Hurry up! I want to get out of here before they wake up," he said, pointing to the sleeping bodies sprawled on the floor.

When I told the real estate agent that John wanted to move into Villa Undercliff right away, he said that he was still negotiating the rental agreement with Studio One and that the Luthis would need a few days to move out. He also informed me that there were no limousines in Bermuda, but that he knew a reliable driver whom we could use for the duration of our stay on the island. After checking with John, who insisted that his identity not be revealed to the driver, I hired the man.

George Bourne turned out to be a garrulous, sprightly man in his seventies. He picked us up in a late-model Japanese-built station wagon and drove us to the parade site in Hamilton, all the while giving us a running commentary on the island's flora and other road-side attractions. When George happened to mention that he was a Seventh-Day Adventist, John grew intrigued by the old man. Soon the two were engaged in a lively discussion of religion. John soon tired of the subject. He next asked George about Bermuda's nightlife. When I had described my night out at Disco 40 to John, he had said he "wouldn't be caught dead at a tourist disco." So now he asked George where "the locals" went to hear music and to dance. George told us that there was a black disco named Flavors, but he advised against going there, explaining that is was a notorious den of iniquity. John looked at me sideways, grinning mischievously.

We arrived at Front Street just in time for the twenty-one-gun sa-lute. The setting was nothing short of spectacular. It was a bright, sunny day, and the parade took place against the backdrop of a sur-realistically smooth and gleaming white hull of a huge ocean liner, its decks crowded with tourists. We hoisted Sean onto a windowsill where he could better view the white and red-suited, pith-helmeted honor guard march by to the rhythm of a drum band. The parade route was lined with thousands of people, and John—wearing a white jacket and slacks, a T-shirt, and sunglasses, his shoulder-length hair tucked into a straw hat—was thrilled to be able to blend into the crowd and not be recognized. It was hard to tell who was more ex-cited by the parade, John or Sean. Indeed, John admitted sheepishly that he even felt strings of patriotism and pointed out that among the few things shared by the British and Japanese was a fascination with pomp and ceremony. This was a startling admission from John, who for most of his life had expressed contempt for authority. He remi-nisced about the time the Beatles had smoked a joint in the queen's bathroom in Buckingham Palace when they were awarded the Mem-ber of the Order of the British Empire medal in 1964.

"I didn't take any of it seriously," John said, explaining that he had known all along that the whole thing was a publicity stunt for the government. "I was always aware of the game behind the deed. It made me very cynical." Now, John said, he was learning to appreciate many of the things he had spurned as a rebellious youth.

After the parade, we visited a souvenir shop and brought a few T-shirts before returning to the house for lunch. Then John went into his room to phone Yoko. A few minutes later he informed me that Yoko had rented Villa Undercliff for six weeks, at a cost of twenty-four thousand dollars. John appeared unfazed by the exorbitant rental fee. "I knew we'd end up paying through the nose," he shrugged. "But it'll be worth it."

The only hitch was that payment had to be made by certified check, and because John had no Bermuda bank account, it would take a few extra days to complete the transaction. John was thoroughly vexed by the unexpected delay and told me to figure out some way of speeding things up so that we would move into our new quarters right away. After a round of frantic phone calls, Rolf Luthi agreed to accept payment by personal check, provided he could pick it from John personally.

"Bloody hell!" John fumed when I gave him the good news. "We're paying a fuckin' fortune for the place, and now I have to jump through hoops before they let us move in?" Reluctantly, he consented to meet Luthi that evening after dinner.

The dapper Belgian showed up at the appointed hour, impeccably dressed in a blue blazer, with a beaverish grin on his face. Luthi was thrilled to rub elbows with his internationally famous tenant. He immediately began inviting John to parties and boat cruises. Remaining cold and aloof, John told Luthi that he had come to Bermuda to work, and that he was not interested in socializing. I could tell that John was seething with indignation. He wrote out the check and thrust it contemptuously at Luthi, saying that we intended to move in immediately. When our new landlord asked for another day's time to move out, John would not hear of it. He abruptly disappeared into his room, leaving me with the bewildered Belgian. After a few moments of awkward small talk, Luthi beat a hasty retreat.

The next morning, John awakened me by impatiently tapping my shoulder and gruffly whispering, "C'mon, Fred, we're leaving!" I rubbed my eyes and glanced at my watch. It was a little after 6:00 A.M., John was all packed and ready to go.

Hastily, I collected my things and then helped Uda-san pack our food. John had no intention of leaving anything behind for the Coneyses. Sometimes his pettiness could be astounding. We took off without ever saying good-bye to the sailors.

When we arrived at Villa Undercliff, John met the rest of the Luthi family. The two kids, a young girl and her older brother, appeared somber, almost sullen. No doubt they were less than thrilled by the prospect of having to move out of their house, even if it was for an ex-Beatle. Mr. and Mrs. Luthi, however, were effusive as they proudly showed John the house. First John inspected the kitchen, nervously eyeing a microwave oven. He asked the Luthis to remove it because he worried that it might pose a health hazard. Mrs. Luthi looked stunned for a moment, and when she insisted the oven was absolutely safe, John reluctantly settled for leaving it unplugged.

The Luthis then showed John the living room, where two young men were busy attaching a VCR to a television console. John watched them apprehensively, then directed his attention to the piano, which Mr. Luthi said apologetically had not been used in years and was probably out of tune. Next, John asked about the Sunfish. The Luthis' teenage son showed us how to rig it. Finally, John went up to his room on the second floor to call Yoko. I moved into a small room down the hall from John. Sean and Uda-san took over a large bedroom halfway between the first and second floors. It had two beds and its floor was covered with a fluffy white rug.

Later in the morning the real estate agent showed up with the rental agreement, but John refused to meet him as long as the workmen were still on the premises and he instructed me to sign the contract on his behalf. Luthi was explaining in intricate detail the schedule of water and gas deliveries, and other minutiae of existence on this solitary piece of property, when suddenly John burst into the kitchen. He was extremely agitated, complaining that one of the TV installers, who "looked like a hippie," had told him he resembled John Lennon. Alarmed by what he regarded as a shocking "security breach," John demanded that we immediately "get rid of" the hippie.

Luthi looked flabbergasted, and even I was somewhat taken aback by John's paranoid outburst. I quickly pointed out that if we overreacted it would simply confirm the young man's suspicion about John's identity and that John would not get his TV installed in the bedroom. John thought it over for a moment and then decided to cool his heels in the sun room, a cozy, sunken den beyond the living room. It had a sofa, an easy chair, and a coffee table. "If I'd known it would be like this," John grumbled, anxiously puffing on a Gitane, "I'd have stuck it out with the crew for another day."

By the time the workmen were done it was early afternoon, and now John ordered me to "get rid of" Rolf Luthi so we could eat lunch by ourselves in the kitchen. As tactfully as possible, I explained to the landlord that John's nerves were frayed and he was in desperate need of privacy. Luthi said he wanted to have John over for tea at his new residence some afternoon. I promised to arrange it. As soon as he and the workers were gone, John came to the kitchen and began to relax. We sat down at a large, circular wooden table in a corner of the room near large windows—John said it reminded him of the butcher-block table in the Dakota kitchen—and ate vegetables and brown rice.

After lunch, John decided he wanted to go shopping. George drove us to Hamilton's major shopping center, a modern, multilevel arcade. John was delighted to find a health food store, and we bought brown rice and various "goodies" such as dried bananas and carob-covered peanuts. Next, he bought a leather valise and some T-shirts and post-cards at a souvenir shop. Exhausted from shopping, John and I took a pie and coffee break at a small café. As we were eating our apple pie, three teenagers began flirting in loud, vulgar tones with the waitress, and John grew anxious.

"They'll beat us up just to impress her," John said, only half in jest.

He appeared to be most intimidated by a handsome, athletic kid whose "deliberate moves" reminded John of Pete Best, the Beatles' drummer who was replaced by Ringo Starr in 1962. John hinted that it was Paul's jealousy that led to Best being fired from the Beatles. "Pete gave Paul competition in the pretty-face department."

As the youths became more boisterous, John grew more anxious. He abruptly stopped talking and ordered me to pay so that we could leave before things got too "heavy." John had been eyeing a nearby record store with growing curiosity, and I could tell he wanted to go inside. He told me he had not set foot in a record store in years because the risk of being recognized was too great.

"I always get spotted in record stores," he said resignedly. "That's where the Beatle freaks like to hang out." I suggested we give it a shot, this being Bermuda. As we approached the glass door, John suddenly froze in his tracks. He had noticed a colorful Beatles poster, and de-cided not to go inside. "We have to watch our step," he whispered nervously. "Mother warned me that this is a high-risk period. I have to cool it until she lets me come out of hiding." He said that he hoped to "go public again" in the fall.

A few days after we moved to Undercliff, John asked me to buy a top-of-the-line radio-cassette recorder and some reggae recordings by local musicians. I went to Stuart's, a hi-fi store, and bought a top-of-the-line silver metallic Sony boom box. When I stopped by the record store and asked about local reggae groups I was told that there were none, so I picked up a handful of tapes by Bob Marley and Jacob Miller.

Back at the house, John excitedly examined the "ghetto blaster." He asked me to set it up on the terrace and said he would join me after his nap. I loaded the boom box with batteries and made my way to the red brick terrace, which was hidden from view by a picket fence and trees. I opened the wooden gate and walked down a short flight of stone steps to the terrace situated about ten feet above water level and overlooking a green bay dotted with white villas.

I sat down on a beach chair and placed the Sony and the reggae tapes on the foot-high wall that surrounded the terrace. I had begun to doze off when John showed up around mid-afternoon wearing cut-off jeans. He reported happily that he had just been on the phone to Yoko, who had promised him that she would visit us that weekend.

"I can't wait to show her this place!" John said, surveying the breathtaking view of the harbor. He said that we might stay in Bermuda until the end of July, maybe even longer. "I told Mother that if she didn't get over here soon, I'll have to nick some teenage tourist pussy!" he said, grinning lecherously. John's high-seas adventure had stimulated his libido. He confided to me that he could not even remember when he had last gotten "laid."

He closely scrutinized the boom box, holding back his long hair with one hand while studying the knobs and dials. Then he asked me if I had been able to learn anything about the local reggae scene. He looked skeptical when I told him there were no local reggae bands. "You didn't ask the right person," he scolded. "These white kids don't know what's happening. I bet you anything there are some local reggae or calypso bands. We'll have to ask some of the hip local people."

John looked over the handful of tapes I had bought. Suddenly, his face lit up. He grabbed a Marley tape, lurched toward the Sony box, swiftly inserted the cassette, and then stood back with an expectant grin on his face as the first song came on: "Get Up, Stand Up." He turned up the volume and recoiled with delight. "Sounds great!" he exclaimed. He fiddled with the volume, bass, and treble controls, marveling at the clear, booming sound, which did not grow distorted even at a loud volume. "We can serenade the entire bay from here," he chuckled gleefully. We could hear a mile away the sounds of a constant party, judging from the voices and loud rock music—Led Zeppelin and the Who—that drifted across the bay. "Now we can compete!" he said, rubbing his hands together as he turned up the volume another notch. "This is one of my all-time favorite pieces of music," said John of Marley's classic 1973 recording, *Burnin'*. He positioned himself a few feet away from the tape machine. His chin began to peck on the downbeat, while elbows underscored the less obvious accents.

John told me about the first time he heard it, during his Lost Weekend in Los Angeles. He had been visiting a recording studio, tripping on acid, and an engineer had sat him down between two giant studio speakers and played him Marley's album. John said it had sent chills down his spine. He got the same spine-tingling excitement from Bob Marley as when he first heard Elvis and Little Richard, his early heroes.

John fished a fat joint from a pocket in his jeans. "Tyler's sinsemilla," he said, grinning mischievously. "I've been saving it for a special occasion. Here's to our good buddy, Tyler!" John said with a devilish cackle as he fired up the joint. He inhaled deeply, then exhaled with a frightful cough. We passed the joint back and forth for a few minutes and then gradually became absorbed in the music. John turned up the volume another notch and pointed out that the drums and bass "jumped out" at the listener. He particularly admired the sinewy, dancing bass line. "You can't get this kind of sound in New York," he said, speculating about the possibility of hiring some local reggae musicians to make demo recordings. As John spoke, a song called, "Hallelujah Time" played in the background. It was a mournful, gospel-tinged ballad sung in a plaintive falsetto voice. John grew silent and focused his attention on it.

He was spellbound by the song, which included the lines "We got to keep on living, / Living on borrowed time." As soon as the song ended, he leapt to his feet, rewound the tape, and listened to it again. His face expressed fierce concentration.

"That's it!" he suddenly exclaimed. "That's going to be my first song: 'Living on Borrowed Time.' That's the phrase I've been looking for! I've had this song in my head for ages. It'll have a reggae beat, and I'll write the words around the theme of living on borrowed time, which is exactly what I'm doing. Or, come to think of it, what we're all doing, even though most of us don't like to face it. And that includes you and me, my dear." He ran off to call Yoko, leaving me sitting there, stoned and excited. He and Yoko had made vague, tentative plans to record again, and John was eager to let her know that he was ready to resume his songwriting.

John had brought along a small white canvas carryall containing a collection of tapes with unfinished songs, song fragments, and song ideas going back ten years. He had told me that he planned to sift through this stash of old tapes to see if there was anything "worthwhile." And now, even before he had a chance to use his leftover material, he had been inspired to write a brand-new song. The man who wrote some of the classic hits of the sixties was not going to be silent forever. He had not been burned out; he had been in suspended animation.

By dinnertime, John had written a rough version of the song. We returned to the terrace after the meal to watch the sunset and smoke what was left of the joint. John described how he had matched up his autobiographical lyrics with a reggae beat. Then he sat back in his chair and played me a few more verses of his new song, a plaintive ballad lamenting the lost innocence and optimism of his youth. He was still missing some words, and he filled in the gaps by humming or improvising nonsense syllables. The song's melody revolved around two notes, giving it an insistent, obsessively repetitive quality that was a metaphor for John's recent life, which, up until now, had been in a holding pattern. I was thrilled by the thought that all that was about to change.

"What do you think?" John asked when he finished his performance. I told him it was a wonderful song and also complimented him on his amazingly fast work. "Yeah, it's not bad for a first take," he acknowledged modestly. "I can't wait to play it for Mother!"

John was under the impression that Yoko would be arriving with Helen that weekend, but I had spoken to my aunt before dinner and she had told me that no travel arrangements had been made for Yoko. I did not want to upset John with the bad news, so I kept this information to myself.

As the sun dipped into the blue-green Bermuda waters, we listened to another Marley tape, Survival. John talked about his admiration for Marley, whom he regarded as the greatest musician of the seventies. He revered Marley as a brilliant, mystical poet, who was able to convey through his songs messages of universal truth. He likewise admired Marley's uncompromising political stand and his ability to translate that commitment into powerful, incendiary musical statements.

A song titled "Ambush in the Night" came on and John pointed out that it dealt with Marley's brush with death in 1976, when he took sides in a political contest and a gang of gunmen broke into his house and tried to assassinate him. John had read an article about it in a magazine, and now he described how everyone in Marley's entourage ran for cover, but how Marley himself refused to hide. He was wounded, but he survived, and continued his political activities, refusing to be intimidated by guns and the threat of physical violence. John admired Marley's courage and the strength of conviction that came from his absolute faith in the Rastafarian religion.

"I don't know about this business of worshiping Haile Selassie as God and looking upon Ethiopia as the promised land," John chuckled, "but I guess it doesn't really matter what fuels your faith. The main thing is to believe in something." It was dark now, and the sky had become a dazzling spectacle of stars. John stood up and asked me to set up the recorder in the sun room. He stayed up late into the night, working on the new song.

In the morning, I could hear John playing the guitar in his room, refining the lyrics to "Living on Borrowed Time." When I came back from a trip to Hamilton, I found him sitting at the piano in the living room, still working on the song. I had never seen John doing any serious work as a musician, and it was amazing to witness his transformation from a restless, chronically bored man into a hard-working songwriter whose discipline and tenacity as a musician were nothing short of astounding. He could strum the guitar or sit at the piano for hours, doggedly playing the same chords and singing the same lyrics over and over until he was able to "fill in the blanks."

That same afternoon he recorded a complete take on the piano, with all the lyrics in place. John told me that he wanted to add a rhythm track, and he asked me to have his drum machine sent from the Dakota.

After I relayed the request to the office, I went to the terrace and began reading newspapers, but I had a difficult time focusing on world events. I felt disconnected from the real world. My ruminations were interrupted by a phone call from Aunt Helen, who called to let me know that she would be arriving the next day, but that Yoko's promised trip to visit John and Sean had been postponed indefinitely. I felt bad for John, who so much looked forward to serenading Yoko with his new song, and I hoped that her change of plans would not have a negative impact on John's renewed songwriting activity. I had just begun to doze off when John came bounding down the steps to the terrace, carrying his guitar in one hand and the boom box— playing Marley's *Survival*—in the other.

"I love this stuff!" he exclaimed. "The more I think about it, the more I'd like to go to Jamaica and check out their recording studios. Maybe I can talk Mother into going there with me for a weekend." I still could not bring myself to give John the bad news, that Yoko had canceled her planned visit.

When the tape stopped, John picked up his guitar and began strumming an insistent two-chord riff. "Check this out," he said, playing a new song titled "Face It." Although John had trouble remembering all the words to the song, I heard enough to realize that it was a powerful, autobiographical number that went to the heart of his conflict over fame versus anonymity. John said that he would overdub a "barrage" of guitars in the studio, and that he planned to make this rendition his new album's hardest-rocking piece. Shielding his eyes with his hand, John suddenly got up out of his chair and surveyed the harbor. He squinted at the small island a few hundred feet from the terrace.

"Why don't we launch the Sunfish?" he suggested. "I've been dying to go sailing."

We walked to the nearby shed where the small sailboat was stored and carried it to the sandbank below the terrace. With the help of a stiff breeze, John steered the small craft around the bay while belting out sea ditties at the top of his lungs.

"Don't you just love it?" he cried. "This is the life!"

Just then we heard shouts from the terrace, and turned to see Uda-san calling and Sean jumping up and down beside her.

"Yoko calling!" hollered Uda-san.

"It's Mommy!" screamed Sean.

"Okay!" John shouted back. "Fuck a pig!" he muttered under his breath. "Mother's timing is off."

He complained about Yoko's erratic phone calls as we began the complicated process of turning the boat around. "I keep asking her to call me after dinner, but the past few days she's been calling during dinner, and now before dinner. I'd rather talk to her afterward, because if there's bad news, my stomach gets all tense." As we approached the terrace, he said hopefully, "She's probably calling to tell us what flight she'll be on. We'll have to get some gifts and flowers on the way to the airport. Wait till she sees this place! Maybe she can find a way to buy it."

John grew silent while we struggled to maneuver the boat back to shore. We had drifted a good hundred yards away from the house, and John skillfully guided the boat toward the small sandy area at the foot of the terrace. When we were close enough to shore, I jumped out and waded to the sandbank, pulling the Sunfish behind me. We carried it up the steep flight of stairs and then John rushed into the house. By the time he got inside, however, Sean had spoken with Yoko and she had hung up. He looked dejected as we sat down to eat.

"Mommy can't come." Sean blurted out.

"What?" John bellowed. "But she promised!"

Leaping up from his chair, he ran to the phone and dialed, then had to redial, becoming more angry and frustrated as he fumbled with the phone. Suddenly, all the calm skill, the measured control he had exhibited earlier on the ocean and while playing music, had vanished. He was like a puppet: When Yoko decided to jerk the strings, John danced madly.

"Where is she?" John shouted into the phone when he finally got through. "No, it can't wait!" he screamed. "I don't care if she's in a meeting, you get her on the phone *now!*" There was a pause, and I could envision Rich, all flustered, calling Yoko on the intercom. "Okay, you tell her to call me back on the bedroom extension right away!" John's voice quivered with rage. He slammed the phone down and then vaulted up the stairs to his room, two at a time, leaving behind the meal he had barely begun to eat. The house shook as he fired the bedroom door shut. Dinner was a depressing affair. Sean threw a tantrum, and Uda-san was unable to appease him.

"I want my mommy!" he wailed. When reminded that Helen would be arriving the next day, he hollered, "I want Helen now!"

I helped Uda-san clean up and then went to the terrace. The sun was smoldering on the horizon when John came out.

"Well, folks, she ain't coming," he said with a sad, resigned smile, and collapsed into his chair. "She's got a a date to go the theater with Sam—I didn't even ask her which Sam. Tomorrow she's meeting some record company bigwigs. She thinks we should do the album in Nashville. Can you imagine?" he guffawed. "Maybe we can record some basic rhythm tracks in Jamaica and then finish it off in Nashville. I could start a new style—country reggae. The critics would freak!" He laughed softly, shaking his head. "I warned Mother that if she didn't get over here soon, I might go bonkers and she'll read about it in the papers." I thought he was kidding, but John was up to something. "Since she's going out tonight, I told her I would go out, too," he said defiantly. "Let's check out that black disco, you know, the one George told us to avoid. Mother told me that someone would try to sell me hash, but she warned me that it would be shit."

Then John began to consider how we should dress. "We don't want to look too conspicuous," he said, "but we have to distinguish ourselves from the tourist masses." Eventually he settled on a black suit, boots, and a baseball cap, under which he tucked his long hair. He cut a striking figure. I decided to wear a white outfit, for contrast.

George picked us up a little after 10:00 P.M., and John chattered nervously as we rattled along the Bermuda streets, headed for iniquity with hope in our hearts. "This is my first visit to a disco in years," John babbled. His excitement was palpable. He began speculating about the possibility of meeting girls and made crude remarks about "scoring teenage pussy." George silently squirmed in the front seat and I sensed that he did not approve of John's vulgarisms. Very protective of us, he also did not like the idea of our going to the black disco. He tried to convince John that we would be better off visiting the more wholesome Disco 40. But John remained intent on visiting Flavors. He had gotten it into his head that the hip local blacks went there, and even had some vague notions of trying to recruit local musicians for a band. Reluctantly, George dropped us off.

It was so dark inside that it was hard to tell the size of the crowd. Diana Ross's single "I'm Coming Out" blasted from powerful speakers. The whole floor vibrated. John sat down at a table on the edge of the dance floor while I went to the bar to get us beers. Once our eyes had adjusted to the darkness, we saw that the place was not crowded at all. There were a few black couples, as well as a sprinkling of older white tourists. They looked bewildered.

"I guess the hotel staff sent them to the 'disco around the corner' and they were expecting something more sedate, eh?" John snickered. "This stuff sounds so much better when played loud over studio speakers," he screamed into my ear over the din of the music. "You can really hear all the different instruments."

At one point he became so absorbed in the music that he raised his arms and pretended he was conducting a live orchestra, attracting curious stares from the young black couples who began to fill up the place. John said he felt like dancing, but there appeared to be a shortage of single females. He began to grow bored with the increasingly bland disco music that blasted out of the speakers. When John had had enough he asked me to find a cab. I thought he wanted to head back to the house, but he suggested paying a visit to Disco 40 instead.

When we got there, a sea of mopeds out front indicated that the place was packed. I paid our admission and we went inside. The club was crowded with teenagers, and John began seeking out a likely dance partner. But every girl he asked turned him down. "They must think I'm weird or something," John said dejectedly.

We staked out a place at the bar and drank a beer. At one point "Rock Lobster," a popular song by the B-52's, came blasting over the speakers. John was amazed to hear one of the group's female singers do a high-pitched yodeling sound reminiscent of Yoko's screaming vocals.

"Can you believe it?" he exclaimed. "They're doing Yoko!"

Suddenly galvanized by the discovery that Yoko's vocal mannerisms had influenced a new-wave group, John began speculating about "selling" Yoko as an underrecognized talent who had been ahead of her time. "Mother will love it!" he enthused. "She's always complaining that no one takes her seriously as a rock singer. I can't wait to tell her she's finally arrived!"

In fact, I had made John a tape of the B-52's first album when it first came out, but he'd never bothered to listen to it. Now his curiosity was piqued and he made plans to go shopping for tapes first thing on Monday, to find out if any other new-wave groups were "doing Yoko." John's enthusiastic chatter was cut short by the approach of three young men who had been eyeing us for some time across the room. John stiffened, and a look of alarm crossed his face. I braced myself for the inevitable.

"Excuse me," a ruggedly handsome young man said deferentially, "are you by any chance John Lennon?" John, who had probably feared that the guys were coming over to pick a fight, looked relieved and gamely acknowledged his identity. "What are you doing here in Bermuda, of all places?" one of the interlopers asked, wide-eyed with amazement. Coming in the wake of his rejection as a dance partner, John now warmed to the attention of these strangers.

"The wife sent me here on a working vacation," he said, boasting that he had sailed over from Newport. The guys looked impressed, and I almost expected John to tell them about how he had steered the *Megan Jaye* through the vicious storm. But when the leader of the trio introduced himself as a reporter for a local newspaper, John groaned and threw me a worried look. A few hours earlier he had told Yoko that he might make a spectacle of himself in public, and now he was well on the way to blowing his cover. John grabbed the reporter's arm and said urgently, "Listen, ah, I'm incognito, you know, and I would really appreciate it if you guys didn't tell anyone that I'm here." The reporter nodded his agreement and promised not to write an article announcing John's stay in Bermuda, in exchange for a promise of an exclusive interview at some future date. John told him that he was working on a new album, and assured the scribe that when the time came to go public, he would make sure that he got the news ahead of anyone else. I dutifully took down the reporter's name and phone number, and then bought the guys a round of beers at John's request. Sipping his third beer for the night, John launched into an animated discussion of new-wave and reggae music. The journalists bought the next round of beers, and after consuming another brew, John's eyes began to glaze over and the color drained from his face. "You better find us a cab," he said at 2:00 A.M. "It's way past our bedtime."

I rushed downstairs and hailed a taxi, then ran back upstairs to rescue John. His face was white and he kept moaning that he should have known better than to drink so many beers. The three men formed a flying wedge as I spirited John out of the crowded disco and into the waiting cab. During the ride to Villa Undercliff, he threw his head back and groaned that he wasn't feeling well. When we reached our destination, John struggled to his feet and took a few unsteady steps toward the house. Then he doubled over and vomited. Meanwhile I discovered that the front door was locked. John began cursing under his breath, while I made my way to the kitchen entrance. It, too, was locked, but fortunately one of the windows was ajar, and I could crawl inside to open the door for John.

"Don't be alarmed if you hear strange noises coming from the bathroom," he whispered as we crept up the stairs to our rooms on the second floor.

When I ran into John in the hallway the next day, he said that he had spent "half the night" throwing up, and he complained of having a hangover and a headache. Meanwhile, Sean buzzed around the house, ecstatic that Helen was flying in from New York that afternoon. John apologized for not being able to accompany us to the airport because he was still feeling hung over. He told me that our wild night out had not been wasted, because he had been inspired to write a new song, titled "Steppin' Out."

"As long as I get a song out of it," John smiled feebly, "it'll be worth the agony." Before disappearing back into his room, he asked me to be discreet with Helen and Uda-san. "They don't need to know everything," he said. Knowing John, I anticipated that he would experience so much guilt and remorse that he would waste no time in spilling his guts to Yoko, and would confess everything in detail.

During the drive to the airport, Sean bounced wildly up and down on the backseat. It took a great deal of effort on my part to keep the little dynamo from hurting himself or damaging the car's interior. Helen's plane arrived right on schedule, but we had to wait for her to clear customs. Finally, Sean spotted her at the other end of the terminal, and he ran toward her, screaming at the top of his lungs. The two had an exuberant reunion. Soon we were on our way back to the house, where Uda-san had prepared a late lunch. John stopped by the kitchen to welcome Helen, but he did not go near the food. He said sheepishly that he would be "back in action" the next day, and promised to take us all to Sunday brunch at a restaurant in the Bermuda Botanical Gardens.

Dressed all in white, treading the paths of the gardens, we must have looked like a religious order led by John, the guru. He looked like an emaciated ascetic with his hair pulled back in a ponytail. Helen, the aspirant, looked after the imp Sean, who buzzed around us, in and out of the flower beds. Uda-san was the aged nun, hands clasped to her abdomen in silent prayer. I suppose I was the acolyte. We had come to lunch at the Italian restaurant in the gardens, then to wander the aromatic lanes, where we were intoxicated by exotic sights and smells. The day was typical of Bermuda weather—sunny with a dazzling blue sky, temperatures in the eighties, cooled by a fresh breeze.

Uda-san, Sean, and Helen stopped to watch the small monkeys leaping through the branches of trees. John and I strolled along, bending down to read the small signs posted amid the profuse, brilliantly colored flowers. Finally we came to an area planted with irises that sported names such as *Angel Wings, Purple Imperator, Bronze Queen,* and *White Excelsior.* In one area were the freesia, where John stopped, bending low in front of a small patch of flowers. He stared at a small rectangular sign that had the words *Double Fantasy* engraved in white letters against a black background.

"Double Fantasy," he said softly. He looked pensive for a moment. Then his face lit up. "That's it!" he exclaimed suddenly. "That's the album title I've been looking for!"

The album had already evolved into a double act designed to revive not only John's career but also his marriage. As they had done after they married, John and Yoko would once again go public with their love, singing to each other for all the world to hear. John had been searching for a title and, suddenly, here it was, handed to him on a horticulturalist's tag. It was one of those cosmic moments he spoke of.

"I can't wait to tell Mother that I've found the perfect album title," he kept saying as he trotted up and down the fragrant, colorful paths in his white-on-white suit, dashing around in the sunshine and the glorious floral explosions of pink and blue and purple and orange. It was like something out of a fable in which the hero wakes up to a new dream of living. John was clearly gaining creative momentum. He had written several new songs and had rewritten some old ones. His Compurhythm drum machine had arrived, and he now decided to set up a makeshift recording studio. He wanted to buy a second tape recorder and a microphone so that he could start recording two-track demo tapes. Being unfamiliar with basic recording technique, I asked John what he meant. He explained that by using a second recorder he would be able to "double-track" his demos—play back a tape while simultaneously adding a second "live" track, and then record everything on the second cassette machine.

One morning late in June, John asked me to take along some extra cash and instructed George to take us to the store where I had bought the Sony recorder the previous week.

Wearing his usual white outfit, with the faded green image of Marilyn Monroe's face adorning his white T-shirt, John gingerly marched into Stuart's, which resembled a Times Square discount shop crammed full of the latest hi-fi equipment and electronic gadgets. I followed him as he went from counter to counter, twirling knobs and telescoping antennas, until a salesman approached.

"Are you looking for anything in particular?" the young black man politely asked us. John ran down the list of things he wanted to buy: a tape recorder, blank tapes, headphones, and maybe a microphone. "Are you guys in a band?" the salesman asked, eyeing John with growing curiosity.

"Yeah, sort of," John said, grinning broadly. The salesman asked John what kind of music we played. "All kinds," John replied, tiring of the charade. "We're just mellowing out between engagements. Do you know of good places to hear live music?"

The young man said that there wasn't much of a music scene in Bermuda, except for cabaret-style shows at the major hotels.

"That's not what we had in mind," said John.

"Well, what kind of music are you looking for?"

"Reggae."

"If you want reggae," the young man replied, "you have to go to Jamaica."

"That might not be such a bad idea," John said. "Maybe I can talk Mother into it."

He then directed his attention toward the various radio-cassette recorders on display in the store, checking out different models and eventually settling on a large black Panasonic recorder. He also bought blank tapes and a set of headphones. When it was time to pay, John said that he wanted to "check out the local jailbait," and would wait for me outside.

John was in no mood to head back to our villa. We dropped off the recorder with George and then paid another visit to the shopping arcade we had visited once before. John wanted to pick up some tapes of local bands. He told me he was interested in hiring local musicians to make some demo tapes. We went to the record store with the Beatles poster in the window. This time John did not flinch. Digging his hands into his pockets, he resolutely walked up to a salesman and inquired about recordings by local reggae bands. The salesman threw us a puzzled look and said that there was no local reggae, but that the store had a fair selection of imported reggae music. He recommended a tape by a new Jamaican group, Matumbi. John eagerly snapped it up, along with recordings by Jacob Miller and Bob Marley's latest release, titled *Uprising*.

We rushed back. At the house I hauled the new recorder into the sun room. Soon John busied himself overdubbing tapes. He added a guitar track to a piano version of "Serve Yerself!" and seemed delighted with the result. Next, he worked on a new song he had written for Sean, titled "Beautiful Boy." It was a tender ballad whose lyrics expressed an idealized picture of the father-son relationship and contained the profound, if somewhat fatalistic, statement, "Life is what happens to you while you're busy making other plans."

Anxious to add some "miscellaneous percussion" to his latest demo, John suggested that I should buy myself a pair of bongos and a tambourine and to also buy him a music stand while I was at it. I wasted no time in visiting a musical instrument shop. One night after our customary sunset watch, John said he was ready to record a definitive demo of "Beautiful Boy." He asked me to get the bongos and join him in the sun room. He loaded a blank tape into one of the recorders, played a few arpeggios, and tuned his guitar a little. I sat a few feet away, waiting expectantly with the bongos wedged between my knees.

"We'll use those later," John said, instructing me to clap a reggae rhythm. I told him I would do my best. "Just play it by ear, Fred," he said, sensing my trepidation.

He pressed the "record" button on the Sony, leaned forward with the guitar pressed against his ribs, and began strumming the gentle melody. I clapped a simple beat and looked to John for further directions, but he simply nodded his approval and closed his eyes. We did the song without a hitch, and afterward John rewound the tape and listened to the recording. In addition to my clapping and John's guitar and voice, a third sound was distinctly audible on the tape: a loud chorus of frogs. They serenaded Villa Undercliff every night.

"Not bad for a first take," said John, cuing the tape again. This time, I was allowed to play bongos. After a few bars, he stopped the tape and complained that I was playing too loud. "Just keep it down, Fred," he said, admonishing me to "stay in the background." I assured

John I had no intention whatsoever of competing with him as a musician. We did several takes while I beat the bongo drums, and as I heard the song unfold, I could feel it as I had never felt music before. The takes were crude, my playing off the beat, but John dug it. It was as if I were watching John mine ore that would subsequently be refined, washed, treated, then cast into something beautiful.

After a few takes, John suggested that instead of beating the bongos with my hands I tap out the rhythm with a pen. I drummed a few beats that way, and John nodded his approval. "Singing lullabies!" he said as I counted off the downbeat. He played back our first "hand-clap take" on the Panasonic recorder, while recording "live" with the Sony.

By now, I was familiar enough with the song to be able to add a few subtle accents, although I took great pains not to play too much or too loud. At the very end of the song I allowed myself a forceful roll, and John did not seem to mind. Playing back the "double-track demo," John complimented me and said that in the studio he would use a conga drum to duplicate my offbeat rhythmic pattern. He said he might even let me play a tambourine or cowbell on the album. I was thrilled. Not in my wildest dreams had I ever imagined I would someday make music with John Lennon.

The next morning John played "Beautiful Boy" for Sean, who danced around the sun room, overjoyed that his father had written a song for him. As usual, John was feeling guilty that he didn't spend more time with Sean, who was out of the house most days, roaming around Bermuda with Helen.

John soon moved his makeshift recording studio to a spare room on the second floor. His repertoire, which already included "Borrowed Time," "Beautiful Boy," "Steppin' Out," and "Serve Yerself!" was expanding rapidly. John had several other songs that he was struggling to complete before Yoko's visit, scheduled for the last weekend in June. Among them was a Dylanesque autobiographical ballad, "Watching the Wheels," that had evolved out of an earlier demo song titled "Watching the Flowers Grow."

John took great care in crafting the lyrics to "Watching the Wheels." He sat at the piano in the living room before lunch or dinner and played it until he sank into a deep, trancelike state where the missing words just came to him from "above." He explained that the trick was to make the mind blank, which was a prerequisite for being able to receive input from "a higher power."

"The best songs," he said, "are the ones that come to you in the middle of the night and you have to get up and write them down so you can go back to sleep." He told me these "inspired" songs were usually far superior to "formula songs," the kind he and Paul McCartney had churned out in great quantity during the early years of the Beatles. "Writing formula songs," John told me, "is like painting by numbers."

John's approach to songwriting was very methodical. He would construct the basic chords on the piano, while sometimes simultaneously working on the lyrics. When he had a rough version of a song, he would use his guitar to refine the melody. Lastly, he would add a rhythm. John was skilled at programming his drum machine, and he would usually try different tempos until be found one that "clicked." John always had a tape recorder running when he worked, and he would double-track his favorite demos of a song—combining guitar, piano, rhythm, and voice tracks—until he produced a "master demo" that pleased him.

During meals, John talked about marketing the record. Some of the new-wave music we were listening to, particularly the B-52's, reminded him of Yoko's early work, and he thought that she ought to consider doing that sort of thing on *Double Fantasy*. The album had not started out as a double act. John at first had hoped that only he would sing on the album. But Yoko had her own plans. She saw the new album as a way to rekindle her short-lived career as a rock singer, and she broke the news to John gradually, bearing down on him until he agreed to share the record with her equally. The John Lennon solo album became at first two separate records, his and hers, in one packet. Then it evolved into a single disk. Once he had resigned himself to the inevitability of Yoko's participation on the record, he began to think of ways to strengthen her contribution. John knew that even though he was an ex-Beatle, he could not take the market for granted. Not having made a record in more than five years, John worried that he would have to prove himself all over again. He was determined to make his record commercial enough to reach the high end of the charts. It would be his reentry into the marketplace, and he wanted it to be an auspicious event. If Yoko were going to be on the album, he wanted her songs to be hits, too. He did not want to swim with anvils strapped to his ankles.

On Friday, June 27, there was a delay in Yoko's arrival. A wave of panic rolled through the house, but we were assured she would come on a later flight. Rich called at regular intervals to say Yoko had canceled a flight and would be on the next one. The tension mounted throughout the day as Yoko canceled one flight after another. By mid-afternoon, no one believed she was coming. Yet word came that she would arrive on the last flight from New York, at 9:30 that evening.

After dinner, John could not sit still. Even though it was too early to leave, he had George drive us to a tavern near the airport just to kill time. He insisted that we split a beer, fearful that if he consumed more than that he would get a hangover. He was so excited about Yoko's arrival that he could not stop talking and the subject on his mind was sex. He said that working always made him very "horny" and that he could not wait to "jump Mother's bones." He told me that when he appeared on stage with the Beatles, he would often demand that a female fan be held in the wings so that he could have a "knee-trembler"—which was Liverpool slang for quick stand-up sex—before or after the performance (or, occasionally, even between songs). "I was always obsessed with sex," John confessed. "I'd run after girls and feel them up, put them up against a wall, that sort of thing."

He said he lost his virginity at age fifteen with his first girlfriend, Barbara Baker, a buxom, buck-toothed beauty. John then described the deflowering. "Barb wasn't wet and I had a hell of a time shoving it in," he said nonchalantly. "I was frantic to get inside her, and when I couldn't, I got so frustrated and angry that I started to curse her: 'You dumb cow, what's wrong with you? You're tight as a rat's ear!' " John paused, shook his head and smiled. "It wasn't her fault, of course. But what did I know? I was just a weird, psychotic kid covering up my insecurity with a macho facade."

Ruminating about his clumsy, often violent approach to love-making, he said that he never used to engage in foreplay; he would immediately attempt penetration. "I had no idea you were supposed to take your time," he laughed nervously. "I thought the idea was to get in and out as quickly as possible." He also told me that he would sometimes write his girlfriends erotic letters. "I wouldn't be surprised if they show up one of these days, hopefully after I'm dead."

John paused briefly to sip the beer and light a fresh Gitane. "I think after my mother was killed, I felt betrayed by all womankind," he continued. "I used to have fantasies about torturing women to death. I still have a lot of violent fantasies, but I manage to keep them under control."

He said that if he let his imagination run wild, he would imagine crucifying women, actually nailing them to a cross, and then disemboweling them. "It wasn't until I met Yoko that I realized that men didn't have to be aggressive, didn't have to be macho, that men could be gentle and tender. That's the lesson Yoko taught me."

John then talked about his early ideal of womanhood, Brigitte Bardot, and the irony of winding up with Yoko. He speculated that he and Yoko were Egyptian royalty in a previous life, and that fate had cast them as an upper-class Japanese avant-garde businesswoman and a working-class British poet, "to see if we could make a go of it in this life. She's my soulmate," he concluded matter-of-factly.

I had grown used to being John's listener, but the substance of what he said never ceased to fascinate me. His psychosexual analysis of himself was no exception. Which is why, when I glanced down at my watch, I leapt from my bar stool in horror. Yoko's plane was arriving at that very moment.

By the time we arrived at the airport the plane had landed, and Yoko was nowhere to be found. Near the gate we found a janitor who was sweeping up, and we grilled him. Yes, he said, he had seen a little Japanese woman with long hair wandering around looking lost and confused. John went into shock as the janitor gave us the grim details. It seemed Yoko had been waiting all alone for a long time, standing in a corner of the terminal while anxiously searching the hall with her eyes, apparently looking for John. I could see his face drain of all color as he envisioned Yoko's wrath at being abandoned at night in a foreign country.

I called the house and discovered that Yoko had arrived there and was fuming. "Better come quick," said Uda-san in her understated manner.

During the ride back to the villa, John went through torture trying to figure out a way out of avoiding the blame for being late. He was mortified. He knew the truth would not sit well with Yoko. ("Well, um, Mother dear, we were in a bar, talking about my old girlfriends, and I lost track of time!")

"There's only one way out of this," he announced finally as our cab careened along Fairylands Drive. "You'll have to take the blame. Tell her that you talked me into having a couple of beers. She'll want to fire you, of course, but don't worry, I'll save your ass."

It did not turn out as badly as it might have. John spent some time in the bedroom with Yoko. When they came out, she was sulking, but he looked relieved. We had set the tape recorders up in the sun room, and John now led Yoko there and started taping himself playing for her. He led off with "Serve Yerself!" which he played at a furious tempo, throwing in a few extra curse words to get more of a reaction from Yoko. She sat cross-legged opposite John, expressionless. He serenaded her with virtually his entire repertoire. Finally, he played her some of the new-wave, ska, and reggae music we had been listening to, suggesting that she should use some of these rhythms for her own songs. "They're doing you, Mother!" John said emphatically. "So it's okay if you use some of their stuff."

While the music played, he began petting Yoko, touching her, coming on to her sweetly. But Yoko remained as impassive as a sphinx. John seemed so pleased just to be with her that he did not even appear to mind the rejection. He was happy as a puppy.

When they went to bed that night I could hear them arguing in their room. After that the television went on, and then I could hear Yoko talking on the phone.

Yoko spent Saturday talking on the telephone in the bedroom. When she came down for dinner John brought up the subject of visiting Jamaica to look at recording studios. Yoko said that was out of the question because she had to go back to New York on Sunday. John looked at her with disbelief. Then he became enraged.

"Why don't you spend some time with Sean and me?" he bellowed. "What's so important that it can't wait?" He was furious. She had only just arrived and was already planning her getaway. Yoko whined something about real estate deals. Then she and John had an argument over Sean imitating Yoko's habit of pouring honey on her melon. John scolded her for setting a bad example.

Looking peeved, Yoko returned to the bedroom. She did not even bother putting Sean to bed, but had Helen do it instead. John was incensed. Sunday morning, Yoko said she was going back to New York. Sean, quite naturally, wanted to see his mother off at the airport, but Yoko told Helen to take him somewhere to keep him out of the way. John was livid. He warned her that her neglect of Sean would come back to haunt her one day. When Sean got older, John warned, he would try to get back at her somehow. "I'll probably pay a price, too," he said, "but at least I'm trying."

He accused Yoko of copping out of her responsibilities by insisting she lacked the maternal instinct. It wasn't an instinct, John insisted, it was a job, a responsibility that had to be accepted, and her excuse was just "macho bullshit." Yoko ignored the substance of John's remarks and tried to appease him, saying that as soon as the record was done, she would buy him a house in Bermuda and they would all come back and relax for a while before going on tour. That caught John's interest—buying a house in Bermuda.

At the airport, Yoko was utterly helpless. Papers, visas, passports, customs—they left her trembling with confusion. Finally, after a hasty good-bye, she disappeared into the crowd of tourists heading back stateside. On the way back to Fairylands, John had George drop us off at the Italian restaurant in the botanical gardens. We had cappuccinos, and John let off a little more steam. He was deeply hurt. He complained bitterly that what Yoko had been doing on the phone was selling a prize holstein cow from their farm upstate at an auction—it was a record sale, at around $250,000—and that as a result he had not gotten laid.

John also resented the fact that he had hardly had a chance to discuss the record with her. He worried that Yoko had not made any serious efforts to organize a recording session. "If she doesn't get on the ball soon, there ain't gonna be no album!" he fumed. "She's supposed to be writing songs, checking out studios, and looking for a producer, but she's not doing anything except selling cows! I mean, if she can sell a cow over the phone, she can bloody well set up a recording deal over the phone! Instead, she's locked into that useless lifestyle in New York, selling bloody cows and buying antiques and God knows what." He said that they had talked briefly about producers, and that Yoko had mentioned Jack Douglas as a likely candidate. Douglas had worked as an engineer on many of his and Yoko's recording sessions in the 1970s, and had gone on to produce Aerosmith and Cheap Trick.

Even as John spoke, sipping his cappuccino and chain-smoking Gitanes, he took in the room around us. A number of women in the place had clearly recognized him, and John was beginning to get a little anxious. It was well past lunchtime; Uda-san was going to be upset with us for being late. I left enough for the tab and tip, and we made a quick exit from the restaurant. On the way home we stopped by the freesia section so that John could look again at *Double Fantasy*.

John did not let Yoko's foot-dragging slow him down. He kept working on the album, refining songs and coming up with new ones. He joked that he was becoming more and more like Paul McCartney, whose prodigious musical output had sometimes been a source of friction in their relationship. John wondered if Yoko might be feeling intimidated by his current period of fertility, just as he had once been intimidated by Paul's greater musical productivity. Still, John kept up the pressure on Yoko over the phone, playing her his songs and encouraging her to play hers for him.

One day in early July, John was unable to get Yoko on the phone. He called her private line at dawn and found it busy. He called the office and got no answer. Finally he locked himself into his room and I began to hear the dissonant slapping of guitar chords. he flailed away for several hours. When he came down for dinner, he had written "I'm Losing You," a mournful, angry blues. Then he ordered me to go to New York to find out what was going on.

In order to demonstrate his progress, John prepared a special tape for Yoko. It included the obligatory tribute to his beloved, "Dear Yoko," as well as the entire repertoire he had developed for *Double Fantasy*.

John also ordered me to deliver a cedarwood box to Yoko. He had cut off a lock of his hair, wrapped it in a brand-new handkerchief, and put it in the box. If a customs inspector wanted to look inside, I was to say that ancient Japanese custom dictated that the box not be opened. "If it's opened," he warned, "the magic of the ritual is spoiled."

The day before I left, John and Yoko finally spoke on the phone, and she tried to talk him out of sending me to New York. John, however, was adamant. He even made up a story that I was being evicted from my apartment and had to go back for a few days to take care of it.

Finally, John asked me to take the new clothes he had bought back to New York. We purchased an enormous suitcase and Uda-san packed everything away. We had been told that there was a duty to be paid on clothes bought in Bermuda, which struck John as absurd. He instructed Uda-san to remove the price tags and told me that I should tell the customs agent that they were my clothes. But when the agents searched through the suitcase full of sweaters they doubted my story and I was forced to pay a fine for attempting to smuggle clothes out of the country. Fortunately, they did not ask me to open John's cedarwood box.

When I arrived in New York on Friday, July 4, I took a cab straight to the Dakota. I was not prepared for the scene of chaos and debauchery that greeted me. Yoko's office was strewn with papers, her dirty clothes were all over the floor, and on her table there were half-eaten plates of sushi in advanced states of decay. The kitchenette in Studio One was piled high with caked, dirty dishes.

Things did not look any better upstairs. I was astounded to find numerous bottles of scotch and vodka in the kitchen. From the look of it, the apartment had not been cleaned properly in weeks. Myoko, the maid, looked haggard and complained that she was overworked. While taking John's suitcase into the clothes room I ran into Luciano Sparacino, Sam Havadtoy's boyfriend, who had been hired to renovate the room. When I pumped Luciano for information, he told me matter-of-factly that Yoko planned to divorce John. Luciano said that John was supposed to move into Apartment 71 upon his return, and that he had been instructed to move John's furniture, clothes, and stereo equipment next door.

Saturday, I met with Yoko in her office. When I handed her the box with John's lock of hair, she opened it up and said, "How sweet of John, isn't it?" I marveled at how happy and relaxed she looked. I could not help but notice the low-cut black silk blouse she wore, emphasizing her large breasts. Her provocative outfit would have been daring if worn by a woman half her age. In fact, I detected in Yoko a youthful exuberance that belied her forty-seven-years.

As I flew back to Bermuda, I decided that I could not describe to John the sordid details about life at the Dakota, certainly not at a time when his work was going so well. I saw no point in alarming him by telling him about the rumors that Yoko planned to divorce him. I worried that the shock might send him reeling back into seclusion and terminal depression. As it turned out, John did not press me for details of Yoko's life at the Dakota. Instead, he talked in vaguely optimistic terms about his partnership with Yoko. He was convinced that working together was the best way to lift their marriage out of its rut. He told me that Yoko had played him some of her new material over the phone and that some of it made his songs seem "shallow" by comparison. I wondered if this was something Yoko had told him.

He next expressed concern that Yoko was not giving the album her undivided attention because of the many "distractions" she faced in New York, and even made a snide reference to her being surrounded by "useless sycophants." He again likened their situation to his old songwriting partnership with Paul McCartney, who had always been the more prolific writer and had frequently prodded John to come up with new material.

"Paul never stopped working," John said with grudging admiration. "We'd finish one album and I'd go off and get stoned and forget about writing new stuff, but he'd start working on new material right away, and as soon as he had enough songs he'd want to begin recording again. I would have to scramble to come up with songs of my own. I wrote some of my best songs under that kind of pressure." Although it remained unsaid, I got the distinct impression that John believed his spontaneous emissions were better than Paul's meticulously crafted material.

John fired up a Gitane—I had imported a fresh supply from New York—and looked at me with a mischievous glint in his eyes. "I don't suppose you brought anything interesting to smoke, snort, or chew?" he asked hopefully. In fact, I had brought with me the magic mushrooms I had stashed away the previous month. John was delighted to have a chance to "clear the head."

"I'll think of an excuse to send Uda-san and Helen away after lunch so we can spend a quiet afternoon," he said, suggesting that we eat a light lunch and skip dinner altogether. "It's better to take the mushrooms on an empty stomach. That way the body absorbs them more quickly and you have a more intense high."

After lunch John told Uda-san and Helen to take Sean out to dinner in Hamilton. He asked me to call George and instruct him not to return before sundown. When Uda-san protested this sudden break in her routine, John dismissed her feeble objections. "I'm giving you the evening off, Uda-san!" he said firmly. "Why can't you just enjoy it instead of complaining?" He shook his head, exasperated. Then he went upstairs to call Yoko, whispering conspiratorially, "Call me when the coast is clear."

As soon as George picked up the others, John and I sat at the wooden table in the kitchen and examined the twisted brown fungi in the plastic bag. I poured them onto the table and moisture began to condense onto their frozen surfaces. I picked one up and handed it to John. He examined it cautiously. I popped one into my mouth, and he did the same. We ate several stems and one cap apiece. Then we went out onto the terrace overlooking the blue water, which shimmered in the sunlight.

We sank into white plastic deck chairs. John talked aimlessly for a while. He told me about a new song he had written using a line of Robert Browning's poetry, "Grow Old Along with Me." He asked me to get his guitar so he could play it for me. I got up and sauntered toward the house. I felt as if I were walking on a cushion of air. When I returned, I found John pacing around the terrace with strange determination, a lopsided grin on his face. "Well, I'm definitely feeling something," he announced in a peculiar drawl. "I'm not quite sure what it is, but I like it."

He grabbed the guitar and strummed the plaintive ballad. He said he would like to tape it, but when I offered to get the recorder, he waved me off. "Never mind," he said. "I'll get it." He lurched toward the house, returning after a while with the machine plus a bag of tapes. He inserted a Marley tape and started dancing slowly, with his eyes closed, swinging his arms, twisting his skinny frame in the sunlight. Beyond him were light years of blue sky, blue sea, and a warm breeze that shattered the water into a trillion tiny mirrors.

When the tape stopped, I thought I heard an eerie high-pitched sound drifting across the bay. I assumed I was hallucinating. John sat down with a puzzled expression on his face. "Do you hear something, too?" he asked. I found it astonishing that we both seemed to be experiencing the same auditory hallucination. "It sounds like bagpipes!" John said, enthralled.

He asked me to find out who the mysterious bagpipe player was so that we might express our appreciation by presenting him with a bottle of whiskey as a gift. I nodded gravely and began to ponder this difficult assignment. Perhaps I could place an ad in the newspaper or, better yet, conduct a door-to-door search. My musings were interrupted by John, who stood up and wobbled down the steps leading to the sandbank below the terrace. Slowly, he waded into the ocean until he was chest-deep in the water.

"This is like a huge tranquility tank," he marveled. "Let's float!"

I joined him in the water, feeling an intense and involuntary muscular vibration caused by the psilocybin mushrooms. We had passed the peak of the effect, but I knew it would be quite a while before we would feel normal again. Soon we heard the sound of a car, and in a little while Sean exploded from the house wearing swimming trunks and a big grin. He leapt into the water, and crystals spun in the sunlight, shattering water against blue sky. Four-year-old Sean swam like a beaver toward his father and the two of them frolicked together in the water until it was time to get ready for dinner.

During the second week in July, as John's songwriting wound down, he commissioned a portrait of himself and Sean from Nancy Gosnell, an American painter who resided in Bermuda part of the year and had done a large oil portrait of the Luthis that had captured John's interest. John and Sean would spend hours posing for their portrait in Gosnell's house, which was a short drive from our villa. John enjoyed these sessions because the painter was an intelligent, well-read and well-traveled woman, someone he could relate to.

When John and Sean returned from their sitting on Friday afternoon, July 18, John was in an expansive mood, and during lunch he began talking about a subject he generally avoided—his childhood.

"When I was your age," he told Sean, "I had to decide if I wanted to live with my mommy or my daddy." John told Sean that paralyzed with dread, he chose his father. But when his mother started to leave, he became hysterical and ran after her, crying and screaming. He couldn't stand the thought of being without her. As John narrated this story for Sean, he acted out the heartbreaking scene. Then he stopped and smiled. "That's why Daddy is so strange sometimes," he said. "To this day I hate having to make decisions," he continued, turning to me. "I get a headache when confronted with a choice. Even if Mother only asks me to choose between black or white marble."

Next, John told Sean about life with Julia, his mother. John said she often went out until the early-morning hours, leaving John to fend for himself. John said he often had trouble sleeping when Julia was out. "One night," John whispered to Sean, "I saw a ghost just outside the window and screamed with terror until the neighbors came round to investigate."

John also talked about the time his father, Freddie, showed up unexpectedly while Julia was entertaining another man in her apartment. As John watched from behind velvet curtains, a brawl ensued.

Life with Julia became so difficult that John began to run away to his Aunt Mimi's more and more frequently. Sean sat fascinated as John recalled long walks to kindergarten and trolley rides to Mimi's. John said, "I learned to recognize the right trolley by the quality of the black leather seat. To this day I'm fond of black leather. I find it comforting." Sometimes strangers, thinking him a lost or abandoned child, would take him to the local police station. "I could never find the right words to explain my situation," he continued. Laying out several chopsticks on the round kitchen table, John illustrated for us the route from Newcastle Street to Penny Lane. He pointed out the barbershop, the bank, the firehouse where the "clean machine" sat, the chapel, and so on.

John sat back, exhausted from the exertion of reliving so much of his childhood. But Sean, who loved hearing John talk about his past, danced around the kitchen, demanding to hear more. Finally John relented. He told Sean that when he was five or six years old he threw a cat into the air. "When I looked up and saw this helpless kitten up in the air with a terrified expression on its face, I thought to myself: 'This is evil.' " It was, he said, the first time he was able to distinguish between right and wrong.

John's talk was interrupted by a phone call from Yoko. He rushed to the phone and immediately launched into a enthusiastic description of his and Sean's portrait. Cut off in mid-sentence, he spent a few seconds listening quietly. When John returned to the table, his mood was subdued, and he announced that Yoko was going to a party at Sam Green's Fire Island house. Then he went up to his room for a nap. Sean and Helen went off to visit a ceramics workshop. I made myself comfortable on the living room couch and watched "One Day at a Time" on TV.

Later that afternoon, John and I went out on the terrace to sunbathe. I lay on a beach chair while John sat crosslegged a few feet in front of me, with his back to the sun. His face, chest, arms and legs were lightly bronzed, and he had been working on getting an even tan. Although he sat calmly in the lotus position, I could tell he was upset. His jaw was clenched and his mouth was set in a thin line. After a few tense minutes, John continued talking about life with Julia. Even at the early age of four, John said bitterly, he had been aware of Julia's promiscuity and suspected her of prostituting herself, "not for money, but for silk stockings." I expected John to launch into an angry monologue about his mother, but suddenly he became self-conscious and switched gears abruptly. He asserted that we subconsciously choose our childhood traumas. "We don't like to admit it," he said, "but we are responsible for our miserable childhood. Of course, it's easier to blame it on Mommy and Daddy, Mother Cosmos, or whatever, but the older I get, the more I understand and accept that we are ultimately responsible for everything that happens to us, whether we like it or not."

I sensed that John was daring me to disagree with him, because he was in an argumentative mood. Although I was skeptical about his theory, I was not about to take the bait. Arguing with John, I had learned in my first few weeks with him, was an exercise in futility. Even when he was in a good mood, John Lennon was not someone to disagree with. He rarely tolerated a dissenting opinion and always insisted on having the last word.

We spent the rest of the afternoon roasting languidly in the intense Bermuda sun with Bob Marley playing softly in the background. By the time Sean and Helen returned, around 5:00 P.M., John appeared to be in a more relaxed state. Sean proudly displayed several glazed clay objects he had made that afternoon: an ashtray, a turtle, and two small vases—"one for Mommy and one for Daddy!"—all expertly crafted. John was overwhelmed. "You made these all by yourself?" he asked. "They're so beautiful!"

Sean beamed and said, "I'm so proud of myself!"

John was thrilled by Sean's ceramic works, and he even suggested sending them to Yoko by messenger. Then he remembered that she was on Fire Island with Sam Green, and his face became taut again.

After dinner John and I returned to the terrace. We had not been there long when the phone rang. Uda-san came running and told John that Sam Havadtoy wished to speak to him. John rolled his eyes. Havadtoy had called the previous day to inform him that the wrong kind of marble had been delivered for the new bathroom/sauna he was constructing in Apartment 72. "He probably wants to tell me about the latest catastrophe on the home front," John snickered as he went to take the call. Normally John would not be bothered with such minor details. I gathered that Havadtoy, who had enjoyed almost unlimited access to Yoko, was calling John because he was unable to reach her. I could imagine how Havadtoy felt now that Yoko

John and Sean aboard the *Megan Jaye*. June 1980.

John and Sean in Bermuda, June 1980.

L-R: Ellen, Tyler, and Kevin Coneys, John and Sean,
Gretchen the Celestial Navigator, and Captain Hank.
Bermuda, June 13, 1980.

John playing his Ovation guitar in Bermuda.

hn working in his makeshift studio at Villa Undercliffe,
rmuda. July 1980.

John at the Hit Factory. August 1980.

John and Yoko with musicians who played on *Double
Fantasy.* Back row Left-Right: guitarist Hugh McCracken,
drummer Andy Newmark, John, Yoko, producer Jack
Douglas, percussionist Arthur Jenkins, Jr.; sitting on the
floor: bassist Tony Levin, guitarist Earl Slick and
keyboardist George Small. (Hit Factory, August 1980)

John and Sean at the Hit Factory.

John and Earl Slick at the Hit Factory.

Left-Right: Yoko, assistant engineer Jon Smith, John, assistant
engineer Julie Last, chief engineer Lee DeCarlo and
producer Jack Douglas in the control room of the studio.

John and Yoko take a dinner break.

John and Sean celebrating their birthdays
in the kitchen of the Dakota, October 9, 1980.

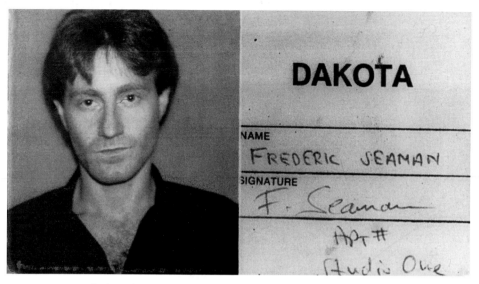

Dakota ID card issued to author on December 1980.

Yoko and constant companion Sam Havadtoy, celebrate her 48th birthday, February 1981.

John and Sean, Bermuda.

seemed to be spending virtually all her time with his rival, Sam Green.

John confirmed my surmise a few minutes later when he told me that Havadtoy had tried to pump him for information regarding Yoko's whereabouts. Although John tried to shrug off Havadtoy's call, I could tell that he was furious. John could see that Yoko was playing the two Sams against each another, and he resented being caught in the middle. He contemptuously referred to both men as "useless sycophants" and "calculating hustlers," as well as "groupies who're ripping us off."

He considered Havadtoy the more mercenary of the two Sams, describing him as an ambitious "pretty boy" who was using Yoko to build a career. Although he had been hired originally to decorate Studio One, Havadtoy subsequantly got Yoko to help him buy a building, finance an art gallery, and start an antique and interior decorating business. And now Havadtoy had hired a large number of workers to renovate Cannon Hill and Irongate, as well as to build a sauna in Apartment 72. "I'm afraid to even ask Yoko how much this is all costing us!" John said, exasperated. I doubted that Yoko would have been able to answer the question.

John next vented his spleen at Sam Green, whom he described as a "would-be WASP" and a "Warhol groupie." Still, John respected Green for his wit and charm. He told me that the patrician art dealer had arranged a trip to the Pyramids in January of 1979. During the return flight their plane flew into a blizzard and was forced to circle JFK airport for hours, while *Sgt. Pepper's Lonely Hearts Club Band*—a mediocre film starring Peter Frampton—played on the plane's movie screen.

"It was one of those exquisitely surreal moments in life," John chuckled. He said that his sense of humor had made it possible to endure the airborne ordeal, but that Yoko was hysterical because she was convinced the plane would crash. Fortunately, Sam Green managed to calm her by distracting her with an endless string of entertaining chatter. John admired Green Sam's gift of gab.

I wondered how much John knew about Sam's current relationship with Yoko. Almost as if reading my mind, John next told me that he did not feel threatened by Yoko's relationship with Sam Green and Havadtoy because he thought they were both gay. He believed that Yoko needed them as a "distraction," and did not regard them as love rivals. John asserted that the real test of his and Yoko's relationship came when he took off with May Pang in 1973. He viewed this eighteen-month period of separation from Yoko as his "seven-year itch."

"I almost blew it then," he said dramatically. "Yoko and I almost broke up, but I was damn lucky. Damn lucky! If you don't choose a partner and stick to the relationship, you'll just slide into promiscuity and still love your ex anyway. Look at Sonny and Cher—deep down they still love each other. Or Liz Taylor and Richard Burton; even though they're not able to live together, they're still in love. It's hard work to keep a marriage going. That's why I think twice about sticking it into somebody on impulse. There's too much at stake!"

John fell silent as he struggled to light a cigarette on the windy terrace. When he finally suceeded, he took a deep drag and exhaled a white cloud of smoke, coughing frightfully.

"Yoko has to fight these impulses, too," he continued. "She's a woman, and of course she's flattered when she gets a younger man's attention. We all need our flings."

I had grown used to John's amazing ability to rationalize away unpleasant realities, but now it took an effort on my part not to look too surprised. John's nonchalance was astounding. I wondered once more if he had any idea just how serious Yoko's "fling" with Sam Green was, and I asked myself if I might be doing him a disservice by not being more forthcoming. I was afraid of John's reaction if I told him details of Yoko's romantic infatuation with Sam Green. I doubted that he would believe me it I told him that Yoko was behaving like a love-struck adolescent. Nor could I imagine confronting John with the rumors I'd picked up about Yoko wanting to divorce him. Perhaps he would have turned on me, the messenger, for bringing him such alarming news. Or maybe deep down he realized that Yoko had abandoned him emotionally, but could not face the devastating truth and thus chose to deny it.

As it was getting dark, John and I walked to the kitchen entrance, which was closer to the terrace than the front door. When he found the kitchen door locked, John flew into a rage and accused Uda-san of "playing games." He was certain that she had locked the kitchen door on purpose to frustrate him.

"I should smash the glass!" he said furiously. I suggested we try the front door. As we walked around the house, John kept cursing Uda-san. He and Usa-san had locked horns over his fanatical supervision of her cooking, and their bickering had escalated steadily since our arrival in Bermuda a month earlier. John saw the locked kitchen door as the latest example of Uda-san's campaign to make his life difficult. "If Yoko were around, she wouldn't get away with it," he said angrily. Fortunately, the front door was open. Walking up the stairs to our rooms on the second floor, John whispered to me that he planned to replace Uda-san in October, but that he hoped to stay on good terms with her so that he and Yoko could avail themselves of her services when they visited Japan the next summer.

During the third week in July, John began handing me handwritten lyrics that he asked me to type and send to New York. John was finished writing songs. Now it was time to start recording. However, Yoko insisted that he stay put in Bermuda until she set up the recording session. We were told that she was deep in conference with her psychics, attempting to find a record label. She had already checked the birth dates of various record company presidents. Buddha Records was a prime contender. Atlantic was out because Ahmet Ertegun's numbers didn't wash. Capitol, the old Beatles label, was rejected because John detested its executives.

John also told me that *Double Fantasy* would be a "concept album."

"We'll probably alternate tracks and create a kind of dialogue," he said. "It'll the be first vinyl soap opera."

It was Yoko's idea and it had grown out of their previous phone conversations, in which they had played their new songs over the phone to each other. John at first had assumed they would each fill one side of the record, but Yoko insisted on alternating his and her songs, creating a "dialogue." It sounded pretty bizarre to me. I wondered how the fans would react.

The recording session was to take place at New York's Hit Factory early in August, and Douglas would recruit a band consisting of top-notch session players. Yoko had promised John that the album would be released on his fortieth birthday, October 9.

"As soon as we finish recording, we'll do a media blitz like you've never seen," he continued, expressing confidence in his ability to reenter the marketplace after a five-year absence from the music scene. "And then we'll start working on a Broadway show. I already have the outline worked out. It'll open with me meeting Yoko at her gallery show in London, then cut to Yoko in Paris and me in India boogying with the Maharishi and working on the *White Album*. Then the Bea-tle sessions and our marriage in Gibraltar, the bed-ins—oh, it'll be great!" Listening to John's enthusiastic chatter, it was impossible not to share his excitement.

While waiting for Yoko's psychics to find us a suitable date on which to return to New York, John resumed his tourist routine. He joined Sean and Helen on their sightseeing excursions, and we even went horseback riding. John developed an interest in the local gastro-nomical scene, and I accompanied him on a tour of the island's best restaurants. We also visited Hamilton's numerous antique stores, where John bought thousands of dollars worth of Victorian furniture and Wedgwood china that had to be shipped to the Dakota. Tiring of his anonymity, John even began using his American Express card.

The last week of July Yoko told John that her numerologist had suggested that we should fly back to New York on the 29th, a Tuesday. A few days before our planned departure, Peter Sellers' death sent John into a sudden funk. John had idolized the brilliant, eccentric British comedian since his teens, when he grew up listening to Sellers on "The Goon Show," a popular British radio program consisting of bizarre skits. (Sellers died when his pacemaker failed while he was attending a "Goon Show" reunion in London.) John said that it was Sellers who had first made him aware that it was possible to use one's weirdness to make a living.

"If Sellers hadn't made it in show business, he would have died in the nutty bin," John declared somberly. "If you're a nobody and are as crazy as he was, they lock you up. But if you're famous, then you're simply considered eccentric."

John felt a certain kinship with Sellers, who in recent years had sunk into obscurity, but had made a comeback earlier that year in *Being There*, a movie based on Jerzy Kosinski's parable of a simple gardener whose only knowledge of the outside world comes from watching TV and who becomes a political prophet by merely uttering a few monosyllabic allusions to gardening. It was a stunning return to form for Sellers, who had spent much of the previous decade cranking out predictable *Pink Panther* sequels. John recalled with satisfaction that Sellers had won universal acclaim for *Being There*, and remarked that it was a perfect swan song for his erratic career.

"At least he went out with a hit," John mused. "It sure beats fading from public view with a whimper." He added that there was nothing worse for a once-successful entertainer than to die in obscurity, and he then instructed me to buy as many British and U.S. newspapers as I could find because he wanted to read Sellers' obituary. John was fascinated by obituaries. Usually, it was the first section he turned to in newspapers. Earlier that summer, he had come across an obituary of Bert Kaempfert, the German bandleader and A&R man who had hired the Beatles to back British singer Tony Sheridan on a record that was recorded in Hamburg in 1961. John had pinned the obituary notice to the bulletin board in the kitchen of Villa Undercliff.

Before returning to New York, I accompanied John on a final trip to St. George, the small village where he had landed six weeks earlier. Our driver, George, pointed out a simple, whitewashed building on Duke of York Street and mentioned that this was St. Peter's, one of the oldest churches in Bermuda. John said he wanted to go inside. The old Anglican church had highly polished cedar doors, floors, and pews. The walls were lined with memorial tablets of well-known Bermudians. The pulpit and altar, George had told us, dated from the early seventeenth century. What most fascinated John, however, was the small graveyard behind the building. I followed him as he walked among the graves.

Finally, John knelt by a large tombstone shaped like a crucifix. He rested his head against the massive stone and closed his eyes as if in prayer. Feeling like an intruder, I waited for John in a corner of the graveyard.

On our last evening in Bermuda, John played me his final demo tape out on the terrace. It included the double-tracked version of "Beautiful Boy" on which I had added handclaps and bongos. The tape also included "Woman," a plaintive love song, whose lyrics painted a scenario in which John was the errant child, Yoko the ever-forgiving mother; Yoko was the sorceress, John the apprentice; Yoko was right, John was wrong. John, it struck me, was in a constant process of atonement for guilty feelings going back twenty, thirty years.

Now inserting Bob Marley's *Exodus* into the boom box, John handed me the demo cassette we had just heard and told me I was welcome to make myself a copy when we got back to New York. He also asked me to mail Julian a copy. He had spoken to his seventeen-year-old son a few days earlier, and, as usual, their conversations had been fraught with tension. Julian had mentioned to John that he and Cynthia were paid a surprise visit by John's childhood friend, Pete Schotton.

John told me that Schotton had been his close friend, but that their relationship soured after John bought him a supermarket. "I tried to look after him when I made it big, but it was useless," he said, explaining that the business venture had failed. "You're not doing people a favor when you simply hand them a business, give them money, or whatever, just so you don't have to feel guilty for being rich and successful. They just end up resenting you more."

John also told me that he and Schotton had lost their virginity around the same time, a fact John had felt compelled to share with Julian. "It's good for Julian to know I was a virgin once, too!" said John earnestly. "I don't want him the think of me as just some weird, mythical dad." John said he was curious if Julian was still a virgin, but that he could not bring himself to ask his son such an intimate question. "Maybe he's still trying to figure out his sexual identity and he'll be offended if he turns out to be gay and thinks I disapprove," he said.

I assured John that based on the time I had spent with Julian in Palm Beach the previous year, I could attest to the fact that his son had a healthy interest in the opposite sex. John remained unconvinced. "Time will tell," he said.

John asked me to remind him to ask Ms. Gosnell, the painter, if she could work from a photo. John's idea was to present Julian with a father and son portrait for his birthday. Looking sad and pensive, John lamented the fact that he and Julian had not seen each other in over a year, and he worried that he might never be able to have a normal relationship with his firstborn son. He said that he hoped Julian would some day read his journals and maybe then he would understand John better. I recalled that in Palm Beach John had once told me the same thing. "I want Julian to know everything about me," said John enigmatically. "There is stuff I could never talk to him about in person. It would be too awkward. If anything happens to me," he said solemnly, "I want you to see to it that Julian gets my journals."

Next, John talked about "weird" recurring dreams in which he suffered a violent death. Sounding grim and apprehensive, John said that he assumed that because he had led a life filled with violence, both in thought and in deed, he was destined to die a violent death.

He told me he often fantasized about getting shot, which, he said, was a modern form of crucifixion, a rather elegant means of moving on to the next life with a clean karmic slate. He was very serious, very impersonal, and spoke without any visible feelings—it was if he were thinking out loud.

Darkness came quickly and the moon emerged among a sprinkling of first stars. John tried to identify the stars, but became confused. The only one he was certain about was Venus, which seemed brighter than the rest. As the sky grew darker, another star appeared to shine even more brightly than Venus, and John speculated that it could be Mars. "Ah, Venus and Mars," he laughed softly. "Sounds like an album title."

Relieved that John seemed to have regained his sense of humor, I joined him in laughter. The tape that had been playing in the background stopped and now John searched for something new. He loaded Marley's latest release, *Uprising*, into the tape player. We sat in silence for a long time, taking in Marley's hypnotic music. The last piece on the tape, titled "Redemption Song," was an acoustic ballad eerily reminiscent of some of John's demos. As the song ended, John got up and stood at the edge of the terrace. I stole a sideways glance at his face, which was illuminated faintly by the moon, giving it a ghostly pallor. John motioned me to stand next to him.

"Well, Fred," he said, placing his arm around my shoulder, "I guess it's time to say good-bye to paradise." I was surprised by his intimate gesture. Standing silently in the moonlight, listening to the waves lapping at the foot of the terrace, I felt close to John. I sensed that his heart was heavy and I wished there were a way to ease his pain.

He took one last fierce drag on his Gitane and then tossed the cigarette butt into the dark waters. John abruptly walked back to the house, leaving me to ponder his strange behavior as I stood frozen at the edge of the terrace. Although I had grown accustomed to his morbid talk, there was something profoundly disturbing in John's solemn demeanor that night.

We left Bermuda on Tuesday, July 29. John's return was unlike any of our other homecomings. There was no more business as usual, no sinking back into the old days of lying around the bedroom killing time.

11

Hit Factory

Back at the Dakota, I found the staff in a state of chaos. Rich De-Palma was on a vacation in the Catskills, and his temporary replacement, a young accountant named Tom Minogue, was perpetually bewildered. Myoko was also on vacation. Her duties were taken over by two new Japanese servants, a petite live-in maid, Harumi, and a part-time gofer named Toshi. The apartment and office were messier than usual, but it was nothing like the squalid scene I had witnessed during my visit in early July.

I was also relieved to learn that Yoko had abandoned her plans to divorce John. Luciano told me that shortly before our return from Bermuda he had been ordered to move John's clothes, books, furniture, TV and stereo equipment back into Apartment 72.

On Thursday, July 31, John and Yoko met with producer Jack Douglas, a tall, soft-spoken man of about thirty years of age. Following Yoko's orders he had contracted a band made up of top session musicians and booked the Lennons into the Hit Factory studios for Friday afternoon. However, John thought this was premature, because Yoko's material needed "work," as he diplomatically put it. Yoko appeared unconcerned. She had a few songs left over from a 1974 session that Douglas had engineered, and she was prepared to recycle these.

By Friday morning, August 1, life at the Dakota was in full, frantic swing as John and Yoko immersed themselves in some last-minute songwriting. John had been working on "Forgive Me, My Little

190

Flower Princess," a song he had written for May Pang, and he rang me on the intercom complaining that the lyric sheet had vanished.

"Do me a favor and look around the office," he said. "Maybe Mother knows where it is."

I found the missing song on Yoko's piano. She told me that she had "borrowed" John's song and turned it into one of her own, titled "Forgive Me."

"John is always asking me to forgive him," she grinned, "so as a joke I decided to use it as the title for one of my songs."

A meeting had been scheduled that afternoon with Douglas to discuss the finer points of his contract. At 4:00 P.M. John came downstairs with a fresh batch of handwritten lyrics that he wanted me to type. He made a point of asking me to keep them in a safe place. "We wouldn't want Mother to borrow them," he said. John hung around the office waiting for Douglas, and when the producer failed to show, he went back upstairs. Douglas finally arrived at 6:00 P.M., mumbling apologies for being so late. He had been on the phone for hours rescheduling the start of the recording session to August 7.

Soon he and Yoko were engaged in heated negotiations over his contract. The major sticking point was the Lennons' demand to co-produce the album. Douglas at first protested vehemently, then dropped his objections when Yoko agreed to pay him five percentage points of the album's gross profit, an amount almost double the customary producer's share. At 7:00 P.M. Yoko asked me to make out a twenty-five-thousand-dollar check to Douglas' company, Waterfront Productions.

When I reminded her that the checkbooks were locked in the accountant's desk, she ordered me to break open the drawers. Fortunately, a search of the office turned up an errant Bankers Trust checkbook with a nifty sailboat design. I made out the check and gave it to Yoko to sign. She asked me how much money was in the account. I told her I had no idea. "Fucking hell!" Yoko hissed. She signed the check anyway, worrying that it might bounce. Still cursing under her breath, she handed the check to Douglas, who nervously examined it on his way out of the office.

On Saturday morning I got a call from Yoko informing me that I was needed at the Dakota. She asked me to call John as soon as I was ready to leave my apartment, because he wanted me to pick up some records along the way. She told me that she and John planned to have a practice session with Douglas and some musicians that afternoon, and I was expected to set up a rehearsal studio in Apartment 71.

I jumped into the shower and made some coffee. When I called John, he reeled off a list of records he wanted me to buy him, including Olivia Newton-John's hit single "Magic" and a song by Kate Bush titled "Babooshka." I was also to bring a tape by Lene Lovich that I had played for John the previous spring. He told me he needed everything by noon.

I rushed out of my West Forty-nine Street apartment and ran to Colony Records on Broadway, where I bought the records. It was a hot, humid day, and by the time I hopped a cab to the Dakota, I was drenched in sweat.

John was in the bedroom playing the piano, looking glum. He accompanied Yoko as she sang one of her songs, a maudlin ballad titled "I'm Your Angel." When I walked into the room, John leapt up and snatched the bag of records and tapes from my hands. He fished out the Lene Lovich cassette, *Stateless*, and inserted it into his tape deck. "When you hear this," he told Yoko, "you'll understand why you can't get away with your stuff!"

We listened to the tape for a while, and John pointed out that while Lovich appeared to have been influenced by Yoko's distinctive vocal style—her high-pitched whoops and wordless screams—Yoko could learn a few lessons from him with regard to the superb overall production. The recording had an outstanding instrumental track as well as an irresistible rhythm. John urged Yoko to pay close attention, but she simply smirked and affected indifference. This infuriated John. Exasperated, he turned off the music and told me to start setting up the makeshift rehearsal studio in Apartment 71. John's Yamaha electric piano was already there, as were most of his guitars. There was also a closetful of miscellaneous musical equipment—amplifiers, microphones, and all kinds of electronic gadgets John had accumulated over the years. I set it all up as best as I could, and when I was finished, a loud electrical hum filled the room.

When I returned to the bedroom to fetch John's drum machine, I found him deeply engrossed in a record by Noël Coward. Captivated by the singer's plaintive falsetto, he turned to Yoko, who sat at a wicker desk on the other side of the bed.

"Listen . . . ." John said. "He's crying!"

Yoko was furiously scribbling lyrics and ignored John.

Jack Douglas arrived a short while later. He was accompanied by three bearded musicians—guitarist Hugh McCracken, keyboard player George Small, and arranger Tony Davilio. John cheerfully greeted the musicians and tried to put them at ease.

"Welcome to our humble abode, my dears," John said exuberantly. "I've been waiting for you for five years!" He shook hands with Mc-Cracken, a veteran of previous Lennon-Ono recording sessions, John broke the ice by reminiscing about the last time he and McCracken had worked together. "I really don't remember what went on," John laughed. "I was too bombed most of the time. Of course, we're older and much wiser now, right?"

There was uneasy laughter among the musicians, who seemed intimidated by John. George Small had a nervous grin fixed on his face and looked at John expectantly. Davilio, an earnest young man whose face was hidden behind a black beard, handed me a batch of scores consisting of transcriptions of John's demo tapes. I photocopied the sheet music in the office and distributed it to everyone. A brief discussion of the arrangements and instrumentation ensued. John knew exactly how his songs should sound, but his limited knowledge of music theory made it difficult for him to express himself in terms musicians understood. Douglas and Davilio helped John formulate his ideas.

The session soon turned into a chaotic jam, as John began to sing, hum, and whistle songs while Douglas pounded the beat on his thighs, McCracken strummed his guitar, and Small played tentative chords on the electric piano. John and Jack sat cross-legged on the floor, while Yoko squatted right behind them. Less than an hour into the rehearsal, Yoko who had been quietly observing John and the band, suddenly broke her silence and announced in a shrill voice that she wanted to do one of her songs.

"Yes, Mother dearest," John said submissively. "We haven't forgotten about you." There was a trace of mockery in his voice.

As John and the group were getting ready to play "I'm Your Angel," Yoko took me aside and whispered in my ear that I should bring her a glass of vodka.

"It'll relax my voice, you know," she said earnestly. I nodded gravely. "But nobody should know I'm drinking vodka," she continued. "So you have to make it look like it's water."

I found a bottle of Stolichnaya in the office refrigerator, brought it upstairs, and poured Yoko a stiff drink. When I handed her the vodka, she took a quick sip and then resumed her high-pitched warbling. Yoko's voice cracked repeatedly in the upper register and she appeared to have great difficulty staying in key. As she struggled through the song, Douglas offered encouragement while exchanging worried looks with the musicians. John grimaced a lot but said very little. After two painfully embarrassing attempts to rehearse "I'm Your Angel," he decided that it was time to move on. Now Yoko said she was hungry and suggested ordering a great quantity of sushi for everybody. John agreed reluctantly. He did not like dinner breaks when he was working.

Next, John played a tape by Matumbi, a reggae group we had listened to in Bermuda. He used it as an example of the kind of "reggae groove" he was aiming for on "Beautiful Boy" and "Living on Borrowed Time." As soon as he heard the music, he jumped up and moved to the beat, pointing out what he liked about Matumbi's smooth blend of reggae rhythms and lush horn arrangements. He even assigned side two of the recording to the musicians as "homework."

At 6:00 P.M., I went to pick up dinner. When I returned with two giant plates of sushi and chicken teriyaki, the session was in full swing. John and the band were jamming "Living on Borrowed Time." John completely ignored the food. But the band had worked up an appetite, and John soon allowed a dinner break. Yoko ate a few pieces of sushi and then asked me to get her a bar of chocolate and another glass of "water."

After dinner, John picked up his futuristic-looking guitar and began strumming furiously. Fired by John's unflagging energy and enthusiasm, the band was soon in full flight again. Occasionally, John played weird chord progressions that left everyone baffled. Douglas or McCracken would then tactfully explain to John what he was doing "wrong." John would listen with slight embarrassment, occasionally throwing in a bit of self-deprecating humor. Sometimes his "mistakes" actually improved the song, and Davilio would promptly revise the score to reflect the change.

At one point during the rehearsal, John drifted into a strange key and Douglas, Davilio, and McCracken began analyzing what he had done. Looking bewildered, John struggled to comprehend the convoluted talk. "You should explain it to her," he said, pointing to Yoko. "She understands this stuff much better than I do."

As if on cue, McCracken spontaneously began playing a familiar-sounding riff from "(I Want You) She's So Heavy," John's ode to Yoko on the Beatles' *Abbey Road*.

"That's the first song I wrote about her!" John bubbled. "Most of my songs are about her, you know," he said, smiling affectionately at Yoko, who acknowledged John's compliment with a frosty smile.

When the band began rehearsing "Beautiful Boy," Yoko called me to her side and whispered that she wanted to leave, but was too drunk to get up. I summoned Toshi, her gofer, who escorted her out of the room. John looked startled. He casually took a sip from Yoko's glass of "water" and shuddered. "Jesus," he said with a grimace, "I didn't know what that was."

On Monday afternoon, August 4, John, Yoko, and Sean came back from spending the weekend with Sam Green at his Fire Island house. John was in a foul mood and disappeared into the bedroom, sulking. Yoko immediately closeted herself in the inner sanctum with Sam Havadtoy, whose birthday it was. He had hired an armored truck to transport some precious gems he was planning to sell to Yoko. His substantial commission would be Yoko's birthday gift to him.

"This is bullshit!" John grumbled when I told him about Havadtoy's birthday and the armored truck. "First she drags me and Sean out to Fire Island, where there's absolutely nothing for us to do, and now she's throwing money away on stuff she'll never wear."

John next informed me that a second rehearsal was to take place in the White Room that evening and he asked me to move the makeshift studio in there. He also said that he wanted his bedroom piano moved to the White Room, which already had a white grand piano, so that he and Yoko could work in tandem. After spending a couple of hours with Havadtoy, Yoko joined John upstairs late in the afternoon.

They changed into matching khaki outfits and then began rehearsing one of her songs, titled "Kiss Kiss Kiss." I had a chance to observe the Lennons at work as I hauled John's drum machine, a ghetto blaster, and several music stands into the room. Sitting at the black upright piano, Yoko mumbled the lyrics to her song as John played the melody on the white grand. Soon, he winced and motioned her to stop. Insisting that the song required a "lively backbeat" to compensate for its lack of melodic variety, John suggested trying a ska beat. He asked me to bring him a tape of Selecter, a British ska group that we had listened to on Long Island. I scrambled to make a cassette copy of the Selecter album in the kitchen, where Sam Havadtoy sat on a sofa, looking forlorn. Yoko had invited him to observe the rehearsal, but John had declared the session closed.

"Do you think it would be cool to go in and just say hello?" Havadtoy asked hopefully. I advised him against it. He soon left.

When I brought John the Selecter tape, he played it at loud volume while fiddling with his drum machine, attempting to duplicate the frenetic beat of a song titled "Too Much Pressure." John snapped his fingers and tried desperately to sell Yoko on the idea of incorporating the fast tempo into her song, but she would not hear of it. She demanded that John turn off the tape player and rhythm box. Gnashing his teeth in frustration, John complied.

At about 6:30 P.M., Douglas, Davilio, and Small trooped into the White Room, where Yoko performed bits and pieces of her songs on the white grand piano. The lyrics sounded like bad nursery rhymes, but she acted as if her songs were masterpieces.

"Don't you think they're great?" Yoko asked Douglas.

Jack was quick to offer words of encouragement, but this forced show of optimism had no effect on Yoko's harshest critic, John. When he asked Jack if he had any ideas for "spicing up" Yoko's material, Douglas turned to Davilio, who looked stumped. Douglas then suggested working on another of Yoko's songs, "Every Man Has a Woman Who Loves Him." John grabbed his Yamaha acoustic guitar and George Small sat down at the black piano.

After a torturous attempt to perform the song, John asked Douglas, "Did you have a chance to work on this one?"

Jack said he needed more time.

Next, they jammed "I'm Moving On." Yoko and Small built some momentum improvising chords on their keyboards while John energetically strummed his guitar, and Jack Douglas played imaginary drums. Davilio struggled to write down the melody as it developed. Everyone agreed that the song had a lot of potential.

At 10:00 P.M. John decided to call it a night. However, he spent another hour discussing the recording session scheduled for Thursday, August 7. He asked countless questions about the instruments and recording equipment they would be using. Whenever Douglas mentioned some sophisticated musical equipment, for instance a digital sequencer, John would inquire if it was something Paul McCartney had used on his latest album. John wanted his record to be a state-of-the-art production, just like Paul's. At one point Douglas said that after the basic tracks were recorded he wanted to mix them at the Record Plant in Los Angeles, his favorite studio. When Yoko agreed with Jack's suggestion, John threw her an angry, disapproving look.

Later, when everyone had gone, I joined John and Yoko in the kitchen for tea and leftover sushi. Yoko seemed pleased with the day's progress, but John was not in a self-congratulatory mood. "Don't kid yourself," he bluntly told her. "Your stuff needs a lot of work." He also scolded her for supporting Douglas' proposal to do the postproduction work in Los Angeles. Yoko assumed that John simply did not wish to go to the West Coast, and said innocently, "We don't have to go with him, you know."

"Are you serious?" he cried in a sudden burst of fury. "No way, Yoko! You must be out of your fuckin' mind!"

Yoko might as well have suggested giving Sean to Jack to raise. I had rarely seen John this upset. He was a perfectionist, and he intended to be involved in the production of the album from beginning to end.

Thursday afternoon, John strode confidently out of the Dakota, guitar case in hand, wearing a black cowboy suit, complete with embroidered shirt and brimmed hat. Yoko's outfit consisted of a blue hot pants suit, high heels, and a baseball cap. The Lennons rode in a limousine to the Hit Factory and I followed in the Mercedes, which was loaded with food supplies and several of John's guitars.

The Hit Factory occupied three floors in a nondescript commercial building on West Forty-eighth Street, less than two blocks from my apartment. We took over the sixth floor, which was declared off-limits to all except the Lennons and their staff, musicians, and sound engineers. The labyrinthine space included a softly lit, cavernous room with a Steinway grand, little electronic keyboards, and fat microphones on gleaming chrome stands. Davilio's sheet music was spread over everything.

The nerve center of the studio was the control room, a smaller area behind a glass enclosure. It had an impressive array of equipment that looked as though it might have come from NASA, and a lot of wood paneling to make up for the cold, high-tech feel of the place. Black speakers the size of refrigerators hung from the walls. Thick cables crisscrossed the floor, which was covered with brown industrial carpeting that took stains well: coffee, beer, soda, ground-in peanuts, chewing gum.

John immediately began inspecting the twenty-four-track board with its spectrum displays for all tracks, faders, equalizers, limiter-compressors, and countless other features, including some that he had never before seen or even heard of. This installation was a far cry from the four-track studio at Abbey Road where the Beatles had recorded their albums. John enthusiastically examined each piece of equipment, demanding to know its function. Jack Douglas and his chief engineer, Lee DeCarlo, gladly obliged. Two assistant engineers, Jon Smith and Julie Last, remained silently in the background.

Behind the control room was a tiny lounge with a small refrigerator that I stocked with the staples of the Lennons' studio diet: chocolate, honey bran biscuits, sunflower seeds and raisins, instant coffee, and a large variety of teas. Yoko immediately began to complain about having to share this tiny space with the musicians and recording staff. She asked me to summon the Hit Factory's owner, Eddie Germano, who assured me that he was prepared to do anything to fulfill John and Yoko's every wish.

"Anything they want, Freddie," he said. "You just let me know and I'll take care of it." For starters, Yoko demanded a private lounge. Germano cleared out a large room, and Sam Green furnished it with plush wall-to-wall green carpeting, shrubs, a piano, lamps, and antique furniture from his extensive collection.

By mid-afternoon, the band was fully assembled. The drummer was Andy Newmark, a boyish, extroverted musician who had played with everybody from Sly and the Family Stone to George Harrison and, most recently, Roxy Music. Percussionist Arthur Jenkins was a veteran of John's *Rock 'n' Roll* and *Walls and Bridges* albums. Bassist Tony Levin was a bald and mustachioed man who had recorded and toured with Paul Simon and Peter Gabriel. Guitarist Earl Slick, the youngest band member, had played with David Bowie.

Much of the first day at the studio was spent setting up equipment and doing sound checks. Finally, late in the afternoon, the band recorded its first take, "Stepping Out." John sat in the control booth, working closely with Douglas. At first, John appeared to be insecure.

He bounced around the studio talking nervously, trying to get to know the musicians. John had not fronted a band in almost six years, but it did not take him long to take charge. Like a king returning from a long exile, John soon assumed command of his troops. Some of the band members—particularly Slick and Newmark—were anxious to impress John and gain his approval. John soon locked horns with drummer Newmark, who tried to loosen things up with humorous talk. But John had no time for idle chatter. He regarded Newmark's friendly banter as impertinent and tried to ignore it. John was also annoyed by the drummer's frequent trips to the bathroom.

"Andy!" John shouted at one point, his voice booming from the studio monitors, "get yer cock out here!"

John loathed "grandstanding." If a band member talked too much or played a flashy solo, John would issue a stinging rebuke.

He liked to keep the musicians on a short leash. He insisted that the band play precisely what he wanted when he wanted it, nothing more and nothing less. John bullied, joked, cajoled, lectured, ridiculed, and insulted the musicians—anything to get them to play what he had in mind. I had never seen John so driven.

On Friday, the band played John's song "Strange Days" and Yoko's "Kiss Kiss Kiss." Before recording her number, Yoko snorted cocaine in front of everybody and conspicuously wiped the residue of white powder from her nostrils. The session wound down at 9:00 P.M. and the musicians streamed into the control room to listen to a playback of the day's work. John passed around his tiny, long-stemmed pot pipe while dispensing some good-natured banter.

The session bogged down on Saturday, as Yoko repeatedly flubbed the bridge on her reggae song, "Don't Be Scared." After several unsuccessful attempts to record the vocals, John lost patience with her and cried, "Remember the Bridge on the River Kwai, you fuck!"

There was stunned silence in the studio. Yoko pretended not to hear John's angry outburst, and Douglas let her off the hook by asserting that the flawed vocals could be "fixed" later. During the first three days in the studio, a total of six tracks had been recorded. The band was amazed at the speed with which John worked. One of the reasons he was in such a hurry to record the album was to cut costs. The Lennons did not have a record company footing the bill for the session. Every day in the studio cost John and Yoko thousands of dollars.

The second week at the Hit Factory, two members of the rock group Cheap Trick—guitarist Rick Nielsen and drummer Bun E. Carlos— were scheduled to back John on "I'm Losing You." John was using them as a favor to Douglas, who had produced Cheap Trick's early albums. He asked me to bring him as many of their recordings as I could find. When we listened to the tapes on Tuesday morning, August 12, John observed that the group had borrowed freely from the Beatles. That in itself was no cause for alarm. What bothered John was that the lead singer appeared to emulate Paul McCartney. He also worried that Nielsen's guitar style was "too heavy metal."

Douglas had told John that Nielsen was an avid collector of electric guitars, and John decided to show off some of his classic instruments from the sixties. We stopped by the guitar room in 71, where John picked out his famous black and white Rickenbacker, a battered blue Vincent Bell, and two classic Fender electric guitars.

When I dropped off the instruments at the studio, Douglas introduced me to the two members of Cheap Trick. The slender, boyish Nielsen, an unabashed Beatle fan, could scarcely contain his excitement at the prospect of meeting John. He handed me a guitar-shaped pin. His bandmate, Bun E. Carlos, was a shy, chubby, bespectacled man sporting a droopy black mustache. When John showed up at 2:00 P.M., Nielsen presented him with a custom-made guitar. John politely thanked the guitarist and invited him to examine his famous Beatle instruments. Nielsen wanted desperately to engage John in friendly conversation, but John remained businesslike, aloof, and distant. Nielsen appeared crushed.

There was a quick sound check, followed by a brief rehearsal with Nielsen and Carlos, plus George Small and bassist Tony Levin. John guided the quartet through several takes of "Losing You"—a song he described as " 'Cold Turkey' rides again," a reference to his gutwrenching 1969 rendition about the agony of heroin withdrawal. As soon as the session was over, John joined Yoko in the Green Room, avoiding further contact with the two Cheap Trick musicians, whose manager discreetly handed me an invoice for three thousand dollars.

When I showed it to Yoko, she had a fit. "Can you believe it?" she fumed. "They should pay *us* for the honor of working with John!"

That evening after dinner, the regular band recorded "Beautiful Boy." I was thrilled when John asked percussionist Arthur Jenkins to duplicate the off-beat rhythmic accents that I had played on the Bermuda demo tape. It took the band about ninety minutes to record a satisfactory take, and afterward we all crowded into the control room to listen to the playback. John passed his pot pipe to Arthur and me. We each took a small puff, and then John put the pipe away.

The next day, George Harrison called the Dakota and left a message for John. Winnie, the concierge, handed me a piece of paper on which she had written: "PLEASE CALL GEORGE—HE'S VERY ANX-IOUS TO TALK TO YOU AFTER AN ABSENCE OF TEN YEARS!" When I gave John the message, he was less than thrilled. "Well, it's kind of George to call after forgetting to mention me in his book," he snickered. He gave me back the note and told me to "let Mother deal with it."

I understood how John felt. Some months earlier, Harrison had written a book, *I, Me, Mine*. John had been stunned that George had avoided any mention of him and felt that he at least deserved credit for having launched George's career. He regarded his former protégé's behavior as a mortal insult.

Also around this time, there was a message from Paul McCartney wishing John luck. When I told Yoko that Paul had called, she looked alarmed. "You better not tell John," she said, worrying that Paul would want to get in on the session.

Late on the evening of August 13, John recorded "Cleanup Time," a danceable tune built on a sleek funk vamp. It was reminiscent of "Fame," a song John had written with David Bowie in the early 1970s. John shuttled back and forth between the band and the control room, both conducting and playing. Yoko spent most of the evening lying on a couch in the Green Room talking to Sam Green on the phone. When I looked in on her, she asked me to cover her with a blanket. "Tell John I'm not feeling well and ask him to visit me," she said faintly.

When I relayed Yoko's message, John was annoyed. "Tell Mother to come out here and listen to the playbacks!" he snapped impatiently.

Thursday, August 14, Rich DePalma returned from his two-week vacation. I was glad to have him back. I had been doing double duty in the office and the recordings studio, and I was feeling completely overwhelmed. I filled in the accountant on the events of the last two weeks. When Rich went over the books he was dismayed by the Lennons' expenditures. Among the incidental expenses for the recording session were a $5,000-per-month hotel suite for Earl Slick and Lee

DeCarlo, who had been brought in from Los Angeles. My own expense account had soared to more than $4,000 per week.

Later in the morning I went upstairs to give John a collection of recordings by Tito Puente, Ray Barretto, and other Latin artists. Anxious to expand Yoko's limited repertoire of rhythms, he had asked me to bring him some salsa music. I found him sitting on the bed, surrounded by a sea of tapes. He was furiously puffing on a Gitane.

"What's Mother up to this morning?" he asked. I told him that she had gone out with Sam Green. John nodded, looking sad and pensive for a moment, but his face brightened when I played him a few cuts from the Tito Puente LP. "If push comes to shove, we'll divide up rhythms," he chuckled. "I'll do fund and reggae, Mother can do ska and salsa."

A little after 1:00 P.M. he asked me to drive him to the Hit Factory. We were the only ones there.

"Where is everybody?" John asked. When I reminded him that the official starting time for the session was 2:00 P.M., he grumbled, "Why can't they all be as eager to get to work as I am?" Then he stretched out on a sofa at the foot of the control board and said, "Wake me up when there's some action."

John's mood did not improve when Yoko showed up with Sam Green later in the afternoon. As John would not allow Sam into the control room, Sam and Yoko stayed out of sight in the Green Room while John recorded "Flower Princess."

At noon the next day, John strode resolutely into the office.

"Mother busy?" he asked, peeking into the inner sanctum.

When he saw that Yoko was on the phone, John called her on the intercom, complaining loudly that he was starving and that unless she was ready to go out to lunch right away, he would go without her. Yoko told him to go right ahead. "C'mon, Fred," John said through clenched teeth, "let's split!"

I grabbed my coat and followed him out the door. We went to the garage, picked up the Mercedes, and drove two blocks to La Fortuna. Over cappuccino and pastries, John worried that Yoko had not made any progress in her efforts to find a record company. Most of the twenty-two basic tracks were recorded, and John thought it was high time that they get a record deal. In fact, numerous labels had expressed interest in signing John, but had backed off when Yoko explained that she and John would alternate tracks.

That afternoon at the Hit Factory, Yoko and the band struggled through several lackluster takes of "Beautiful Boys," a dirgelike number that was intended as her retort to John's song "Beautiful Boy." After numerous failed attempts to record the vocal track, Yoko began to pester Douglas to add "war sounds" to the track. Jack looked at her blankly. "You know," Yoko said impatiently, "machine gun fire, bombs dropping, et cetera." When Jack remained noncommittal and insisted on finishing the basic track first, Yoko threw the producer a withering look. With every unsuccessful take, tension in the studio mounted.

At 5:30 P.M., I left to pick up dinner. I was glad to get away. The thrill of being in the studio with the Lennons was rapidly wearing off. I guzzled hot sake while waiting for the sushi chef to assemble our ritual dinner of sushi and chicken teriyaki.

When I returned to the studio an hour later, Sam Green showed up carrying a stack of books about tropical plants. Apparently John and Yoko had argued about the correct spelling of "freesia," and Yoko had asked Sam to find a picture of the flower with its proper spelling. Suddenly Yoko appeared and shooed Sam into the Green Room. When he was gone, she told me that John was in a "funny mood" and wanted Sam to leave. "John is very jealous, you know," she giggled. Yoko wanted me to drive Sam home, but she worried that his feelings would be hurt. "Don't make it seem like we're kicking him out," she said. Sam was glad to be able to make a discreet exit. "I feel I'm in the way," he said sheepishly.

At 8:30 P.M. on Monday, August 18, I was on my way back to the recording studio after returning the dinner plates to the restaurant. I shared the elevator with a familiar-looking man wearing thick spectacles and a goatee. As we made our way to the sixth floor, I realized that he was Ahmet Ertegun, the legendary boss of Atlantic Records. I assumed that he had come to visit Dr. John, who was recording for Atlantic Records elsewhere in the building. When the elevator reached the sixth floor, I rushed off to the rear lounge to make some calls. Suddenly I heard a commotion in the control room. Apparently Yoko had intercepted Ertegun just as he was about to wander into the session, and she was in a state of hysteria over this stunning breach of security.

"Where's Eddie Germano?" she screeched. "I want Eddie right now!"

Moments later, Germano came running into the studio, and Yoko subjected him to a savage tongue-lashing. The stocky owner of the Hit Factory stood there, out of breath and sweating profusely, with an alarmed expression on his beet-red face. He mumbled apologies, but Yoko ignored these and kept threatening to move the sessions to the rival Record Plant.

The big mystery, of course, was how Ertegun had managed to gain access to the sixth floor, which could only be reached with a special elevator key. When I confessed that he had been in the elevator with me and that I had assumed he would go back down in the elevator, Yoko vented her fury at me. "Are you crazy?" she hollered. "How could you let him up here?"

As she continued her diatribe, John bolted from his chair and fled to the bathroom. Everyone else remained frozen in their tracks, as if transfixed by Yoko's tantrum. I had witnessed similar outbursts in the past and I knew that she would go on like this for a while. Yoko enjoyed throwing tantrums. It gave her a feeling of power, and, in this case, surrounded by a captive audience, it made her the center of attention.

Yoko raged on, blaming me for "almost sabotaging" the session. She maintained that Ertegun had come to "spy" on us and intimated that if she had not intervened, he would have most likely walked off with the master tapes of her and John's songs. This accusation was so ludicrous that I had to struggle to keep a straight face. As I looked around the room, I could see that many of the musicians and engineers were also on the verge of laughing. The rest looked puzzled, except Eddie Germano, who appeared as if he were about to suffer a heart attack. In a desperate attempt to appease Yoko, he promised to post a guard in the elevator. Finally, Yoko ordered Germano and me to search the building and make sure Ertegun was not hiding somewhere. We were glad to escape her fury.

Later that evening, things became even more tense. Yoko had hired a video crew to film John working in the studio. She directed the cameraman to shoot numerous close-ups of John's face from all angles. I felt bad for John, who had once told me that he hated to have his face filmed up close. Like a trapped animal, he jumped around and sang himself hoarse. He had been snorting cocaine, and he was so wired that he was ready to jump out of his skin. It was painful to watch. The session lasted until 3:30 A.M. and was sheer torture for all involved, except Yoko, who seemed to enjoy herself thoroughly.

By Tuesday, August 19, all the basic tracks had been recorded, except one, Yoko's gospel-tinged ballad, "Hard Times Are Over." John showed up at the studio wearing a dark suit and tie, his hair freshly cut. The band and recording staff were in a celebratory mood. I had made reservations for all of us at a trendy Chinese restaurant. The plan was for us to go there as soon as Yoko's song was recorded.

It took Yoko four hours to record her vocals. As time wore on, everyone grew more and more frustrated and consumed more and more drugs. Sam Green and I spent the time in the private lounge, where he had laid out a small amount of cocaine on a table. Cocaine was not a drug that I went out of my way to get, but when it was offered, I helped myself. Once in a while I would poke my head into the studio to see how Yoko was doing.

It was slow going. Yoko's voice cracked as usual and wandered all over the place. Douglas patiently guided her through the song, with John sitting at his side looking bored and frustrated. There was a documentary about the Beatles on Channel Thirteen but John had covered the TV screen with a photo of Sean and refused to give in to suggestions that we turn the set on.

When Yoko finally finished recording the vocals for "Hard Times," I took a group photo of the band and recording staff. Finally, at 10:00 P.M. we all went to the restaurant, where a long banquet table had been reserved for our group of twenty.

The next phase of the recording session involved fixing mistakes in the vocals and instrumental performances, as well as adding new vocal and instrumental tracks. Musicians were called in singly or in groups to redo their parts or add new instrumental tracks. In John's case it meant multitracking his voice by piling vocal track upon vocal track to create a subtle distortion. There was no real need to do this, but John was so insecure about the natural sound of his voice that he insisted on masking it by adding one layer of voice on top of another until he achieved a subtle echo effect.

"The more insecure I am," he candidly told me, "the more I put on a track."

After a five-year hiatus from the music scene John was feeling extremely insecure. Whenever he heard something that he liked by the "competition," he would question his own work. For instance, when John saw David Bowie's video of "Ashes to Ashes," he liked the song-video so much that he sank into a depression. "He's doing what I should be doing," John confided to me. He then talked about doing a video, but what he had in mind was not exactly suited to *Double Fantasy*. His idea was to portray himself as a flying monster.

In Yoko's case the overdubbing process became a nightmare, because she was incapable of singing in key. The solution was to record up to a dozen or more vocal takes and then patch together a final version note by note. It was a laborious, time-consuming process, and it kept the Lennons in the studio until the early-morning hours, day in and day out. Soon, Yoko began to worry that Douglas would conspire with John to eliminate some of her songs. "I think Jack is trying to kick my songs off the album," she would whisper to me after a particularly grueling evening of overdubs.

The only relief from the tedious studio work was provided by an occasional photo session. Yoko had lined up a succession of photographers who took shots of the Lennons in the studio and in other settings around town. The photos were intended for the media as well as for the cover of the album. As the session dragged on into September, John grew increasingly anxious about the fact that he was still without a record deal. Yoko was still "talking" to various labels, but she appeared unwilling to make a decision.

Making matters worse for John was the arrival of Elliot Mintz, Yoko's Los Angeles-based troubleshooter. Mintz was supposed to "keep John company." The only problem was that John did not want him around. When Mintz sat down next to John in the control room, John ignored him completely. Eventually, Mintz realized that he was not welcome and began to spend most of his time with Yoko in the Green Room discussing the business of promoting her. She told Mintz to play up her role as businesswoman and to publicize her reliance on psychics. Mintz had once told me that he did not think that press reports about Yoko's confidence in psychics were good for her image. I was therefore astonished when he now agreed with everything Yoko said. He was a consummate sycophant.

On Friday, September 5, an impressive group of horn players arrived at the Hit Factory to record elaborate horn arrangements Davilio had written for "Losing You," "Cleanup Time," and several other songs. The sessions was thrilling to witness, as the horn section included some world-class musicians. Howard Johnson, the tuba player, was a veteran of many classic jazz sessions as well as previous Lennon-Ono recordings. Some of the other well-known players were saxophonists George Young, J. D. Parran, and Dave Tofani, as well as trumpet player Seldon Powell. The ensemble's razor-sharp playing was breathtaking.

As midnight approached, John asked me to buy four hundred dollars' worth of cocaine from one of the musicians' dealers. When I broached the subject of how to explain this expenditure on my expense account, John blithely instructed me to write it off as "candy." I was whisked by limousine to a West Fifty-seventh Street address, where I collected four grams of cocaine. Back at the studio, the horn players were getting ready to record "I'm Your Angel." Yoko, who had been resting in the Green Room all evening, did not come out to hear their work and John was angered and embarrassed by her absence. "Has anyone seen my wife?" he asked in a mocking tone of voice.

Fueled by cocaine, the session lasted into the early morning.

A few days after the horn session, Douglas assembled a large gospel choir at A&R studios on West Fifty-second Street. The choir, made up largely of black teenage girls, added a rousing gospel chorus to Yoko's song "Hard Times Are Over." At first they were nervous, and their conductor struggled to keep them in key. After a few trial runs, the choir warmed up and sang with great strength and self-assurance. Douglas recorded several dozen choruses of the choir singing "Hard Times Are Over" at full throttle. Afterward, John asked the group to chant "One World, One People," which he intended to use as a kind of coda to the album. When the music was recorded, the conductor asked John if he would care to hear some more. When John said yes, the choir sang its standard gospel repertoire. John was enthralled by the choir's powerful singing. He grinned from ear to ear and his body swayed with the music.

John instructed me to take down the names and addresses of each singer so that he could send each an autographed copy of the album. As I wrote down the information I discovered that quite a few of them were fans. "My friends aren't going to believe I recorded with one of the Beatles!" exclaimed one singer. But things got slightly out of hand on our way out of the studio, when some of the exuberant teenagers grabbed John while emitting squeals of excitement. Panic-stricken, John fled to the elevator.

Ever since the Lennons' recording session had been announced in the media late in August, John and Yoko had been besieged with requests for interviews. During the second week of September, they embarked on a campaign to hype their album, even though they still had not found a record label. The procedure for deciding to whom to grant the interviews involved Yoko doing her customary astrological checkup. In most cases, Yoko also insisted on approving the copy as well as appearing on the cover. In their eagerness to have access to the Lennons, most publications acceded to Yoko's demands.

The first journalist to interview John for a major publication was *Newsweek*'s Barbara Graustark. After talking to Yoko, Graustark approached me seeking confirmation of some of the things Yoko had told her. Was it true, Graustark asked, that the Lennons had a yacht named *Isis* moored off their Long Island estate, as well as a private seaplane? Apparently, Yoko had greatly exaggerated the size of the boat, and made up the business about owning a plane. When I told Graustark the truth, Yoko accused me of undermining her media relations. "How dare you contradict me in public?" she fumed. When I tried to defend myself, saying that it was not fair that I should be put in a position of having to lie, Yoko dismissed my objections as "naive."

The second major interview was granted to *Playboy*. The magazine sent David Sheff, a dark-haired, handsome young man. Trembling with excitement, Sheff showed up at the office on Thursday, September 11, and immediately let it be known that he was not only a Beatle fan, but also a great Yoko Ono fan. I knew right away that the Lennons would have a field day with him.

As the Lennons' media campaign was getting into high gear, John was growing frantic, because he still had no record deal. After either rejecting or being rejected by most of the major labels—many of the major record companies had been eager to sign John, but backed off when they learned that half of *Double Fantasy* would consist of Yoko's music—Yoko had begun to solicit offers from some of the smaller record companies.

On Friday morning, September 19, she met with David Geffen, who a few months earlier had started his own record company. Geffen had made a name for himself in the late 1960s as a successful artist manager representing Laura Nyro and Crosby, Stills & Nash. In 1970 he founded his own record label, Asylum, whose artist roster included Jackson Browne, Linda Ronstadt, Joni Mitchell, and the Eagles. He retired from the music scene in the mid-1970s. At the age of thirty-seven, Geffen had reentered the business, signing Elton John and Donna Summer to his new label, Geffen Records. And now he appeared on the verge of signing the Lennons. I could tell his meeting with Yoko was going well, because I heard frequent laughter coming from her office. When Geffen emerged from the inner sanctum, his tanned, boyish face exuded self-confidence.

As soon as he left, John was summoned from the bedroom. He spent a few minutes with Yoko and then announced, "You'll be pleased to know we have a record deal."

Yoko told John that she had chosen Geffen Records to release *Double Fantasy* because, she said, Geffen's numbers were "perfect." In actuality, she signed with Geffen because he did not flinch when Yoko announced that half the album would consist of her songs. There was considerable irony in the fact that Yoko chose Geffen, because Geffen's mentor in the record business had been Ahmet Ertegun, whom Yoko had ejected from the studio a month earlier.

Although John was relieved that he finally had a record deal, he was also apprehensive about entrusting his comeback album to a small, brand-new company. He was further troubled by the fact that Geffen Records was distributed by the giant Warner Brothers conglomerate. "I want to make sure we're dealing with a real record company," he said, and asked me to get him a copy of Donna Summer's new Geffen single, a remake of Dion DiMucci's "The Wanderer." When I showed John the Donna Summer record, he carefully examined the Geffen logo on the record sleeve and announced that he and Yoko should have their own logo. He asked me to get him reproductions of the British and Japanese flags. John's idea was to create a logo by superimposing the two flags.

On Monday, September 22, *Newsweek* published its Lennon interview, and soon the office was in an uproar. Rich was incensed over a comment John had made about being surrounded by "sycophant slaves."

"I ain't no fuckin' slave man," the accountant griped. "If that's the way John thinks of us, I'm quitting!" I managed to calm Rich down by pointing out that the remark was made in the context of a discussion of John's Beatle years, and that we ought not to take it as a personal insult.

Meanwhile, Yoko was in a panic because Jerry Rubin, the Yippie revolutionary turned Wall Street banker, had called, threatening to make scandalous revelations about her and John unless John apologized for an insulting reference to him in the interview. (Explaining why he had turned away from political activism, John had said: "What the hell was I doing fighting the American government just because Jerry Rubin couldn't get what he always wanted—a nice, cushy job.")

Rubin called several times that morning, demanding to speak to John, who refused to take the call. "John and Jerry were very close," Yoko said, "and he's threatening to say bad things about John." She told me that if Rubin called again I should "try to appease him" by saying that the Lennons had not seen the interview yet, but that we were sure John was quoted out of context. When Rubin called the office that afternoon and angrily demanded to know why John had not gotten back to him, I assured him that John had only the highest regard for him and was anxious to clear up the misunderstanding. "If John Lennon cares enough about me to make derogatory statements to the press," snapped Rubin, "the least he can do is talk to me!" I promised we would get back to him.

No sooner did I get off the phone with Jerry Rubin than Sid Bernstein called. Bernstein had organized the Beatles' first American concert at Carnegie Hall. Ever since the Beatles broke up in 1970, he had pursued his dream of reuniting the group, even going so far as to take out full-page newspaper ads badgering the Beatles to play benefit concerts for charity. Now Bernstein raved on about how excited he was to learn that John was making a comeback and how this was the ideal time for a Beatles reunion, which he—the man who brought the Beatles to America—would be honored to organize. I promised to pass along his proposal to the Lennons.

The final step in the recording process consisted of mixing all the tracks to achieve the optimum sound balance. For some time, Douglas had complained that the Hit Factory's studio monitors lacked "bass definition," suggesting that the Record Plant was better suited for mixing the album. Suddenly, on September 24, Yoko decided to grant Jack's request. She ordered me to round up our staff and to swoop down on the Hit Factory without any prior notice. Once there, we were to collect the master tapes of the session, as well as all of the Lennons' belongings.

I rushed to the Hit Factory with Rich, Mike Tree, Jerry Caron (a Havadtoy assistant who had joined our staff), and Yoko's gofer, Toshi. Everything was quiet on the sixth floor, where a bleary-eyed Lee De-Carlo was already at work. When Douglas informed his chief engineer that we were moving to the Record Plant, DeCarlo buried his head in his hands. "Why does stuff like this always happen when I'm not feeling well?" he moaned. As the Hit Factory staff looked on in disbelief, Rich began collecting the master tapes of the session, Toshi emptied out the small refrigerator and gathered up the Lennons' provisions from the back lounge, Jerry Caron filled shopping bags with Yoko's clothes, while Mike Tree and I assembled John's guitars in the elevator lobby. Everything was then loaded into the Mercedes, which I drove the few blocks to the Record Plant.

At noon on Friday, September 26, Eddie Germano showed up at Studio One hoping to persuade Yoko to return to the Hit Factory. Pleading his case over the intercom because Yoko had locked herself in the inner sanctum, Germano suggested that Douglas had been bribed by the Record Plant and that his complaint about the Hit Factory's speakers lacking bass definition was a mere pretext. When he left, Yoko emerged from her office and announced that we might move back to the Hit Factory. That evening at the Record Plant, Douglas began working on the final mix of "Starting Over" and "Kiss Kiss Kiss," which would be released as a single. We worked through the night, and I did not get to bed until 9:00 A.M. At about 4:00 P.M. John woke me up with a phone call from the Record Plant asking me to bring a Tibetan "wishing bell" to the recording studio. He wanted to add the sound of the bell ringing at the very beginning of "Starting Over." I rushed to the Dakota, found the bell in Apartment 71, and delivered it to the studio.

Although John had said that I was free to go out if I wanted to, I chose to stay. For the first time in a long while, the mood in the studio was happy and relaxed. Yoko chatted amiably with DeCarlo, who told her that his mother consulted psychics. Always on the lookout for new advisors, Yoko asked DeCarlo to get their names and phone numbers. After mentioning that it was crucial to finish the song before a "significant moon change" occurred at 7:00 P.M., Yoko went off to call Mrs. DeCarlo's psychics while Jack and Lee rushed to finish "Starting Over." Miraculously, the song was completed seconds before Yoko's 7:00 P.M. deadline.

2

On Monday, we moved from the tenth floor to a studio on the ground floor of the Record Plant. While Douglas was mixing side two of the album, John Belushi was horsing around with his bodyguard in a lounge just beyond our studio. When someone introduced me as Lennon's assistant, Belushi's face lit up and he asked if it would be "cool" to "hang out" with John for a while. I told him I would ask. John admired Belushi's brilliant and bizarre brand of humor on *Saturday Night Live* and was tempted to invite the comedian into the studio. Yoko, who did not know who Belushi was, vetoed the suggestion.

Later that evening, John decided to add incidental sound effects between the first two tracks on the album's second side, "Watching the Wheels" and "I'm Your Angel." I was sent out with Jon Smith, the assistant engineer, to record the sounds John had in mind. We were instructed to record random street noise, then to proceed to Central Park South and record the hooves of the carriage horses, and, finally, to tape the musicians performing in the Palm Court of the Plaza Hotel. Armed with a four-thousand-dollar Nagra tape recorder I had bought a few weeks earlier, Smith and I set out on our mission. We walked up Eighth Avenue and across Central Park South, where we went alongside the horse-drawn carriages pointing the huge microphone at the horses' hooves, followed by suspicious glances from tourists and doormen. Next, we entered the Plaza Hotel and took a table near the small stage of the Palm Court, where a violin and piano duo were playing classical music for a handful of people scattered around the lavish enclosure. We placed the huge microphone on the table and concealed the Nagra on an empty seat between us. Then we ordered coffee and dessert and sat back, hoping the waiter would not become suspicious.

Around midnight we played back our tape in the studio; the sound quality was superb and John was ecstatic. He worked with Douglas all night to create a short audio collage consisting of John's voice babbling incoherently, street noise, the sound of the horses' hooves, footsteps, a creaky door closing, and, finally, the piano-violin duo from the Palm Court. This strange blend of sounds concluded with a few bars of piano, then segued into Tony Levin's whistled introduction to "I'm Your Angel."

I went to bed at 7:00 A.M. and slept until noon. When I arrived at the office at 2:00 P.M. on Tuesday, I was astounded to see the Lennons eating cheeseburgers with Eddie Germano. Apparently we were going to move back to the Hit Factory as soon as Douglas finished mixing Yoko's song "Every Man Has a Woman Who Loves Him." Yoko ordered Rich to remain on call in the office.

At 10:00 P.M. the accountant called me at the Record Plant. "What's going on?" he asked wearily. I told him that we were still working on Yoko's song and that it was impossible to predict when it would be done. "This sucks!" Rich said. "I'm goin' home."

Yoko's song was completed at 6:00 A.M. As the Lennons prepared to leave, I called Eddie Germano and told him to send his people. Then I faced the unpleasant task of informing the Record Plant's night manager, a cheerful young man named Billy, that we were about to move back to the Hit Factory. "You're joking, right?" Billy said, smiling hopefully.

Grimly, I shook my head and told him that I had been ordered to collect all the Lennons' master tapes. Billy's face turned pale. Sputtering something about the tapes being locked in a vault on the tenth floor, he went off to call his boss, Roy Cicala. A short while later I found myself talking to the irate owner of the Record Plant. "Yoko lied to me!" Cicala screamed into the phone, choking with anger. "I can't believe this is happening." I did not know what to say.

Just then Rich showed up, looking tired and miserable. Yoko had called him at home and ordered him to report to the Record Plant on the double. Rich soon managed to persuade Cicala to turn over the master tapes in exchange for a fee to be negotiated. At 8:30 A.M. three employees from the Hit Factory helped Rich and me load the Lennons' equipment and provisions into the Mercedes.

By 11:00 A.M. we had collected everything except the master tapes. Rich now handed me a blank check and asked me to wait in the office while he negotiated with Cicala the release of the tapes. He called me at noon and instructed me to make out the check to the Record Plant for the sum of $14,612.74. Yoko signed it without batting an eyelash. I delivered the check to the Record Plant and the tapes were loaded into the Mercedes.

When I arrived at the Hit Factory, I was told that Roberta Flack, the Lennons' Dakota neighbor, would be using the sixth-floor studio until 9:00 P.M. Yoko ordered me to see to it that Flack vacated "our" studio immediately. I managed to convince her that this was not realistic. I also reminded her that I had been up for thirty hours and asked her if it was okay to go home and sleep. "Yes, you may," Yoko said, thanking me.

Emboldened by her friendly words, I asked for a raise. She agreed to increase my weekly salary to three hundred dollars.

12

Walking on Thin Ice

Early in October, Yoko told me that John wanted to take a brief vacation when the album was finished, and she asked me to look into renting Villa Undercliff again. When I contacted Rolf Luthi, he told me that we could have the house for the last two weeks of the month. This was welcome news. The frantic pace of the session had taken its toll. We all looked haggard and were in a state of chronic exhaustion. The following week, the mixing session ground to a virtual standstill due to equipment problems. Having used up all twenty-four tracks, Douglas and DeCarlo had decided to connect two twenty-four-track consoles in order to create a forty-eight-track capability. However, the complicated setup still had a few kinks in it, and as a result the work on the album would drag on into its third month.

Meanwhile, as John's fortieth birthday approached, droves of fans began to gather in front of the Dakota and the Hit Factory. The number of people lying in wait for John had been steadily increasing since the last week of September, when Yoko gave an interview to the *Daily News* in which she had discussed her and John's studio schedule in detail and even described the route they took back and forth to the studio every day. Alarmed by the dangerous indiscretion, Sean's bodyguard, Doug MacDougall, had met with Yoko to discuss how to beef up security.

"It's bad enough that half the world knows where John is recording," the usually unflappable ex-FBI agent had told me when he'd showed up for his September 25 meeting with Yoko. Announcing

John's work schedule, Doug worried, was "an open invitation to every wacko in the country to come after them."

Yoko had granted the bodyguard a five-minute audience in her bathroom, as she was in the midst of an important meeting in the inner sanctum with two Geffen-Warner record executives. Doug's suggestion that an armed guard ride with the Lennons in their limousine was quickly rejected because it was deemed too intrusive. MacDougall then proposed that a guard escort her and John to and from their limousine. When Yoko rejected this option as well, Doug had warned her that she was asking for trouble. Yoko had abruptly ended their meeting by informing Doug that her main concern was not security, but selling records. Doug's response had been to the effect that if Yoko was looking to get herself and John killed, it was her business, but that he did not wish to go down in history as the bodyguard who had failed to protect John Lennon. After his acrimonious meeting with Yoko, Doug went on a leave of absence.

When John and Yoko left for the studio on Wednesday, October 8, the small mob of fans came alive. "Happy birthday, John!" a girl shouted as John walked to his limousine.

"Thanks," he replied wearily, "but we're not there yet."

There was another group of fans and curiosity-seekers waiting at the entrance to the Hit Factory. As the Lennons' limo pulled up in front of the entrance, the crowd surged toward the car. Cameras clicked and people began shouting, "Hi, John!" and "When's the album coming out?"

"Soon, I hope," John said as he rushed into the building, flanked by Yoko and me.

Approaching the Dakota on the morning of October 9, I was instantly besieged by a dozen fans, some of whom handed me cards and packages for John. One Lennon look-alike, who had been following me around for days, suddenly grabbed my arm and demanded to know how I got my job. He looked so frantic that I was seized by a sudden impulse to run away. But I did not allow myself to show any outward signs of fear. I worried that if I started to panic, it might set into motion an irreversible slide into paranoia, and that was a luxury I could ill afford. I stared angrily into the fan's eyes, which were obscured by tinted Lennon-style granny glasses, and said firmly, "Let go of my arm!"

Back in the office, I took a call from Sam Havadtoy, who informed me that he had hired a plane to write a birthday greeting for John and Sean in the sky over Central Park at noon. When I told him that the Lennons were still at the studio, Havadtoy worried that they would miss the big event and decided to postpone the skywriting until 3:00 P.M., which would also allow more time for media coverage. Around noon I got a call from the Hit Factory saying that John and Yoko were on their way back to the Dakota. When I went out to the driveway to meet their car, the number of fans had swelled to two dozen and a banner proclaimed, "HAPPY BIRTHDAY JOHN AND SEAN." Soon the Lennons' limousine rounded the corner of Seventy-second Street and Central Park West. As the car pulled into the Dakota driveway, the fans swarmed around the vehicle. The doorman and I formed a protective wedge around John and Yoko as they rushed into the building. The fans were deeply disappointed that John did not acknowledge their birthday greetings, and I soon found myself apologizing for him.

Yoko then called a staff meeting in which she discussed the birthday schedule. There was to be an "outside event"—the skywriting—followed by an "inside event" consisting of a small party for John and Sean in the kitchen. Yoko asked me to document both events with my camera. She instructed John and the staff to watch the "outside event" from the roof of the Dakota.

I asked her if she planned to join us on the roof. "Are you kidding?" she said.

As it turned out, John shared her sentiment. He told me that he resented the circuslike atmosphere surrounding his birthday and that he planned to skip the "outside event" so that he could get some sleep. Sean, meanwhile, was jumping up and down with excitement. At 2:30 P.M., the staff began assembling on the roof of the Dakota. I took the elevator to the ninth floor and walked up the narrow flight of stairs leading to the roof. It was a cloudless day and the sky was a dazzling blue. When I looked down at the street below, I saw clusters of fans looking up at the sky. The skywriting event had been announced on WNEW-FM, which had been playing John's music all day, along with that of birthday boys John Entwistle and Jackson Browne.

Helen showed up with Sean, and when he leaned over the side of the roof the crowd on the street began serenading him. Afterward some of the fans shouted, "Where's John?"

"He can't come," Sean yelled back. "He's sleeping!"

Soon a small plane appeared over Central Park emitting short bursts of smoke spelling: "HAPPY BIRTHDAY JOHN AND SEAN. LOVE YOKO."

I took some photos and played with Sean until 4:30 P.M., when we were summoned to the kitchen for the "inside event." Yoko sat at the butcher-block table, glued to the phone. There was a large cake and a basket with fruit and candy on the table. John showed up wearing a blue denim shirt and a day's growth of beard. He looked tired and scruffy as he donned a hat Helen had fashioned from a brown paper bag. The figure "40" was written on it in orange tape. I took some photos as John and Sean blew out the candles on their birthday cake. Then John stood behind Sean and guided his son's hand as he cut the cake. Finally, Sean opened his gifts, mostly videotapes of cartoons John had asked me to buy. When the birthday party was over, John suggested I take a big basket of candy and some balloons to the fans downstairs.

Friday, October 10, was my twenty-eighth birthday. A friend who produced plays presented me with a black T-shirt with the words "SYCOPHANT SLAVE" emblazoned in white letters. I wore it to the recording studio, where I was presented with a bottle of champagne and a giant birthday card from the Hit Factory staff. There was little else to do except kill time, as the session was once again at a near-standstill due to equipment problems. John was so angry and frustrated that he made everyone around him nervous. I spent the evening partying on the fifth floor with the Hit Factory's pretty secretaries, one of whom had a prescription for Quaaludes.

Saturday afternoon, Yoko called me at home to complain that John had been embarrassed by my "SYCOPHANT SLAVE" T-shirt. She asked me not to wear it anymore. Next, she instructed me to deliver a copy of her book, *Grapefruit*, to David Geffen. She was concerned that Geffen did not take her seriously as an artist and she wanted to impress on him the fact that she was not just a singer-songwriter, but also a published author. I stopped by Geffen's Fifth Avenue apartment on my way to the Hit Factory. When I handed him Yoko's book, he looked puzzled. "I hope I won't be quizzed on this," he then joked wearily.

On Sunday, I went out to an after-hours club with my friend Victoria, a photographer I had met the previous year and dated off and on (mostly off, given my schedule). Victoria had made up my face with black eye-liner and mascara. We stayed out all night. The next day was John and Sean's official birthday party at Tavern on the Green; John turned forty, and Sean five. Guests included Sean's classmates from kindergarten, his playmates and their parents, including Kay LeRoy and Marnie Hair, and friends such as Loraine and Peter Boyle. At one point during the party John sidled up to me and said, "Love your eye makeup, honey!" Meanwhile, Peter Boyle, who was taking photos, told Marnie Hair he would pay her ten dollars if she would kiss John.

"Here's a picture that's worth a lot more," John said. He then kissed me on the mouth.

Stunned and embarrassed, I returned to the Hit Factory, where Lee DeCarlo and Jon Smith were making some last-minute adjustments in the final mix of the album. Yoko had asked me to set up a sound system at Tavern on the Green so that she could play their album at the party, but by the time I returned to the restaurant with a cassette copy of *Double Fantasy*, the party was over and the Lennons had gone back to the Dakota.

The next morning, Tuesday, October 14, DePalma informed me that Villa Undercliff was ours for two weeks, at a cost of nine-thousand dollars, and that I was booked on a flight to Bermuda the following day. Rich then handed me five-thousand dollars in cash and said that John and Yoko would join me in Fairylands in a few days. I was glad to get away. I had been averaging four hours of sleep each night, and I was thoroughly exhausted. I spent the first few days at Undercliff sleeping and lying in the sun. On Monday, October 20, Rich called to say that the Lennons had finally completed work on *Double Fantasy*, but that there was no indication they were going to join me in Bermuda. I had the house to myself.

When I returned to New York on October 30, Yoko played me a test pressing of *Double Fantasy* and complained that Warner Brothers was pressuring her to choose a photo for the album cover. She simply could not make up her mind about which photo to put on the cover of the album.

"That's no good," Yoko would say time and again. "I look fine, but John doesn't look good." Or, "John looks okay, but I don't look so good."

Faced with Yoko's procrastination, the record company simply used the same cover as the single, a black and white shot of John and Yoko kissing. The back cover showed John and Yoko standing grim-faced on the corner of Central Park West and Seventy-second Street. Both photos had been taken by the Japanese photographer Kishin Shinoyama, who was famous for taking the last photos of Yukio Mishima. (John referred to this prominent Japanese novelist who committed hara-kiri after a failed coup attempt as "that kamikaze writer.")

Friday, November 14, *Double Fantasy* was shipped to reviewers and radio stations around the country. John eagerly scanned the local rock stations and monitored the album's airplay. Meanwhile, Yoko began complaining that Geffen had released the "wrong" version of her song "Beautiful Boys," and she ordered me to go around to all the local radio stations and repossess the promotional copies of the album. When I mentioned this to John, he looked at me with an incredulous expression. Then he rang Yoko on the intercom. "Are you out of your fuckin' mind?" he screamed. "You can't send Fred out there to take back the album. We'll be the laughingstock of the music industry!"

By late November, reviews of the album began to trickle into the office. Yoko was dismayed that most were negative and asked me to find some "positive" reviews to show John. She hoped that the British press might be kinder than the American media, but sadly, the British reviews were particularly scathing. The album was dismissed as self-indulgent, irrelevant, and worse. The European press in general did not welcome John and Yoko's return to the music scene. Offsetting the bad press were a handful of glowing write-ups by several leading music critics, including the *New York Times*'s Robert Palmer and the *Los Angeles Times*'s Robert Hilburn.

Yoko's favorite reviews seemed to be those that praised her while dismissing John—for instance, one by Roy Trakin that appeared in the November 24 issue of the *Daily News*: " . . . Whoever imagined that Japanese lyrics delivered with Yoko's 'she-was-there-long-before-Lene Lovich' vocals could so overshadow John's flabby, sentimental bit of vamping Elvis-isms?"

John was understandably anxious about the lukewarm reviews, but he was even more concerned about album sales. David Geffen had called a few days after the album was released with the reassuring news that *Double Fantasy* was "exploding all over," record-company parlance that meant sales were brisk. Now the big question was whether it would reach the top of the record charts. It was my job to call Geffen-Warners several times a week to learn how the album and the single were advancing.

Yoko, meanwhile, was preoccupied with preparations for a film session scheduled for the last week of November. I first became aware of her plans to produce some kind of promotional film when she instructed me to find a movie she and John made in 1968, titled *Two Virgins*. She told me she planned to use some of the old film footage in conjunction with fresh footage of her and John making love, and she ordered me to keep John in the dark about the planned film. She had hired Ethan Russell—a photographer and filmmaker who had taken still photos of the Lennons during the *Let It Be* sessions in 1969—to direct the film. After numerous delays and postponements, the mysterious shoot finally took place on Wednesday, November 26.

"What's happening?" John inquired anxiously that morning. "Are there a lot of guys with camera running around downstairs?" He told me that Yoko was being so secretive about the shoot that he had given up asking her about it. He anxiously awaited his marching orders while sequestered in the bedroom. Yoko eventually instructed me to tell him that he should come down at 1:30 P.M.

John showed up at the appointed time, wearing blue jeans, a gray turtleneck sweater, and a gray plastic overcoat. He and Yoko left the office accompanied by Ethan Russell and Allan Tannenbaum, a photographer who had taken some photos of Yoko the previous week for a cover article in the *SoHo News*. On her way out, Yoko told me to drive to the Sperone Gallery in SoHo, where the shoot would continue later in the afternoon. I went there with Jerry Caron, who had spent the day rummaging through various closets and storage chests in Apartments 71 and 72 searching for quilts and kimonos Yoko planned to use.

The Sperone Gallery was a spacious loft on the second floor of a dilapidated building on Greene Street. A dozen people were setting up cameras and lights under the supervision of Ethan Russell's production assistant, Jamie Lubarr. An oversized white bed stood in the middle of the gallery. A fake white staircase was propped against a wall and appeared to recede into it. Two sets of venetian blinds were drawn over fake window frames illuminated by floodlights, creating the illusion of sunshine streaming in.

I checked in with Rich at the office. He asked me to pick up one of

John's compact stereo systems and an additional prop for the film, a plastic stand with a banana on it. When I returned to the gallery, the Lennons were standing around impatiently, wearing colorful kimonos. A young assistant walked around the loft with a bucket of incense that emitted thick white smoke. Finally, at 7:00 P.M., Russell commanded, "Action!" and the filming began. John and Yoko approached the bed and circled it slowly. Suddenly, Yoko removed her kimono and stood stark naked by the bed. John stared at her with an astonished expression on his face. Regaining his composure, he pointed at Yoko's large breasts and said sheepishly: "Tits!"

"Come on, my dear, you too!" Yoko said, prodding John to take off his kimono as well.

Reluctantly, John complied. The stripping scene was repeated four times.

The next shot featured John and Yoko embracing naked on the bed. Yoko ordered John to get on top of her, a position he held for a half hour while Yoko conferred with Russell about camera angles and other cinematic details. Meanwhile, Allan Tannenbaum circled the bed, taking photos with numerous cameras. A small transistor radio was positioned on a stool near the bed. Among the songs that it played were "Woman" and "Starting Over," providing an eerie sound track for this bizarre film session.

At 9:00 P.M. the crew took a dinner break and the Lennons put their kimonos back on. Yoko asked me to set up the compact stereo system and cue a tape of *Double Fantasy* to "Kiss Kiss Kiss." When filming resumed, the Lennons disrobed again and I blasted Yoko's song at loud volume. Yoko mouthed the lyrics and feigned orgasm as John dry-humped her with grim determination. Between takes, Caron held a mirror in front of Yoko while Toshi, armed with a bucket of ice water, wiped the sweat from her forehead. By 11:00 P.M. it was all over. John and Yoko posed briefly for a few photos with the film crew, and then make a quick exit. The crew stayed behind for a wine and cheese party.

By early December, "Kiss Kiss Kiss" was "bubbling under" the Top 100 in *Billboard*'s Disco Chart, and Yoko was determined to finally establish herself as a rock star in her own right. On December 3, the *SoHo News* featured Yoko on its cover with a headline caption announcing: "YOKO ONLY." The article inside, written by the paper's music editor, Peter Ochiogrosso, began: "Like many people, I used to hate Yoko Ono." The writer then described why he had grown to respect her. The article included an astonishing assertion by Yoko to the effect that she had kept her "experimental material" off *Double Fantasy* "so that John would have a better chance for a hit record."

That morning, I delivered two copies of the paper to the kitchen, where John and Yoko sat at the butcher-block table in nervous anticipation. "Give it to me first!" Yoko demanded. But before I could do so, John snatched both papers from my hand. He looked at the cover and laughed while Yoko sat there fuming. Then he handed her a copy and they both began to avidly read the article. John later told me that they loved the article and ordered me to buy one hundred copies of the newspaper.

By the end of the first week of December, John and Yoko were again working around the clock. Most mornings they would go to a screening room and work on Yoko's film. Later in the day they would meet Jack Douglas at the Record Plant and supervise the mixing of Yoko's song "Walking on Thin Ice," which was intended to launch her solo career as a rock and roll singer.

"Make sure you get some rest," John told me on Friday night. "Next week's going to be heavy."

I was so drained that by Monday morning I still had not caught up on my sleep, and I overslept. I was suffering not from simple fatigue but from prolonged exhaustion. My steady diet of drugs did not help. I did not know it at the time, but I was running myself very close to the edge.

13

Helter Skelter

Monday afternoon, December 8, Studio One was jammed with people. Aside from the usual faces, there was an RKO Radio crew waiting to interview John and Yoko. Having forgotten all about the appointment, Yoko was upstairs and had left word that she was not to be disturbed. When she finally came down and saw all the strange faces, she was taken aback.

"What's going on?" she asked.

I reminded her of the interview.

"Oh, yes, of course," Yoko giggled. She entered the inner sanctum, followed by the RKO team, who after removing their shoes went in single file, like supplicants to the altar.

When John came down, I was surprised to see that he had his hair cut. The hair was cut short in front, almost forming little bangs, and in back it had been left to curl around behind his ears. John looked over the mail briefly, stopping to examine a card from David Peel, who said he was writing a biography of John and wanted him to check its accuracy. John seemed amused by Peel's request. Shaking his head, he threw the card back on my desk and then went into Yoko's office to join the interview.

Then Doug MacDougall called to confirm an appointment with Yoko for the next day to discuss security arrangements. The bodyguard had been on a leave of absence since late September, when Yoko had brushed off his suggestions for beefing up security. I told the bodyguard that as far as I knew, he was still on for the next day, Tuesday, December 9.

At about 5:00 P.M. John and Yoko emerged with the RKO people, and because the Lennons' car had not arrived yet, they accepted a ride in a limousine rented by the radio crew. I walked out to see them off. If any one of us had forgotten what John Lennon had once been, all we had to do was to step outside the Dakota in those days. A radio was blasting "The Ballad of John and Yoko" on WBAI, which was rebroadcasting an old interview with the Lennons. The fans outside clapped and sang along, blocking traffic, as John came out of the building.

A chubby kid wearing spectacles approached John and held out a copy of *Double Fantasy*.

"Do you want me to sign this?" John asked impatiently. Grinning expectantly, the fan nodded.

John grabbed the album and quickly autographed it. Paul Goresh, the amateur photographer who had sneaked into John's bedroom the previous year, snapped a picture of John with his head bent, scribbling. The fan took back the album and kept his eyes on John as he walked quickly to the waiting limousine. The crowd parted to let it pass, and the black car sped off toward Columbus Avenue, leaving an excited gaggle of fans crowding the sidewalk in front of the building.

Back in the office, I went over the mail and added up some receipts for my expense account. Around 6:00 P.M. John called from the Record Plant, asking me to bring some tapes from a recording session Yoko had done in the early seventies. He told me that Yoko thought the tapes might be in a kitchen cupboard.

I was glad for an excuse to leave. Studio One at sundown could be gloomy.

It took me a while, but I finally located a cardboard box containing the old tapes. On my way to the Mayfair garage, Goresh came up to me in front of the Dakota and introduced me to the guy whose album John had signed earlier.

"This is Dave Chapman," Goresh said. "He came all the way from Hawaii for an autograph. He really scored!" Chapman was clutching his signed copy of *Double Fantasy*. He looked vacant, his eyeglasses reflecting the streetlights.

"Congratulations, man," I said, hurrying off to get the Mercedes.

In front of the elevator at the Record Plant I ran into David Geffen, who had been summoned urgently to the studio.

"You know," Geffen said wearily as the elevator made its way to the tenth floor, "Yoko's a tough customer. One never knows what's really on her mind."

"Yeah, she sure knows how to keep people guessing," I said. "She's a Zen businesswoman."

As we walked into the studio, John gave a thumbs-up signal to Jack Douglas, and "Walking on Thin Ice" began blasting over the giant speakers. It had been remixed with layer upon layer of guitar textures—riffs, chords, overtones, feedback, and echoes that added up to an irresistible whirlpool of sound. And floating on top of this mesmerizing sonic barrage was Yoko's voice, talking, chanting, screaming, and even making retching sounds. It was an amazing piece of music. The studio shook with the pounding beat, and pretty soon Geffen, John, and Jack were bobbing their heads. When it ended, everyone looked around, and John was grinning. Even Yoko smiled. It was the best thing she had ever recorded, and she knew it.

"Isn't it fantastic?" John bubbled. "Let's release it right away!"

"Yes, let's put it out before Christmas!" Yoko gushed.

Geffen frowned and shook his head. "It's impossible to release a single on such short notice," he said firmly.

"David," Yoko bellowed, "you're just being negative!"

Geffen finally left the argument at an impasse, saying he would see what could be done.

They were going to tinker with the song a bit more and look for a B-side in the box of outtakes I had brought with me, songs recorded by Yoko with guitarist David Spinozza in 1974. I took my leave to pick up Victoria.

We went to the St. Marks Cinema to see *The Idolmaker*, a film about the rise and fall of a rock star. When it ended, a little after 11:00 P.M., we walked south on Second Avenue. As we passed a newsstand on the corner of St. Marks Place and Second Avenue, I noticed a long-haired young man holding up a copy of the *SoHo News*, with its cover photo of Yoko and the bold banner headline: "YOKO ONLY."

The hippie stared at the cover. Tears were streaming down his cheeks. He was shaking his head and looked upset. Usually, I would not think of walking up to a stranger on the street in Manhattan and asking him what was the matter, but I went right up to this guy and said, "What's wrong?" He pointed to the *SoHo News* cover and mumbled, "Isn't it ironic, now that John's been shot?"

"What do you mean, *shot?*" I gasped.

"They shot John in front of the Dakota just a short while ago," said the hippie softly, placing a hand in front of his face.

Surely the guy had to be hallucinating, I thought, as my heart began to pound madly. I ran to the nearest phone booth and dialed the Dakota. The line was busy. I tried another extension. It, too, was busy. All the lines were busy—Yoko's private line, John's private line, all the desk lines. Finally, I took out my phone book and tried to think of who else I could call. I dialed Rich DePalma's home number. His wife, Debbie, answered. I did not have to ask.

"Fred, I'm so sorry!" she cried. She told me that John had been taken to Roosevelt Hospital, where he had been pronounced dead. Rich had been at the hospital with Yoko, who was unharmed. Now everyone was back at the Dakota, and Debbie urged me to get there as fast as possible. Stunned, I hung up the phone and stood there frozen with disbelief.

Reflexively, Victoria hailed a taxi. The car's radio confirmed the grim news of John's death. Victoria and I held each other tight in the back of the cab, and she whispered comforting words. But it was no use. Something gave way in my middle, and the streets and people and cars around me, even Victoria, seemed to fold inward and slip away. I felt isolated, afraid, overwhelmed by a growing sense of dread. It was like being in an elevator cut loose at the top—falling, and not knowing when you will hit.

As we approached the corner of Central Park West and Seventy-second Street, I could see that a massive crowd of people had gathered in front of the building, some of them singing "Give Peace a Chance," most of them crying. There were flowers and pictures of John, photos and crude drawings, like effigies in a South American funeral procession, and I thought of John talking about Mayan culture, about where you go when you die, about coming back after learning your lessons. I wondered where he was.

When I finally waded through the crowds of weeping, singing fans and got past the ring of cops that had been deployed in front of the Dakota, I found Rich in Studio One. He was answering the phone, a model of efficiency and professionalism. Wordless and grim, I faced Rich and searched his face for some sign of distress. I saw none. I immediately got the sense that business was the order of the day. Sam

Havadtoy was there, nervously pacing the floor, complaining that Yoko would not see him. Rich told me that Yoko was in the kitchen with the detectives who were investigating John's murder, and that Helen and Sean were upstairs asleep. They had returned earlier in the evening after a trip to Helen's daughter's house in Pennsylvania, and were blissfully unaware of the tragedy. Rich informed me that Yoko had left instructions that Sean should not be told of his father's death because she wanted to tell him herself later, when she was "strong enough."

I took the service elevator to the seventh floor and let myself into the kitchen. Yoko sat on one of the couches, flanked by Geffen and a homicide detective, who was gently asking her questions. Yoko buried her face in her hands and said, "The shock is too great . . . I can't . . . I can't do this right now." Her face was an impenetrable mask, and I wondered if she was feeling what I was feeling. I sat by the door and said nothing. The plaintive sounds of those singing John's songs could be heard drifting up from the street. I felt like I was hallucinating. At one point, Helen came into the room and recoiled with surprise at the sight of the many grim faces. I could not bring myself to tell her that John had been shot. Eventually, someone else did.

When the detectives left, Yoko turned to me and asked: "Is Sam downstairs?" I think I jumped. It was like watching a movie and having one of the characters speak to you. I nodded. Yoko asked me to send him up. I hurried out. When I told Havadtoy that he was wanted upstairs, he lunged for the elevator as if his life depended on it.

I sat down and wanted to help Rich answer the phones, but I was too dazed and upset to function. I turned on the radio on my desk. Nothing but Lennon was playing. I heard John ask, "How Do You Sleep?" and I felt that sharp, inner pain again, a suffocating sense of grief and cold fury. I could feel all control slipping away from me, and I went into Yoko's bathroom to cry. After a few minutes, Rich came in and said, "You better pull yourself together, man, or else you're through here!"

I was hurt and angered by Rich's rebuke. I could not believe the period of mourning was already over. In fact, it had never even started. When I returned to my desk, I noticed that the radio had been turned off. I turned it back on so that John's music would be playing in Studio One—to be listening to his music then was the only thing that seemed right.

At around 3:30 A.M., Geffen came down with a statement from Yoko soliciting donations from the fans and directing them to send their contributions to the Spirit Foundation, a not-for-profit organization that had been set up hastily by Yoko's lawyers. He read the statement to the *Times*, and then Rich called the other daily papers and the wire services and did the same. I went back upstairs and found Yoko still sitting in the same spot in the kitchen, with her head bowed as if in silent prayer. I did not know what to say or do; so I sat by the door, waiting. After a few minutes Yoko got up and said she was going to the bedroom. I stood up and followed her.

"Don't worry," she said. "It's going to be all right. You should get some rest."

I did not know what she was talking about. What was going to be all right? What rest? Perhaps Yoko had made a remarkably quick recovery. But I knew that I was not going to rest for quite some time, and that nothing would ever be all right again—not this week, not this month, not ever.

I went to the White Room and set up the Sony radio-cassette player John and I had bought in Bermuda. I tuned in one of the rock stations and "#9 Dream" came on. I felt as if John were speaking directly to me, and I sat down and cried. As I listened to John's music, a piercing sorrow welled up. I found myself thinking back to the countless conversations about death I had had with John over the past two years. I remembered vividly one particular talk in Bermuda the previous summer in which John had told me that deep down he was an extremely violent man, and that he believed it was his destiny to meet with a violent death. I had often been mystified by the morbid streak in John's personality. Now, as I brooded over John's obsession with death, I wondered if perhaps he had had some kind of premonition. I could imagine John saying, as he had so many times before: "There are no accidents!"

Stunned with grief and gripped by morbid thoughts and emotions, I struggled to regain my composure. I stood up and went out on the wrought-iron balcony outside the White Room. I breathed the icy winter air, hoping that it would help clear my head. Although it was 4:00 A.M., there were still at least a thousand people on the street below, hanging out, singing Beatles music intertwined with John's songs, drinking beer, and smoking pot.

Two police cars positioned themselves in front of the driveway, but no attempt was made to disperse the crowd. Speakers had been set up, and when "Dear Yoko" came on, everyone began singing along. A bizarre, festive atmosphere prevailed, as if John had just *arrived* among the fans, not left them. Down below, someone climbed onto the hood of a police car. The cops made quick work of him. Kids clustered on both sides of the cars. A tense, volatile standoff ensued between the police and the fans. At about 4:15 A.M., the police decided to clear the front of the building and move the fans to the sidewalk across the street. It would not have surprised me if there had been a riot. The crowd quickly regrouped and continued its boisterous vigil.

I went back to the office and found Rich, Havadtoy, Mike Tree, and Doug waiting there. Doug had just arrived. He looked grim.

"The front of the building should be cleared," the bodyguard fumed. "After all, it's the fuckin' fans that got him!"

I told Doug that the cops had managed to move the fans, but his anger and frustration remained palpable. I could imagine how Doug felt. For months he had been badgering Yoko to let him beef up security. If he felt half as useless as I felt, there was no word to describe it. We were all here, working, getting paid. Yet no one had been guarding the king. We had all failed at the one thing we might actually have done for John. I remembered a guy in a Bermuda disco recognizing John and asking me, "What do you do?"

Trying to be cute, I had said glibly, "Keep him out of trouble."

Rich suggested that I stay up in the White Room and look in on Yoko every half hour or so. He seemed worried that she might try to take her life in a fit of despair. I dutifully went back upstairs. When I opened the bedroom door to peek in, I found Yoko on the phone. She did not even look up. I went back to the White Room. The phone was ringing. I answered it. It was Yoko's sister, Setsuko, saying she was coming the next day—or perhaps she meant that day; I had lost track of time. Yoko's mother was coming, too, she said, and her brother as well. Yoko should call them if she did not wish them to come, she said. A little while later Rich buzzed, and I gave him Setsuko's message.

"Fuck Setsuko!" he snapped.

It seemed Yoko had been trying to discourage her relatives from coming to New York, but they kept calling and insisted on flying in anyway.

"Look in on Yoko again, will ya?" Rich asked. It was 5:00 A.M.

I crept into the bedroom once more. Yoko was lying in bed with her eyes closed and the covers pulled up to her neck, the phone dangling near her arm. Slowly, she opened an eye and muttered, "I'm trying to sleep, but the fans are making too much noise. It's terrible, all the noise. Why don't they stop? Can't you do something?" At that moment, I felt tremendous sympathy for Yoko, and in an uncontrollable wave of emotion, I went over to her and tried to hug her. She remained stiff, impassive. It was an awkward, embarrassing moment. When it passed, I stood there wondering what to do.

"If Sean wakes up," Yoko said, "it's okay to bring him into the bedroom, but don't wake him if he's sleeping." I went out and stood in the corridor outside Sean's room. I could hear him coughing in his sleep, and I pushed his door open and looked in. He was sound asleep next to my aunt. Remembering what Yoko had said about the noise, I went downstairs to talk to the fans.

José Perdomo, the friendly, white-haired Cuban doorman who had been on duty when John was shot, stood solemnly before a wall of flowers, banners, ribbons, paper decorations, and images of John that hung on the Dakota gates. I commiserated with José, who had always liked and admired John. The normally jovial doorman was devastated by John's death. He found it incomprehensible that Chapman, with whom he had had a friendly rapport in the hours before the murder, had committed such a brutal and senseless crime. José adamantly rejected the notion that Chapman was simply a crazed fan who went over the top. "Chapman not crazy!" José kept saying.

I told a short, bearded Brazilian, who seemed to be leading the crowd in its chants, that Yoko was trying to sleep and asked if he could tell the crowd to keep it down. He said he would, and there was a brief interlude in which the fans kept a nearly silent vigil, playing their radios softly, holding their lighted candles, passing joints, and drinking beer in the chill air. But as soon as the sun began coming up, the chanting resumed as more people gathered on the street. Back upstairs, I looked in on Yoko again. She was on the phone. I resumed my vigil in the White Room.

When I went to the kitchen to get some coffee, I found Elliot Mintz there. He had just flown in from L.A. and could hardly wait to go into action. He talked excitedly about his experience in "crisis management," boasting that he had been Sal Mineo's friend for thirteen years and that when Mineo had been killed, he had been there to take care of business. At about 7:00 A.M. Yoko came into the kitchen, said hello to Mintz, and made some tea. Then she sat on the couch and put her head in her hands. Mintz went over to her and patted her on the back. "Don't worry, Yoko, it's going to be all right," he said. "We'll take care of you."

Havadtoy buzzed from downstairs, saying that Julian was on the phone.

"I suppose he'll want to come," Yoko said wearily, as she put Elliot on to make the arrangements. "Tell him it's all right if he wants to come. But I don't know what we'll do about Cynthia."

She sipped some tea and then went back to the bedroom, where she met with Havadtoy and Mintz, who helped her draft a statement in response to the media's frantic inquiries regarding John's funeral. Helen and Sean showed up for breakfast, and I realized with a jolt of horror that no one had told Sean. He was very quiet. Maybe he guessed that something terrible had happened. In any case, this normally inquisitive little boy never asked what was going on.

I went downstairs again. Studio One, it seemed, was back to normal. The phones were ringing off the hook with calls, mostly from people wanting to know where the funeral would be and how Yoko was holding up. Press. Fans. Old friends. Jerry Rubin called to say he was heartbroken. Abbie Hoffman called to say that he was good under pressure and would be glad to help. Jack Douglas called offering assistance. May Pang called to offer condolences. There was even a telegram from Yoko's estranged teenage daughter, Kyoko.

By 9:00 A.M. Yoko was dressed and ready for business. There were more meetings with Havadtoy, Mintz, and Geffen. I was asked to type up an announcement. It read:

THERE IS NO FUNERAL FOR JOHN. LATER IN THE WEEK WE WILL SET THE TIME FOR A SILENT VIGIL TO PRAY FOR HIS SOUL. WE INVITE YOU TO PARTIC-IPATE FROM WHEREVER YOU ARE AT THE TIME. WE THANK YOU FOR MANY FLOWERS SENT TO JOHN. BUT IN THE FUTURE, INSTEAD OF FLOWERS, PLEASE CONSIDER SENDING DONATIONS IN HIS

NAME TO THE SPIRIT FOUNDATION, INC., WHICH IS JOHN'S PERSONAL CHARITABLE FOUNDATION. HE WOULD HAVE APPRECIATED IT VERY MUCH. JOHN LOVED AND PRAYED FOR THE HUMAN RACE. PLEASE PRAY THE SAME FOR HIM. LOVE, Yoko & Sean.

At about 10:00 A.M. Ringo Starr showed up with his wife, Barbara Bach. Looking dazed and bewildered, they went upstairs to play with Sean. Suddenly, I remembered that about a year earlier Ringo had visited the Dakota, dressed all in black and looking gravely ill. He and John had posed for a Polaroid photo in the kitchen, John with a self-confident smirk and Ringo with a fierce frown; John's youthful image had stood in marked contrast to Ringo's ghastly appearance. Later, John told me that Ringo had had several feet of intestine removed and nearly died during the complicated surgery. And now John was gone and Ringo was going to comfort Sean, who had not even been told of his Daddy's death. It seemed beyond comprehension.

When they came back down, Mintz and I led them out of the building. Ringo was mobbed by fans. They tried to touch him, to grab his clothes, his hair. It was like Beatlemania all over again. Poor Ringo was like an animal caught in a trap, and we were powerless to stop the hordes if they really decided to take him from us.

Back in the office, Yoko asked me to find John's last will and testament in the files. She was meeting with her lawyers and accountants in the inner sanctum. During the long meeting, she kept buzzing the outer office with requests for caviar—I sent a messenger out to buy an ounce of Beluga Gold at the Caviarteria—and chocolate cake from Mrs. Grimble's.

Meanwhile, Sean developed a fever. I spoke to Helen, who was extremely worried about him and wanted to have a word with Yoko. But Yoko said she was too busy to talk to Helen, and gave no indication of when she planned to talk to her son. Helen found the situation maddening.

At 6:00 P.M., Doug and I left to meet Julian at Kennedy Airport. Doug cheerfully showed me a big revolver in his coat, lest there be any doubts about Julian's safety. It began to rain as Doug and I pushed our way through the curious crowd and went out to meet the car that would take us to the airport. I fantasized Doug pulling out his revolver and nailing a couple of fans as we went. It was hideous—I could not control my imagination anymore. I could see John's body, bones cracking as he went down on his own front steps. I could see him dancing in the Bermuda sun swaying his skinny frame to the reggae sound of Bob Marley and the Wailers. I wanted to cry again, but I did not. Doug chatted merrily during the long ride to the airport, trying to cheer me up.

"The body'll be cremated tomorrow," he said. "I've made all the arrangements."

John's remains would be taken in a bodybag from the morgue to the Frank E. Campbell funeral chapel at Madison Avenue and Eighty-first Street. From there it would go to the Ferncliff Mortuary in Hartsdale, New York. Doug next described his elaborate plan for thwarting the media's attempts to learn the location of John's cremation. He had arranged for several decoy hearses to leave the funeral home in order to befuddle the press. I admired Doug's efficiency.

Julian arrived at 9:30 P.M., wearing a leather jacket and jeans, his hair long, looking so much like John that I could feel my insides start to jump around again. We walked to the car, tense, silent, and I said how sorry I was. It sounded stupid, but I did not know what else to say. Julian said he could not cry anymore—he had cried his heart out on the plane and had run out of tears. Now he was just smoking one cigarette after another. He was calm and resigned. He told me that he had awakened in the middle of the night when his chimney collapsed, leaving a hole in his roof. He had had a terrible sense of foreboding. His mother was away, and his stepfather, John Twist, knew about John being shot but was reluctant to give him the tragic news. When Julian finally emerged from his room, he saw the journalists outside the house, and he knew that his premonition was true. Finally, his stepfather confirmed the tragic news.

"How's Sean handling it?" asked Julian.

I told him that Sean had a fever. I felt odd about telling him that Sean did not know. Or perhaps Sean, too, knew it intuitively, without having to be told.

"Do they know the guy who did it?" Julian asked, his voice sounding pained and angry. "Do they know why?" I told him about Chapman, whose motive for shooting John remained a mystery.

"I hope Dad didn't suffer much," Julian said, and fell silent again. We watched the river of red taillights snaking along the expressway.

After a while, he remarked, "Well, I guess it's better dying like that than in a nuclear war." We agreed John had died a noble death.

At the Dakota, Julian was mobbed by fans and disappeared in a firestorm of flash strobes, screams, and general pandemonium. Julian screamed back, frightened and confused, his hands going up to his face to protect himself, as if he had been dropped into a pit of cobras. Doug shouldered into the mob, putting his linebacker body out front, and Julian and I threw ourselves through a hole in the crowd and ran into the basement of the Dakota. We stood there for a moment, trying to recover our breath, and then took the service elevator to Apartment 72. We went to the White Room and stood on the balcony to watch the amazing scene below. Both sides of the street were covered with litter, flowers, paper, beer cans, trash. The police had set up barricades now. Beyond the blue sawhorses, the crowd surged, forming and reforming, then surged again.

Julian and I went to the kitchen, where we found Helen. She embraced Julian. Mintz showed up and told him, "My lawyer is at your disposal." Julian looked bewildered. Flustered, Mintz added, "Should you have any questions."

Julian asked where Yoko was and how she was holding up. I assured him Yoko was doing fine.

At that very moment she was, in fact, having dinner at a restaurant in Harlem with David Geffen and Calvin Klein. The dinner party returned later that night, and Geffen hung around in the office with Rich, Doug, Havadtoy, and David Warmflash, one of Yoko's lawyers. Geffen and Warmflash busied themselves talking about record sales. There was something eerily festive about their demeanor. Geffen spoke proudly of his career, about all the people he had managed, all the money he was going to make. It seemed that he had taken out a $1 million life insurance policy on John, an amount equal to the advance he paid Yoko for the right to release *Double Fantasy*.

A little before midnight Tuesday I exited the Dakota through the basement, which was filled with flowers sent by fans, and went home. Numb with grief and exhaustion, I collapsed on my bed fully clothed, listening to John on the radio, crying my heart out. Around dawn I drifted into turbulent sleep. I awoke at noon, rising from the lower depths with a sense of infinite sadness and dread, but with no memory of any dream save John's disembodied voice whispering insistently: "There are no accidents." I dragged myself into the shower. I will mourn later, I said to myself. There is work to be done.

I stopped by a newsstand. John's death still dominated the front pages of most newspapers, giving the lie to my hope that yesterday and the day before had been a bad dream. I could not help thinking that John would have been pleased by the universal coverage his death had occasioned. It was the biggest news event of the year, perhaps even of the entire decade. All along Seventy-second Street vendors were hawking John Lennon buttons, photos, and other commemorative trinkets.

Dazed and disoriented by it all, I raced to Studio One, where I found Geffen sitting at my desk, talking on the phone to the West Coast, saying, "Business is booming!" Geffen had hit the jackpot, and he made no effort to hide his satisfaction. Indeed, Double Fantasy had already sold over a million copies and was selling at an unprecedented rate all over the world.

I brought Yoko the morning papers. She was in the kitchen having lunch with Sean, Julian, Helen, and Havadtoy. As I entered, she joked that I reminded her of a dead rock star. "You know," she said, "the one who died in the plane crash."

After a few awkward moments I guessed: "Buddy Holly?"

"Yes," Yoko chirped, "that's the one!"

I must be hallucinating, I thought, staring at her with disbelief. I went down to the office again. To perform the most routine tasks—answering the phones, sorting the mail—required a great effort.

That afternoon, Doug had picked up John's body and took it to be cremated at the Ferncliff Mortuary. At 3:40 P.M. Mike Tree buzzed me from upstairs to say that Yoko wanted me to call Doug and stop the cremation because Sean wanted to see his daddy one last time. When I got a hold of Doug at the crematorium and relayed the message, the bodyguard groaned. "It's too late, kid," he said sadly. "The body's been in the oven for two hours."

Next, Yoko drafted a new statement for the media, announcing a "silent vigil" in lieu of a funeral for John:

I TOLD SEAN WHAT HAPPENED. I SHOWED HIM THE PICTURE OF HIS FATHER ON THE COVER OF THE PAPER AND EXPLAINED THE SITUATION. I TOOK SEAN TO THE SPOT WHERE JOHN LAY AFTER

HE WAS SHOT. SEAN WANTED TO KNOW WHY THE PERSON SHOT JOHN IF HE LIKED JOHN. I EX-PLAINED THAT HE WAS PROBABLY A CONFUSED PERSON. SEAN SAID WE SHOULD FIND OUT IF HE WAS CONFUSED OR IF HE HAD REALLY MEANT TO KILL JOHN. I SAID THAT WAS UP TO THE COURT. HE ASKED WHAT COURT—A TENNIS COURT OR A BAS-KETBALL COURT? THAT'S HOW SEAN USED TO TALK WITH HIS FATHER. THEY WERE BUDDIES. JOHN WOULD HAVE BEEN PROUD OF SEAN IF HE HAD HEARD THIS. SEAN CRIED LATER. HE ALSO SAID "NOW DADDY IS PART OF GOD. I GUESS WHEN YOU DIE YOU BECOME MUCH MORE BIGGER BE-CAUSE YOU'RE PART OF EVERYTHING." I DON'T HAVE MUCH MORE TO ADD TO SEAN'S STATE-MENT. THE SILENT VIGIL WILL TAKE PLACE DECEM-BER 14TH AT 2 P.M. FOR TEN MINUTES. OUR THOUGHTS WILL BE WITH YOU. Love, Yoko & Sean

At 9:00 P.M., Doug showed up with a big gift-wrapped box. I sat there at my desk, mystified, looking at him in the doorway.

"What's that?" I asked.

"That," said Doug with a grim smile, "was once the greatest rock musician in the world."

The bodyguard then described his day-long odyssey. Everything had gone according to plan. Doug noted that when he first picked up the body, John's face had looked relaxed. But just before the body slid into the oven, John's mouth had twisted into a pained, macabre grin, probably due to rigor mortis.

I felt nauseous. When I buzzed Yoko upstairs to let her know that Doug had brought John's ashes, she asked me to deliver the urn to the bedroom. I could not bring myself to do it, and a lawyer took the ashes upstairs instead.

A few minutes later, Yoko summoned me to the bedroom. She was sitting on the bed, talking on the phone. The urn was at the foot of the bed. She indicated that I should place John's ashes under the bed. I gritted my teeth and moved the urn. Trembling, and on the verge of tears, I then asked for a leave of absence. Yoko frowned and inter-rupted her phone conversation.

"These are difficult times for all of us," she said wearily. "Why don't you take a little break. Just don't do anything reckless."

As I turned to leave, she asked me to tell Warmflash to bring Julian and Sean to her. I went downstairs and gave the lawyer Yoko's message. Then I walked out, past the fans, past the images attached to the front gate, the flowers strewn in the street, past the coffee cups and the beer cans crushed by a thousand feet, the cops, cold, bored, mute, breathing fog into the chill, wet air, out of the dark looming Dakota that seemed to glower under the low sky like a gothic nightmare.

Afterword

Thursday, December 11, I woke up feeling lost, helpless, and overwhelmed by a growing sense of dread. I could see that far from being the grief-stricken widow she played for the media and for the detectives investigating John's murder, Yoko was determined to take advantage of this once-in-a-lifetime opportunity to forge a more positive public image and make money. Not wanting to be part of this campaign, I called Yoko and told her that I could no longer work for her. Yoko complained that I was behaving irrationally and needed a break from the pressure of working at the Dakota. She told me that she was sending Julian to Cold Spring Harbor and suggested that I accompany him. Julian and I spent a few tranquil days at Cannon Hill, where we watched the television coverage of the "silent vigil" for John that was held in Central Park on Sunday, December 14. Yoko released the following statement to the media:

BLESS YOU FOR YOUR TEARS AND PRAYERS
I SAW JOHN SMILING IN THE SKY
I SAW SORROW CHANGING INTO CLARITY
I SAW ALL OF US BECOMING ONE MIND
THANK YOU.

LOVE, Yoko

When Julian and I were ordered back to the Dakota, my heart was still heavy with sorrow, and I knew that unlike Yoko, for me there would be no quick recovery. I renewed my request to leave her employment.

Yoko adamantly insisted that I stay on until the summer of 1981. She told me that she needed me to help "spread John's legacy" and that if I abandoned her now, it would be like "deserting John." Yoko said she planned to make several music videos as well as record an entire album of her own music, using the same musicians who had worked on *Double Fantasy*. She made it very clear that she was counting on my support and that she would not take no for an answer. Filled with a constant sense of dread, I resumed my duties at the Dakota as if in a trance. Slowly, my feelings of grief turned into rage— at Yoko and the staff members, lawyers, accountants, psychics, and sycophants for whom John Lennon had already become a faint memory.

On the evening of December 23, Elliot Mintz asked me to help him find a letter of condolence from Bob Dylan that Yoko had misplaced. Although we did not find the letter, Mintz did come across in John's bedroom a familiar-looking New Yorker Diary. It was John's 1980 journal. Mintz said it was too sensitive a document to be left lying around the bedroom. He asked me to take the diary to Yoko in the office. When I showed Yoko the journal, she told me to file it with John's other writings. I was astonished by her apparent lack of interest in the diary. I also remembered the conversation I'd had with John in Bermuda five months earlier, when he told me that if anything happened to him he wanted me to see to it that Julian got his journals.

By January, 1981, Yoko was working frantically to finish a music video for "Woman," the second hit single from *Double Fantasy*. On Friday, January 16, she told me she planned to premiere the video on the BBC's Top of the Pops television program and that she was sending me to England the next day. I was to deliver her video to the BBC and also pay a visit to Julian in North Wales. Yoko was concerned that Julian and his mother, Cynthia, might challenge the provisions of John's will, which appointed Yoko executrix of John's estate and gave her complete control over a $30 million fortune. As I was the only person on her staff who was close to Julian, Yoko needed me to function as a "liaison." Later that day, Yoko asked me to find a cassette tape she had misplaced somewhere in Apartment 72. While searching for the tape in the bedroom, I came across an attaché case containing John's journals for 1974 to 1979.

I decided to deliver the diaries to Julian in England. It would be the last thing I would do for John. There was no doubt in my mind and in my heart that it had been John's wish that his oldest son should have his journals. I also knew that Yoko would strongly disapprove, and therefore I did not ask her permission. She had made it very clear that she did not want the boy to have any of his father's things. She had even countermanded John's instructions to send Julian a copy of his Bermuda demo songs because, she said, she thought the boy might sell them to a record bootlegger.

That evening after work, I walked out of the Dakota with the attaché case containing the Lennon diaries. I felt that I needed to talk to somebody, so I met with a close friend from college who worked for my uncle and discussed with him my decision to give Julian his father's journals. I had become friendly with this fellow six years earlier when I first began writing for CCNY's student newspaper. My friend had been one of the paper's better-known writers, specializing in provocative stream-of-consciousness articles, and I looked up to him. For several years we were also neighbors in Washington Heights. My friend offered to copy the journals overnight while I packed for my trip to London. I would then be able to return the journals to the Dakota in the morning, while keeping a set of copies for Julian. I trusted my friend completely, and gratefully accepted his help. I was shocked when he called me late that evening and announced his intention to use the Lennon diaries as material for a book that he thought he and I should collaborate on.

Stunned and alarmed by my friend's betrayal, I contacted Francis DeBilio, a Brooklyn Heights psychotherapist I initially consulted because I found myself unable to shake the suffocating grief and rage that had built up inside me since John's death. When I told DeBilio about my problem the therapist promised to help me recover the journals. He said that I needed a "troubleshooter," and he knew just the man—Norman Shoenfeld, a wealthy businessman and long-time patient of his. Although I had my doubts about this arrangement, I was desperate to recover John's journals and felt I needed all the help I could get. The alternative was to confess everything to Yoko and throw myself on her mercy. I could not bring myself to do this. I was afraid of how Yoko would react.

Thus, I went along with my therapist's plan, hoping that I would be able to return the journals to the Dakota. The therapist urged me to pay lip service to my friend's proposed collaboration on a Lennon book, and to drop a hint that I might be able to find us a backer. My friend swallowed the bait and demanded to meet this potential backer. Around Christmas, 1981, Shoenfeld told my friend that he was prepared to finance a book about John Lennon, and proposed to hire him as my co-author. Shoenfeld even offered to send my friend on an expenses-paid vacation to a Caribbean island of his choice— provided that he first turn over John's journals. My friend agreed. In January, 1982, shortly after I left Yoko's employment, he surrendered John's journals to Shoenfeld in exchange for a three-month employment contract plus three thousand dollars' spending money for his vacation.

Shoenfeld insisted on keeping the diaries for the time being, promising to figure out a way of returning them to Yoko through an intermediary. When I complained to DeBilio, the therapist said that he trusted Shoenfeld completely and that I should leave it to the businessman to find the best way to return the diaries to Yoko. I simply could not bring myself to contact Yoko myself and face the consequences of my actions. I kept hoping that somehow it would all work out and no harm would be done.

My friend had stashed away copies of the Lennon journals, and when he realized that he had been duped, he attempted to peddle the journals to *Rolling Stone* magazine. Its publisher, Jann Wenner, was friendly with Yoko and told her that he had been approached by someone offering to sell copies of Lennon's diaries. Yoko immediately put Elliot Mintz, her publicist and troubleshooter, on the case. It did not take Mintz long to track down my friend, who in order to get himself off the hook fingered me as the mastermind behind a conspiracy to publish a book based on the Lennon diaries, while also implicating DeBilio and Shoenfeld.

I now felt I had to explain my side of the story to Yoko. I called her at the Dakota in late August, 1981.

"How could you do this to me?" Yoko asked angrily.

I tried to explain that I planned to deliver John's journals to Julian because I firmly believed that was what John would have wanted. I assured Yoko that it had not been my intention to harm her, and that I deeply regretted the trouble I had caused. Yoko did not seem to be particularly receptive to my explanation. She turned over the phone to her chief of security, Dan Mahoney, a New York City police sergeant assigned to an undercover Career Criminal Apprehension Unit.

Mahoney said he wanted to meet with me in order to "straighten out this mess." He asked me to come to the Dakota. When I balked at his suggestion, he said he would meet me at DeBilio's apartment instead. (DeBilio, who had been diagnosed as having cancer of the prostate and had checked himself into a hospital in Boston on August 10, had asked me to move into his Remsen Street apartment and office space for the time being. On August 13, three days after I moved in, the apartment was burglarized. Among the items stolen were two of my journals covering the period of spring and summer of 1980. Luckily, I had made copies of my journals. Also taken were several slide trays containing photos I had taken of the Lennons, as well as Polaroid photos of John and me.)

Mahoney showed up in the company of Rich DePalma, who excused himself after a few minutes, saying that he had to go back to work. Then Mahoney informed me that Shoenfeld had returned John's journals to Yoko for a $60,000 finder's fee. However, Lennon's 1980 diary was not included among the journals that the businessman delivered to the Dakota. Shoenfeld had insisted that he knew nothing about the missing journal. Mahoney told me that the consensus at the Dakota was that I had John's 1980 diary. When I protested that I didn't have it, Mahoney told me that he thought I was bluffing and warned that if I did not "come clean," Sam Havadtoy was ready to "play hardball." Grinning menacingly, Yoko's security chief said: "I like you, Freddie, and I wouldn't want to see you get hurt."

A month after Dan Mahoney's visit I was abducted by Bob Greve and Barry Goldblatt, the two cops who moonlighted as Yoko's bodyguards. (Goldblatt, I later learned, was Dan Mahoney's partner in the NYPD's Career Criminal Apprehension Unit.) After beating me and pointing a gun to my head, Greve searched my pockets and took the keys to my apartment. Then he and Goldblatt drove me to the 20th Precinct station house on West 82nd Street, where I was met by a Detective Lt. Robert Gibbons.

When I told Gibbons angrily that I had been assaulted by two cops who worked privately as Yoko's bodyguards, he informed me that there was a warrant for my arrest, based on a complaint by Sam

Havadtoy. As for my being beaten, the detective told me that it was my word against the cops'. Next, Detective Gibbons said he wanted to have a look at my apartment, just to make sure that I did not have the diary or any of the things that Havadtoy said I had stolen from the Dakota—John's clothes, artwork, stereo equipment, and guitars. Gibbons said that he could get a search warrant, but that it would take time. He reminded me that Yoko's blond guard—who was sitting outside the detective's office—had the keys to my apartment, and raised the possibility that he might decide to search the apartment himself. I saw that I had little choice but to cooperate.

Around 3 A.M., Gibbons and two other detectives drove with me to my Brooklyn Heights studio. After filling several shopping bags with things they thought might belong to Yoko—such as John's shopping lists and other papers from my files; cassettes of John's music, including *Double Fantasy*; copies of Yoko's "Walking on Thin Ice" and "Woman" videotapes; and a framed drawing by Sean that had been given to me by John in 1979—the detectives took me back to the station house.

I was now told to sign a confession that had been written out on a yellow note pad, that said in effect that I had taken things from the Dakota without Yoko's approval. I told the detectives that the only things I had taken without approval were John's journals, which were back in Yoko's possession. The detectives said that they believed me, but insisted that I sign the handwritten scrap of paper anyway, so that they could finish their paperwork. They assured me that the wording would be changed in a subsequent version that they would type up later, and promised that as soon as I signed the statement I could go home. Exhausted from my ordeal, and frightened by the possibility of another attack by Yoko's guards, I once more agreed to cooperate. After I signed the statement, I was locked up overnight.

The next day, I was taken to Central Booking by a grim-faced detective, Bill Mulitz, who had been designated my official arresting officer. I had been in police custody for more than twelve hours, but my rights were never read to me. After being fingerprinted and booked, Mulitz took me to a room where Assistant District Attorney Consuelo Fernandez was waiting to interrogate me in front of a videotape camera, a method normally reserved for homicides. I attempted to tell my side of the story to Fernandez, explaining the bizarre circumstances surrounding the disappearance of Lennon's journals. However, as soon as I mentioned my abduction and beating by Yoko's guards who were also cops, Fernandez abruptly terminated the interrogation. After spending another night in jail I was finally arraigned on Wednesday afternoon, September 29. A preliminary hearing was set for October 28 and I was then released on my own recognizance.

I hired an attorney, John Esposito, who initiated a civil suit against Yoko, Havadtoy, and New York City in connection with my assault. In January, 1983, I filed a complaint with the police department's Internal Affairs unit as well as a notice of claim in State Supreme Court alleging assault, battery, harassment, false arrest, false imprisonment, kidnapping, intentional infliction of mental distress, illegal interrogation, illegal search and seizure, and violation of constitutional and civil rights at the hands of members of the New York Police Department. I retained the law firm of Zelma & Grossman as my criminal attorneys. The firm shared office space with Esposito.

At my October 28 preliminary hearing a representative of the district attorney's office sought an adjournment until December 8. On that date—the second anniversary of Lennon's death—the charges on which I been arraigned in September were dismissed. I assumed this was the end of the criminal case against me. Little did I know that my legal problems were only just beginning.

In a letter dated February 18, 1983, Yoko's fiftieth birthday, Assistant D.A. Fernandez informed me that she was bringing my case before a grand jury. I was being charged with four counts of grand larceny in connection with the theft of Lennon's journals. Having signed a written confession as well as admitted to taking the diaries in my videotaped interrogation, I was promptly indicted by the grand jury.

My lawyers argued that in view of my confession, it would be foolish to insist on a trial. My only hope for an acquittal was to have my confession thrown out, but in order to do that I would have to prove that I was illegally arrested by Goldblatt and Greve, which was virtually impossible because there had been no witnesses to the assault. George Zelma, my chief criminal attorney, assured me that pleading guilty in exchange for a suspended sentence was the only reasonable course of action. A hearing had been scheduled for May 27, and on the advice of my criminal attorneys, I agreed to plead guilty to a reduced charge of criminal possession, a misdemeanor.

On the morning of my May 27 hearing before Judge Jeffrey Atlas, I was presented with a copy of the plea bargain agreement. The words "criminal possession" had been crossed out and replaced with "grand larceny," a felony. I refused to sign the agreement. Judge Atlas suggested I talk it over with my attorney outside the courtroom. Zelma and I went out into the hallway, where the lawyer told me that if I wanted to go to trial, I would have to pay him and his partner more money. Then he unceremoniously placed two papers in front of me—the plea-bargain agreement and a ten-thousand-dollar retainer letter—and insisted I had to sign one of the two. I had already paid Zelma & Grossman a total of ten-thousand-dollars. When I told the lawyer that I had no intention of signing the new retainer agreement, he threatened to walk out.

Feeling trapped, I agreed to plead guilty to one count of grand larceny. I did manage to state for the record that it had not been my intention to profit from the taking of the journals. On July 14, 1983, I was sentenced to five years' probation by Judge Atlas. In October, 1984, I filed a motion to vacate my guilty plea, on the basis of ineffective assistance of counsel. It was denied by Judge Atlas, and a request for permission to appeal was denied by the Appellate Division in 1985. I was granted an early termination from probation in 1986. Having spent close to thirty thousand dollars in legal fees, it was financially impossible for me to pursue my previous legal claim against Yoko, Havadtoy, and New York City.

With ten years' hindsight, I can see that it was irresponsible to take John's journals, regardless of how well-intentioned I was. However misguided my attempt to carry out what I understood to be John's wishes, it was never my intention to steal his diaries. It seems to me that my criminal conviction is largely a result of Yoko's ability to influence overzealous prosecutors.

I have tried to present a fair and honest account of my unique experience as John's assistant. I would like to stress that this book is based entirely on my own journals and recollections. For two years, I compulsively scribbled my diary in everything from small memo pads to massive, leather-bound ledger books. Although more than a decade has passed since John's death, I retain a vivid memory of my life with him. I would like to think that I made John Lennon's isolated, lonely and often tortured life a little easier. Sometimes I thought I was his friend. I hope that I have succeeded in shedding more light on this brilliant, yet tortured soul, who gave so much of himself through his music.

Epilogue

Yoko Ono recorded solo albums in 1982 (*It's Alright*) and 1985 (*Starpeace*), but she abandoned her pursuit of rock and roll stardom after a disastrous world tour ("It's silly to bring out something when there is no demand," she acknowledged). Making the best of a bad situation, she turned her status as Lennon's widow into a licensing and marketing business. As executrix of the Lennon estate, she has exploited John's unissued recordings and song demos, peddled his unpublished manuscripts, and sold his artwork. She is president of Bag One Arts, the estate-owned company that operates the Bag One gallery on West Seventy-ninth Street. In 1990, she commemorated John's fiftieth birthday by organizing tribute concerts in Liverpool and Tokyo.

Sean Ono Lennon attends an exclusive private school in Geneva, Switzerland, where Yoko maintains a second home. He has appeared in Michael Jackson's *Moonwalker* music video and in February, 1991, appeared in an updated version of his father's pacifist anthem, "Give Peace a Chance."

Julian Lennon was signed to a multialbum deal by Ahmet Ertegun, the head of Atlantic Recording Corporation. His first LP, *Valotte*, yielded a Top 40 hit single, "Too Late for Goodbyes." Two follow-up albums, *The Secret Value of Daydreaming* and *Mr. Jordan*, sold poorly.

Cynthia Lennon tried to organize a John Lennon tribute with producer Sid Bernstein, at Berlin's Brandenburg Gate. However, Yoko managed to sabotage the event.

Helen Seaman left Yoko's employment in 1982. She has had no

247

contact with Sean, except for a brief encounter at a Julian Lennon concert in New York's Beacon Theatre on August 2, 1988. She is currently working at a facility for emotionally handicapped children near Brewster, New York.

Norman Seaman still operates a concert/theater club in Manhattan.

Rich DePalma left Yoko's employment in 1982 and now works for a Manhattan accounting firm.

Sam Havadtoy, Yoko's live-in boyfriend since the summer of 1981, has assumed the role of her business manager. He is vice president of Bag One Arts, an estate-owned art gallery specializing in Lennon-related art objects. Havadtoy's ex-boyfriend, Luciano Sparacino, died of AIDS in 1987; his assistant, George Speerin, died of AIDS in 1990.

Uneko Uda, the Lennons' maid and cook (Uda-san), returned to her native Japan in 1983.

Nishi Saimaru, the Japanese photographer who preceded me as John's assistant, published a book of photos, *The John Lennon Family Album*, in 1991.

Sam Green, Yoko's ex-boyfriend, is still a Manhattan art and antique dealer.

John Green (a/k/a Charlie Swan), Yoko's long-time tarot card reader, in 1983 published a book, titled *Dakota Days*.

Jack Douglas sued Yoko for royalties owed him for *Double Fantasy* and *Milk and Honey*, an album consisting of outtakes from the fall, 1980, recording session. In 1983 he was awarded $3.5 million, but he settled for half a million less when Yoko threatened to drag out the case with endless appeals.

Michael Medeiros (a/k/a Mike Tree) works as a free-lance gardener and videotape editor.

Doug MacDougall, Sean's former bodyguard, lives in retirement on Long Island.

May Pang has a son and a daughter by record producer Tony Visconti, whom she married in 1989.

Elliot Mintz, Yoko's publicist and troubleshooter, has added Ringo Starr, Bob Dylan, and Don Johnson to his client roster.

Barry Goldblatt, the cop and Yoko Ono bodyguard who in September 1982 punched me in the face, was assigned as a sergeant to the 112th Precinct in Queens. In March, 1991, a grand jury indicted Sgt. Goldblatt on murder charges in connection with the death of

Frederico Pereira, a teenager found sleeping in a stolen car.

Bob Greve, the other Yoko bodyguard who beat me and threatened to shoot me, is retired from the NYPD and lives near Brewster, N.Y.

Mark David Chapman pled guilty to murdering John Lennon and is serving a sentence of twenty years to life at Attica State Prison, where he is reportedly writing his memoirs.

Index